Europe Undivided

EuropeUndivided

The New Logic
of Peace
in U.S.-Russian
Relations

James E. Goodby

Foreword by Alexander L. George

UNITED STATES INSTITUTE OF PEACE PRESS
Washington, D.C.

INSTITUTE FOR INTERNATIONAL STUDIES,
STANFORD UNIVERSITY
Stanford, California

United States Institute of Peace
1550 M Street NW
Washington, DC 20006

First published 1998

Printed in the United States of America

The paper used in this publication meets the minimum requirements of American National Standards for Information Sciences—Permanence of Paper for Printed Library Materials, ANSI Z39.48-1984.

Library of Congress Cataloging-in-Publication Data
Goodby, James E.
    Europe undivided : the new logic of peace in U.S.-Russian relations / James E. Goodby : foreword by Alexander L. George.
        p. cm.
    Includes bibliographical references and index.
    ISBN 1-878379-75-5 (pbk.)
    1. United States—Foreign relations—Russia (Federation) 2. Russia (Federation)—Foreign relations—United States. 3. United States—Foreign relations—1989– 4. National security—Europe—International cooperation. I. Title
E183.8.R9G635 1998
327.73047—dc21   97-45199
                                                                      CIP

For Priscilla, Sarah, Laurence, and Lucy

Contents

Foreword by Alexander L. George   ix

Preface   xv

Introduction   3
The Logic of Peace

1. **Inventing Rules of Behavior for the Nuclear Era**   13
    Presidential Leadership on the Threshold of a New World

2. **Challenging the Bipolar Order**   37
    *The American Origins of the West's Campaign for
    Human Rights*

3. **Testing the Utility of Nuclear Restraints
    after the Cold War**   65
    *The Bases for Ukraine's Adherence to the
    Nonproliferation Treaty*

4. **Bringing Order Out of Chaos**   93
    U.S.–Russian Cooperation in Blocking Nuclear Terrorism

5. **Principles, Leaders, and the Use of Force**   111
    The Case of Yugoslavia

6. **Transforming Nuclear Deterrence**   141
    Can Strategic Partners Be Nuclear Rivals?

7.   Devising an Interim Security Order in Europe   **159**
Spheres of Interest and Collective Security

8.   Achieving a Stable Peace in Europe   **181**
A Grand Design for the Twenty-First Century

Notes   **205**

Index   **227**

Foreword

E*urope Undivided* is a significant, timely, and unique contribution to the theory and practice of foreign policy. Not only does Ambassador Goodby provide an incisive analysis of the nature of the peace during the Cold War and how it was accomplished, he also presents a sober, realistic identification of the challenges in the post–Cold War era that must be met if we are to construct a new basis for peace in Europe.

Although Goodby modestly refrains from referring to his role in developments leading to the end of the Cold War and in prevention of nuclear proliferation since then, it was a distinguished contribution that superbly qualifies him to be heard regarding the challenges that lie ahead and ways of dealing with them.

The new European security structure that is evolving and the nature of the peace associated with it remain to be decided. The reader may wonder why Goodby and I refer to "the nature of the peace" instead of just "peace." As he states in the introduction to the book, there are several distinctively different types of peace: "precarious peace," "conditional peace," and "stable peace." Precarious peace refers to an acute conflict relationship between two states when "peace" means little more than the temporary absence of war. Such a peace depends not merely on "general deterrence," to use a term Patrick Morgan introduced into the literature some years ago to describe the kind of deterrence that is ever present in the background of a highly conflictful relationship and serves to contain it.[1] To keep war from breaking out in such a relationship also requires frequent resort to "immediate deterrence"—that is, the timely use of threatening actions and warnings in war-threatening crises. The Arab-Israeli relationship, until recent times, is an example of precarious peace.

Conditional peace, on the other hand, describes a less acute, less heated conflict relationship, one in which general deterrence plays the predominant, usually effective role in discouraging policies and actions that might lead to war-threatening crises. As a result of general deterrence, such crises seldom occur. Therefore the parties to the conflict do not often need to resort to immediate deterrence. The U.S.-Soviet relationship during the Cold War qualifies as an example of conditional peace. During the Cold War there were only a few diplomatic crises in which general deterrence had to be supplemented and augmented with immediate deterrence.

Neither in precarious peace nor in conditional peace does either party to the conflict rule out initiating force as an instrument of policy, and deterrent and compellant threats do occur on occasion. In contrast, stable peace is a relationship between two states (or groups of states) in which neither state considers engaging in the use of military force, or even making a threat of force in any dispute between them. Deterrence and compellance backed by military force are simply excluded as instruments of policy. Two states or more states (as in the European Union) that enjoy a relationship of stable peace may continue to have serious disputes, but they deal with them by nonmilitary means. An example of this is the Suez crisis of 1956 in which President Eisenhower made strong, credible threats of economic sanctions to pressure the British government to withdraw its forces from the Suez.

In discussing possible European security structures that may develop in the years ahead, Goodby focuses first on a type of peace that he hopes can be achieved in the midterm, a variant of conditional peace. If it is achieved, general deterrence will suffice. Disputes between the two sides will be managed without war-threatening crises.

Chapter 7 of the book discusses the requirements and modalities for such a new variant of the conditional peace model. I need not summarize his discussion except to call attention to Goodby's forthright, realistic recognition of the tension in such a security system between the two pillars on which it would be based: "collective security" and "spheres of interest." The reader will find particularly interesting the case Goodby makes that these two shopworn models and the practices associated with them need to be reconsidered. Indeed, he provides a significant reconceptualization of both collective security and spheres of interest that, if accomplished in practice, would enable them to coexist and jointly contribute to maintaining conditional peace.

An even more important contribution is to be found in chapter 8. Here Goodby addresses in a novel and creative way the need to look beyond a conditional peace. He examines the prospects and the requirements for a transition to a security system that would provide a stable peace for the entire Euroatlantic community. This community would include Russia and some other countries that formerly lay on the other side of the Iron Curtain.

In this part of the book Goodby provides the architecture for a U.S. foreign policy that would aim at developing stable peace. In the terms used by academic scholars, Goodby engages in a "design exercise."[2] In more familiar language, chapter 8 is an example—all too seldom achieved in the U.S. government—of serious long-range policy planning. Policy planners worth their name are architects of efforts to create a new and better international security system. Franklin Roosevelt referred to his abortive plan for a new post–World War II security system as "the Four Policemen." American leaders, as Goodby indicates in chapters 1 and 2, were the architects of the system that contained communism in ways that avoided war, and American diplomacy deserves credit for some of the critical steps taken in the Helsinki Accord of 1975 and thereafter that helped pave the way for the end of the Cold War. Far less successful was the effort Nixon and Kissinger made to develop a new international system based on a "constructive relationship" with the Soviet Union that would replace or modify the Cold War under the ambiguous term "détente."

A *full-blown* design exercise or long-range policy plan comprises several elements: first, what might be called a "grand design" (the term Roosevelt used in referring to his "Four Policemen" model) that identifies in general terms the essence of a new security system; second, a "grand strategy"—the outlines of a strategic plan for achieving the long-range goal; third, of course, the various "tactics" that have to be improvised to implement different elements of the grand strategy. Chapter 8 provides a skeletal architecture of this kind. Goodby depicts both the grand design and elements of the grand strategy.

Where does Goodby's grand design come from? As he explains in the introduction and in chapter 8, he believes that President Clinton described a grand design when he spoke in October 1996 of "an opportunity to build a peaceful, undivided, and democratic continent" embracing all of Europe. As Goodby notes, the president has repeated a similar phrase on subsequent occasions. In a press conference on March 7, 1997, the president referred to his "vision" of "a united, democratic, and free Europe." He explicitly stated that this "does not rule out even Russian membership in a common security alliance"—eventually, that is.[3]

It is indeed possible to interpret these statements, as Goodby does, as indicating that the president has set as a long-range goal of U.S. policy to try to bring about a stable peace within an enlarged Euroatlantic community. But in fact it is difficult to ascertain to what extent Clinton's vision is as yet a well-considered, well-developed grand design. And it is equally difficult to tell to what extent policy planners within the government have privately articulated some semblance of a grand strategy for achieving this ambitious, difficult goal. Certainly it is fair to say that if the administration has such a long-range goal and strategy, it has made little effort thus far to explain it to Congress or to the public in order to achieve their understanding and support.

Any long-range foreign policy objective such as this one must pass two "tests"—the test of desirability and the test of feasibility. A grand design is desirable if it is considered to be consistent with American values and with basic national interests. Goodby makes a plausible case that a stable peace that includes Russia meets the test of desirability.

The more difficult test is that of feasibility. Is such a security system achievable? Do our policymakers have the motivation and incentives, the knowledge and resources, a good enough grand strategy, and the political and diplomatic skills needed to bring about a transition from conditional peace to stable peace? And, equally important, can our policymakers persuade not only themselves but also enough members of Congress and the public that such a long-range goal is feasible as well as desirable? The reader will find in chapter 8 a realistic discussion of the obstacles that stand in the way of achieving such a goal and of the formidable requirements for doing so. Therein also is a lucid case on behalf of its desirability and feasibility.

Working together with other states, the United States has undertaken a number of initiatives toward developing a new security system for Europe. This is a fluid process. Some steps have already been undertaken—for example, the Partnership for Peace and the NATO-Russia Founding Act. Some additional steps have been determined but not yet ratified—notably, the enlargement of NATO. Discussions have started concerning the enlargement of the European Union to include some states that lie on the other side of the former Iron Curtain. There is also unfinished business, as Goodby reminds us, to develop what might be called a "constitution" for Europe and the Euroatlantic community that will embody appropriate norms, rules, and new or strengthened institutions.

Are these developments part of a coherent, if not yet fully developed and articulated long-range strategy for realizing Clinton's vision? Are they the first, pragmatic "building blocks" designed to lay the basis for an all-embracing Euroatlantic community based on stable peace? Or are the various assurances being offered to Russia damage-limiting tactics—short-term improvisations designed to make NATO enlargement more palatable to the Russians? Alternatively, as Goodby hopes, are they or should they be parts of a transition strategy that aims at eventually bringing Russia into a common security system that achieves stable peace?

If, as seems likely, the administration has not yet undertaken the in-depth policy planning needed to implement its "vision," Ambassador Goodby goes a long way toward filling the vacuum. These are not the musings of a starry-eyed idealist or an impractical dreamer. Quite the opposite: Goodby's analysis is grounded in a serious assessment of the obstacles that stand in the way and what must be done to make a transition to stable peace at least possible. It will require a transformation of NATO so that it provides the basis for a common security system within the Euroatlantic community. As he would be the first to recognize, additional aspects of a grand strategy for achieving this goal need to be addressed; and additional questions regarding its feasibility will be raised and will need to be answered. But to recognize that more hard thought is needed to complete the assessment is not to fail to appreciate fully the value of the framework this book presents and the encouragement it provides to consider with utmost seriousness the concept of an inclusive Euroatlantic security community that would achieve stable peace.

Alexander L. George
Stanford, California

Preface

Writing is said to be a lonely occupation, but many people have shared in the creation of this book; the title page could rightfully be crowded with their names. Their ideas and advice and their critique of the manuscript truly have become a part of it. Their support encouraged me to persevere in a work in which I have been engaged off and on for over a dozen years. But in one important way, of course, this is not a collaborative effort: the author alone is responsible for the way the book has finally turned out.

I wrote and rewrote a substantial portion of the manuscript while I was the Arthur and Frank Payne Distinguished Lecturer for 1996–97 at the Institute for International Studies, Stanford University. The purpose of the Payne Lectureship is "to raise public understanding of the complex policy issues facing the global community today and increase support for informed international cooperation." I tried to do just that in the public lectures I delivered at Stanford. This book, which includes ideas I broached in my lectures, panel discussions, and publications while at Stanford, will reach a wider audience and, I hope, will be a continuing fulfillment over many years to come of my deeply felt obligation to Stanford and to the descendants of Arthur and Frank Payne.

If this book is at all successful in linking the theoretical and the public policy worlds, no one will deserve more credit than Professor Alexander George, Stanford University, author of the foreword and my friend and mentor for many years. He was the inspiration behind the central themes I have sought to develop. More than anyone else, he encouraged me to merge my practitioner's experience with my scholarly aspirations. I owe him a great debt of thanks.

The director of Stanford's Institute for International Affairs, Dr. Walter Falcon, and the deputy director, Dr. Nancy Okimoto, were constantly helpful to me during my year as Payne Lecturer. They were "force multipliers" in the sense that I utilized my time more effectively because of them. Dr. David Holloway and Dr. Michael May, codirectors of Stanford's Center for International Security and Arms Control, did everything possible to make my year in their center an intellectual and a personal pleasure. Janet Weitz was faced with the daunting task of deciphering my early drafts of lectures and chapters of this book, and for her patience I will be forever grateful.

The genesis of the book goes back to 1985 when I became Research Professor of Diplomacy at Georgetown University. Still on leave then from the U.S. Foreign Service, I began to study the influences on American presidents as they made their decisions regarding the acquisition and the potential use of nuclear weapons. I came to realize that behind all the rhetoric there lay the simple recognition that, as Ronald Reagan later put it, a nuclear war could not be won and must never be fought. American presidents had wisely constructed a set of tacit rules that the Soviets had implicitly accepted too, despite Moscow's ideological rigidities at that time. The logic of this system of rules pointed to the nonuse of nuclear weapons. On this foundation rests much of the remainder of the book. My formative year in the world of academia meant a great deal to me, and Ambassador David Newsom, then director of the Institute for the Study of Diplomacy at Georgetown, opened that door for me. He also made it possible through a Pew Grant for me to extend my study of presidential decisionmaking by researching and writing case studies of decisions made by Roosevelt and Reagan. Two of my research assistants in those days were Robert Danin and Janette Hill. They also became my good friends, and still are. This book's publication owes a lot to their work and their continuing interest in the project.

The critical middle years of the book's creation took place at the United States Institute of Peace, Washington, D.C., where I became a Distinguished Fellow in the fall of 1992. My plan was to study and write about rules of international behavior in the post–Cold War period, building on the work I already had done on nuclear rules of behavior in the early part of the Cold War. At the Institute I focused on the origins of the human rights norms sponsored by the U.S. government in the late 1960s in the context of the preparations for the Conference on Security and Cooperation in Europe. I also studied the breakdown of norms and rules in Yugoslavia that had led to war in 1991 and looked into the problem of collective security in the post–Cold War era.

The origins of chapters 5 and 7 date back to this period. Chapter 5 appeared in an earlier version in the *Journal of International Negotiations* 1, no. 3 (1996), and in a still earlier version in *Regional Conflicts: The Challenge to U.S. Russian Cooperation,* edited by J. E. Goodby (SIPRI and Oxford University Press, 1995). The United States Institute of Peace published an earlier version of chapter 7 in *Managing Global Chaos* (1996), edited by Chester A. Crocker and Fen Osler Hampson with Pamela Aall. My discussion of contemporary collective security in chapter 7 was published in an earlier version by the *Journal of International Affairs* 46, no. 2 (1993).

My tenure at the Institute was interrupted in 1993 by a one-year return to duty with the State Department as chief U.S. negotiator for the Safe and Secure Dismantlement of Nuclear Weapons. This experience gave me fresh insights into the role of norms and rules in international affairs since part of my official responsibilities involved negotiating for the dismantlement of nuclear weapons on the territory of Ukraine. I wrote about this experience on my return to the United States Institute of Peace in 1994.

I owe a great deal to the support given to me by the Institute's former president, Sam Lewis, and its current president, Dick Solomon. Sam Lewis made it possible for me to have a productive year of research and writing at the Institute. Dick Solomon endorsed the project and approved the book's publication by the Institute, giving me encouragement through every one of the final steps. Michael Lund, former director of the Jennings Randolph Fellowship Program, and Sally Blair critiqued my efforts and offered me their ideas. Joe Klaits the current director of the Jennings Randolph Fellowship Program, was involved in the take-off and in the landing. I am especially grateful to him for his unfailing confidence in this project. Dan Snodderly, director of the Institute's publications program, has worked with me from my first days at the Institute, seeing it through from gleam in the eye to finished product.

I received magnificent support at the Institute from three wonderful research assistants, Dan O'Connor, Lou Klarevas, and Fred Williams, each of them a Ph.D. candidate at The American University. The academic community can be proud to be represented by such fine young people. Of course, the quality of every book is the result of transactions between its author and its editor. I was very fortunate in working with Nigel Quinney, of the Institute of Peace. Nigel improved the quality of the manuscript significantly. Furthermore, he turned out to be the better diplomat of the two of us. If I felt at times like the bull in a *corrida de toros*, I realized it was for my own good.

The memory of the late Senator John Heinz is very special to me because I was the first winner of the Heinz Award in Public Policy for 1994. Teresa Heinz and the Heinz Family Foundation deserve great credit and the warmest thanks from all of us for what they are doing to encourage us to remember what we owe to others. Because of them and their ideals I pursued the theory and practice of peace for a longer time than I had ever expected, both in my writing and in my career as an American public servant.

Finally, of all the "it would have been impossible withouts," the one that is most heartfelt is my tribute to my wife, Priscilla, who not only put up with this extended effort but also converted it from yellow pads to diskettes, improving the product all the while.

Europe Undivided

Introduction

The Logic of Peace

Statecraft and its exercise in the pursuit of an ordered, predictable, and peaceful international environment during times of transition is the subject of this book. Managing change while remaining constant in the nation's commitment to long-term goals is a challenging task for American statecraft. Essential for success in managing change is the articulation of a clearly defined, overarching strategic concept, a "grand design" from which tactical considerations and moves will naturally follow. During the Cold War the overarching principle was that nuclear war must be avoided. It was self-evident why peace made more sense than war, and why a modus vivendi that set some limits on national behavior was necessary. Norms, rules of acceptable behavior, and institutional structures flowed from this recognition.

Today, we have the chance to move beyond a grand design motivated mainly by the imperative of avoiding nuclear war and toward the promotion of far-reaching and enduring cooperation involving not only "the West" (the well-established democracies of North America and Western and Central Europe), but also the entire "Euroatlantic community" (all the nations of North America and Europe, including Russia). President Clinton provided America with a nascent strategic concept to govern its relations with Europe when he spoke on October 22, 1996, of "an opportunity to build a peaceful, undivided, and democratic continent." He reiterated this ambition in his 1997 State of the Union address, during which he also noted that "the enemy of our time is inaction."[1] It was recorded once again in the documents of the Clinton-Yeltsin Helsinki meeting in March 1997. If Clinton's aim were realized, Russia and the United States would move beyond their present well-armed wariness, an achievement dwarfing even Franco-German reconciliation in its historical importance to Europe and the world.

The argument of this book is that past American engagement with the Soviet Union was instrumental in fostering a "logic of peace," and that contemporary U.S. policymakers—working cooperatively in a sustained engagement with their Russian counterparts during this transition from one epoch to the next—have an opportunity to promote that logic anew. "The logic of peace" refers to a complex of interconnected norms, rules, and structures within the international systems—namely, the West and the Euroatlantic community—that are the focus of this study. The "natural" state of affairs within these systems is assumed to be one where harmony is elusive and disputes are commonplace. The internal logic of these norms, rules, and structures increases the likelihood that disputes within the systems will be addressed without resort to extralegal methods and, if possible, without resort to violence. Sometimes force must be used or threatened to uphold the prevailing norms and rules, but force itself then becomes subject to codes of behavior. The process contributes to an understood order among a set of nations.[2] Nothing is permanent in international relations; rules and structures need revision periodically. This was done infrequently during the Cold War. Now, in response to sweeping change, a process of wholesale revision is under way—but amid the flurry of activity it is hard to discern the organizing principles that should guide the nations engaged in this process.

One fundamental principle, this book argues, is that the logic of future norms, rules, and structures should, over time, work toward establishing or reinforcing a "stable peace." A stable peace is one in which the use of military force between two states is simply not considered, and thus one in which nuclear deterrence has no part. By contrast, a "conditional peace" refers to a situation—like the present time—in which war is possible, although not likely, and deterrence by military means remains a factor in the relationship.[3]

There was no stable peace between the United States and the Soviet Union during the Cold War, but that era's carefully articulated logic of peace did ensure that the two superpowers refrained from direct military conflict in Europe. With the collapse of the Soviet Union and the end of the Cold War, however, many of the central ideas, strategic concepts, and rules of behavior of that period suddenly became irrelevant or at least detached from the circumstances that brought them into being. Consequently, we are faced today with great uncertainty about both the longevity of Cold War creations—will the nuclear restraint regime, for instance, survive?—and the character of the future Euroatlantic region—for example, can Russia and the United States put behind them the bitter rivalry of the Cold War, considering that both are still armed to the teeth with nuclear weapons?

This book aims to stimulate pragmatic consideration of foreign policy options by demonstrating how the logic of peace evolved and functioned during the Cold War, by indicating where in the aftermath of that war it has continued to operate and where it has broken down, and by arguing why it can and should be refashioned to help engender an increasingly close-knit and stable Euroatlantic community. The book is organized around three periods and two issue areas. The three periods are early and late Cold War; early post–Cold War; and the mid- and long-term future. They were chosen because they show how U.S. statecraft responded both conceptually and in a specific tactical sense to major changes in the international system, and how it could do so in a future that is likely to remain in a state of flux for decades. The two issue areas are the management of the nuclear threat and the control of actual or potential conflict within the Euroatlantic system of nations. These were chosen to demonstrate the role of norms, rules, structures, and strategic concepts in dealing with threats to national survival and to international peace. The book progresses chronologically, with nuclear issues dominating the earliest part of each of the three periods (especially the Cold War and early post–Cold War periods), while conflict issues dominate at the end. This shift of emphasis within each period reflects the fact that norms and rules were urgently required to keep the nuclear threat under control. As that task was successfully handled, interstate or intrastate disputes rose to the top of the international agenda. There are signs that the same pattern will repeat itself in the immediate future, as well.

The starting point for this book is the proposition that during the Cold War an order was imprinted on relations between the governments of the United States and the Soviet Union, an order that steered those governments toward decisions that yielded peaceful outcomes to their disputes. The foundations of this order were laid by clear-sighted U.S. leadership, but as its rules were elaborated over time, they came to be well understood by both the United States and the Soviet Union. Chapter 1 discusses the efforts of Truman, Eisenhower, and Kennedy, faced with an unprecedented threat to human existence, to find concepts that would help them frame a policy to achieve the goal of defending Western Europe while avoiding nuclear war. Those efforts were crucial to the formation and character of the entire Cold War order. In the process of defining the role of nuclear weapons in modern warfare, these presidents' administrations devised the strategic concepts of nuclear deterrence and extended nuclear deterrence, both based on the principle of using nuclear weapons first against the Soviet Union, if necessary. Yet all three presidents also saw clearly the absolute need to avoid nuclear war, and this became one of the central norms guiding decision-making during the Cold War. The idea that these weapons should not be used was fixed in people's minds by the early 1960s; this dramatically narrowed the range of risks that political leaders were prepared to accept. Rather more slowly in the Soviet Union than in the United States, similar worries about nuclear weapons were having their effect on Soviet leaders and on rules concerning the use of the new weapons. By 1954, many within the Soviet leadership were in broad agreement with the Americans that a nuclear war could not be won and must never be fought.[4]

The circumstances created by the domination over Central and Eastern Europe that Stalin had achieved by 1948 and the judgments of leaders in Moscow and Washington that nuclear weapons were not usable except in a deterrent sense fostered certain expectations. Chapter 2 begins by describing the terms of the modus vivendi that the United States and the Soviet Union worked out in Europe, an arrangement based essentially on tacit understandings about the use of force and about spheres of interest. As the Cold War declined in intensity, political relations between East and West become more complex. Change was in the air, and new ideas emerged to challenge some elements of the order created in the 1950s and 1960s. One of these new ideas, and perhaps the most powerful, was the issue of human rights. The West presented a fundamental challenge to Moscow's control when, in the 1970s, the West advocated and the Soviet Union accepted the concept that human rights were a matter for international review and negotiation. Through the mechanism of the Helsinki Final Act and the processes that it originated, human rights in the Soviet Union and Eastern Europe became permanently inscribed on the East-West agenda and became legitimate topics for international negotiation and debate. By undermining the implicit assumption that the Soviet government was entitled to a free hand in Eastern Europe and that its treatment of its own citizens was of no consequence to other nations, the idea of human rights accelerated the decline of the bipolar order in Europe.

In chapter 3 we shift to the early post–Cold War period, a time of dramatic change in U.S.-Russian relations and in European affairs in general. Some norms and rules endured the collapse of the order within which they had been created and contributed to the avoidance of conflict in a new era. A case in point, the successful U.S.-Russian-Ukrainian negotiations in 1992–94 concerning Ukraine's nuclear status, is examined in chapter 3. According to neorealist theory, a new nation like Ukraine would insist on being a nuclear power if it had the capacity to become one. Ukraine did not, however. One reason for this result was that in the minds of all the principal actors the norm of nuclear non-proliferation was firmly imprinted. As chapter 3 shows, there were two major reasons for success: active and persistent U.S. diplomacy, and a nuclear restraint regime that was well understood and well entrenched. This regime helped to simplify options for national leaders. There was a familiar logic that they understood and that their peoples understood, and it pointed toward limiting the spread of nuclear weapons. National decisions thus came easily, without much debate, in the United States. Decisions in Ukraine were tougher to make, but there, too, the nuclear restraint regime influenced the outcome. The success of this negotiation meant that the regime of nuclear restraint developed during the Cold War had proved its utility and so had survived—at least in part—the passage to a different era.

After the collapse of the Soviet Union, documented cases of illicit trafficking in fissile materials apparently stolen from what had been the Soviet "atomic archipelago" gave rise to fears of nuclear smuggling and nuclear terrorism. Cold War experience offered little guidance to U.S.

or Russian leaders on how they might work together to thwart substate entities interested in acquiring fissile materials or, worse still, an intact nuclear weapon. The thefts of fissile material that were known to have occurred, the many others rumored, and the deliberate release of nerve gas by the Aum Shinrikyo sect in a Tokyo subway convinced political leaders in Moscow, Washington, and elsewhere that action was overdue. International agreements now are helping to put in place a regime of principles and actions that address the very real threat that weapons of mass destruction can fall into the hands of criminals and terrorists. Rules by definition have little effect on outlaws, but international agreements can galvanize domestic action and foster closer intergovernmental cooperation. Chapter 4 describes how new strategies of cooperation devised jointly by Russia and the United States are attacking the problem at its source: plugging the holes in the internal systems that protect nuclear material. In the process the two countries are tearing down the barriers between foreign and domestic policies, the distinctions that President Clinton has called "the walls in our minds."[5]

Norms and rules of behavior, whether long established (like the nuclear restraint regime) or newly minted (like the evolving measures to guard against nuclear terrorism), are not self-enforcing. They must be enforced either by direct countervailing action, in the cases of the major powers, or by collective action. Sometimes, enforcement requires the threat or use of armed force; indeed, without that possibility, order-building diplomacy will be fatally ineffective. Always, enforcement requires leadership; otherwise, the political, economic, and military costs of ensuring that rules are obeyed will likely deter action on the part of an ambivalent power or a divided group of states. The failure of the West's diplomacy in the former Yugoslavia led to an enormous human tragedy and to a serious erosion of the principles of peaceful settlement of disputes, respect for frontiers, self-determination, and national sovereignty. The disaster resulted not so much from the irrelevance of well-understood norms of international behavior as from the failure of leaders of the West and the Euroatlantic community to take timely and decisive actions to enforce the norms. Striking, however, was the fact that although Russia and the United States saw the problem of the Yugoslav succession from very different angles, they were still able to patch together a collaborative effort. The lessons of Bosnia, discussed in chapter 5, come down to the simple facts that norms and rules are not enough, and that, in the end, leadership in the collective use of force is an essential element in creating and enforcing the rules of a peaceful international order.

Strategic partners, as the United States and Russia could become, and as their leaders have already proclaimed them to be, are likely to have difficulties living up to that role if they are also rivals in nuclear weaponry and locked into mutual nuclear deterrence. Russia and the United States cannot cross the threshold from a conditional to a stable peace while they maintain thousands of nuclear weapons in a posture where prompt launch is available and while they hold many others in reserve "just in case." Chapter 6 suggests that there are possibilities for drastic cuts in nuclear weapons, perhaps down to a few hundred. The reality, however, is that nuclear disarmament has been stalled for several years, and the outlook for dramatic progress through renewed negotiations is uncertain despite the important set of understandings reached by Presidents Clinton and Yeltsin in March 1997. The Russian and U.S. governments have never returned to the ideas about deep reductions in nuclear weaponry that Ronald Reagan and Mikhail Gorbachev voiced a decade ago. They have, however, begun to address nuclear warheads themselves, an encouraging new area for negotiation. Reductions in the number of deployed nuclear missiles constitute only one element in the U.S.-Russian deterrent relationship. Other elements, such as the readiness of missile forces for rapid launch and whether or not excess nuclear warheads are dismantled, also affect the way the two countries interact. The design underlying U.S.-Russian cooperation in the future should be altered to deal with the problem of transforming nuclear deterrence itself. Obligatory reductions of excess nuclear warheads, and measures to make their elimination irreversible, which the U.S.-Russian Helsinki summit of March 1997 encouraged, should be accompanied by changes in the readiness of intercontinental ballistic missiles (ICBMs) for rapid launch and, if possible, the elimination of substrategic nuclear weapons. Transforming nuclear deterrence is an inherent part of a move to a stable peace in the Euroatlantic region.

The final two chapters of this volume deal with the future management of conflict in a time of change in the Euroatlantic region. And they deal with the transition from a conditional to a stable peace.

Chapter 7 looks to the midterm future, in particular to the likely character of concepts and rules that will underpin Euroatlantic security during the next decade. It seems probable that the Euroatlantic security system will be based on the principles of collective security—broadly defined as a multilaterally sanctioned use of force—and of spheres of interest—a recognition that big powers have interests both in their own neighborhoods and in the fate of nations with which they share a common outlook. Under current conditions, neither of these two strategies in its pure form is likely to meet all of Europe's requirements for security. Collective security is flawed because the great powers cannot solve problems between themselves in this fashion. But collective security— a multilateral approach to conflicts like Bosnia—must be an element in a European security system. Internal conflicts in fragmented societies are best dealt with in this way. Strong multilateral organizations and an American presence in Europe are two essential ingredients for the success of a collective security strategy.

Balance-of-power and spheres-of-interest policies have been misused in the past to serve the purposes of national aggrandizement. But spheres of interest are the natural results of strong attractions— geographic proximity, economic ties, and cultural affinities, among them. Spheres of interest need not be, and should not be, equivalent to a zone of hegemonic domination as seen in Eastern Europe in Cold War days. Norms and rules of behavior will help avoid this outcome; structures such as NATO and the Organization for Security and Cooperation in Europe are key to reinforcing rules of acceptable international behavior.

If those are the midterm prospects, what ideas should guide longterm U.S.-Russian security relations in Europe? An American consensus on a framework for U.S. relations with the nations of Europe has not yet appeared. Critics of Clinton administration foreign policy complain that it lacks a unifying concept and is therefore purposeless. Not so in Europe. The president has sketched out repeatedly a strategic concept that could deservedly be called a "grand design" by speaking of "an opportunity to build a peaceful, undivided, and democratic continent." He has suggested that "territorial politics" may be an anachronism. The goal is a lofty one, amounting to the establishment of a stable peace among the nations of the Euroatlantic community. Chapter 8 examines the question of what it will take to achieve the goal of a truly undivided Europe at peace, finally, with itself. The effort will require long-term commitments and a level of tenacity and skill exceeding that shown by the United States during the Cold War—but the goal is not impossible to reach.

The enlargement of NATO really is only one element in a grand strategy to promote the expansion of democracy across the continent of Europe. Strengthening ties among the Western nations in political and economic areas is another essential element because an undivided Europe requires that the West serve as a powerful example of the value of integration. Transforming NATO's agenda so that it can deal effectively with conflict engendered by the fragmentation of societies is part of the process. So must be closer trade ties among the nations of the Euroatlantic community, including Russia, the United States, and the European Union. And global problems, such as crime, terrorism, and the proliferation of weapons of mass destruction, should be the subject of a coordinated attack by the Euroatlantic community. If over the long term a democratic Russia is excluded from membership in broadly based Euroatlantic institutions, including NATO, its exclusion should be the result of a decision of the Russian people, not of anyone else. Contradictions between expanding NATO and strengthening a close and confident relationship between the United States and Russia will be inevitable, and there will be serious quarrels between the two nations unless the ultimate goal is in fact an undivided and democratic Europe.

1

Inventing Rules of Behavior for the Nuclear Era

Presidential Leadership on the Threshold of a New World

Of all the tasks of statecraft in the early days of the Cold War none was more delicate and dangerous than the task of avoiding nuclear war in the midst of a titanic struggle between two antagonistic systems.[1] In those years, expectations that war with the Soviet Union was imminent were widespread. Intellectuals as disparate as Bertrand Russell and Herman Kahn wrote about nuclear war as something that might be just around the corner.[2] Preventive war—a war initiated by the United States to deny the Soviet Union the possibility of acquiring nuclear weapons— was publicly discussed, for the unprecedented horror of a nuclear attack on American cities was seen by some as inevitable unless the United States arranged a showdown with Moscow before the Soviets acquired a nuclear arsenal.[3]

In the United States, three presidents, Truman, Eisenhower, and Kennedy, presided over the dawn of the nuclear age. They had different ideas about nuclear weapons, but they all agreed on two fundamentals: that nuclear weapons should not be used except in the direst circumstances and that preventive war was unthinkable. Truman thought of an atomic monopoly and sequestering nuclear weapons in special storage sites. Eisenhower wanted to dramatize the nuclear deterrent and so he authorized the wide dispersal of nuclear weapons with military units. But at the same time he sought to limit the occasion for the use of

American military force. He thought little about war-fighting options. Kennedy imagined what might happen if deterrence failed, and he sought to arm himself against that possibility with presidentially controlled war-fighting plans and a buildup of conventional forces. The learning curve for American presidents between 1945 and 1965 was very steep. Their decisions blocked a trend toward thinking that nuclear war was inevitable; they provided the guidelines and the precedents for U.S. implementation of the strategic concept of nuclear deterrence and successfully applied the concept without ever detonating a nuclear weapon in a conflict after 1945. Rules of international behavior sprang from these early decisions that helped to consolidate a U.S.-Soviet bipolar order, especially in Europe. The historical record demonstrates some of the cardinal points of statecraft in the nuclear age: do not assume the inevitability of the worst plausible case; do act in time to head off crises; be decisive but never be cornered.

The experiences of Truman, Eisenhower, and Kennedy are a lesson in the need for rules of behavior backed by a grand design and a grand strategy, and never more so than at uncertain times of transition from one era to another—at times like the present. Because these presidents and the key members of their administrations thought coherently and deeply about the destructive force that nuclear energy had made possible, nuclear weapons never became just another instrument of war. These weapons, Truman, Eisenhower, and Kennedy understood, were different. Nuclear weapons had changed the course of history. At the core of the logic of peace of the first American presidents of the nuclear age was the principle, as Reagan later said, that a nuclear war could not be won and, therefore, must never be fought. In time this process built a barrier to thoughts about preventive nuclear war or, indeed, any war that might involve the use of nuclear weapons.

A New World

In the beginning, there was a void. There were no ideas about nuclear weapons and how they should fit into the existing political system. Should nuclear weapons be integrated into the armaments of American military forces? Who authorizes the use of nuclear weapons? What is their strategic purpose? How should governments control their use?

Are they deterrent or true war-fighting instruments? How do nuclear weapons and conventional forces relate to one another?

Because of the struggle between two views of the future of humanity —one championed by the United States, the other by the Soviet Union— other questions came to the fore. Is preventive war justified? Is there a need to settle differences soon or can they be left to the long term? How to react to the acquisition by an adversary of these ultimate weapons? What should nuclear weapons be targeted against? Most of these questions were addressed during the administrations of Truman, Eisenhower, and Kennedy for the first time in human history. Their answers have been guiding us during the nuclear age ever since.

In Truman's time, the main military threat to American interests was the Red Army's presumed ability to overrun Western Europe with relative ease. The Truman administration's National Security Council had adopted a statement of objectives (NSC 68), drafted in 1950, which asserted that Soviet ambitions were "directed toward the domination of the Eurasian land mass."[4] The USSR was seen as an expansionist state with a potentially dangerous nuclear capability. Its actions in Eastern Europe, particularly the coup in Czechoslovakia in 1948 and its blockade of Berlin in 1948, and its acquiescence in and support for the North Korean attack on South Korea in 1950 provided ample evidence of its hostile intentions. Most experts assumed that Moscow wanted to avoid war with the United States, but that it would seek to expand its empire through proxies and at a level of conflict that would not provoke general war. George Kennan had recommended a grand strategy consistent with the basic aim of avoiding nuclear war: containment, a pragmatic mix of policies designed to constrain Soviet expansionism while allowing time for changes favoring American interests. Recipes for the mix varied according to the tastes of the principal policymakers, but Truman's national security policy was rooted in that concept, as were the policies of his successors.[5]

Although the strategy was long term in its essence, the short-term needs of political leaders could not be ignored, and the short term was full of hazards. NSC 68 included a warning—for planning purposes— that a time of peril for the United States was not far off as the Soviet nuclear arsenal grew in strength. The year when the Soviet Union could deliver 100 atomic bombs on target in the United States would be a "critical date," since "100 atomic bombs on targets in the United States would seriously damage this country." This "critical date" was expected to occur in 1954.[6] The idea of a critical date recurred for a long time thereafter and raised the question of whether action should be taken to deal with the anticipated situation. The question sometimes was posed in terms of preventive war, rather than preventive diplomacy.

From Grand Design to Grand Strategy

During the presidency of Dwight Eisenhower, the Cold War was in one of its most dangerous and, at the same time, most promising phases. Joseph Stalin died on March 5, 1953, just forty-four days after Eisenhower's inauguration. Efforts were made by his successors in the Kremlin to reduce tensions in Europe. But in the United States, the impact of the Korean War, the first Soviet nuclear test explosion in 1949, and the national crisis of McCarthyism circumscribed the diplomatic possibilities available to the U.S. leadership. Mistrust of Moscow's intentions was very deep.

Dwight Eisenhower became the first American president to deal with the fact that the American homeland was no longer safe from enemy attack and that Americans were condemned constantly to live only thirty minutes or less from extinction. Eisenhower's position in the history of the American presidency therefore is and always will be unique.

Eisenhower's experience as Supreme Commander in NATO exposed him to European thinking about nuclear deterrence. His own practical, pragmatic view of the world told him that nuclear weapons would never be disinvented and that forevermore they would occupy a key place in strategic relationships. He took office with certain clear views, but before he allowed his administration's national security policy to take its final form, he took steps to build a consensus among his advisers and to show where he stood on the fundamentals. The organizational device he used was the National Security Council (NSC), an inner cabinet that Eisenhower met with frequently throughout his administration. The educational device he used for this was Project Solarium, a remarkable exercise in informing an administration about a president's thinking. Eisenhower approved the outline for a study on U.S. security policy toward the Soviet Union on May 9, 1953. Three strategic options were considered: drawing a no-cross line around the periphery of the communist-dominated lands; rolling back communist gains, especially in Eastern Europe; and containment. The findings of the study were presented to the NSC on July 16, 1953, and discussed again in the NSC on July 30.

When Project Solarium was reviewed at the NSC meeting of July 16, 1953, Eisenhower spoke about his views of nuclear deterrence. Nuclear war was not a policy option he would ever court: in the future the only thing worse than losing a global war, he said, would be winning one. There would be no individual freedom after a nuclear war. But avoiding a nuclear war would require a struggle with the Soviet Union that would be protracted; the willingness of the American people to sustain a defense effort over an indefinite period of time would have to be based on their freely given acknowledgment that it was necessary. Americans, he said, had shown little interest in occupying conquered territory: what would we do with Russia if we should win a global war? He made it clear that he was against unilateral American actions. Allies, the president said, are essential, and their understanding of American objectives must be gained by persuasion.[7]

Andrew J. Goodpaster, then an army lieutenant colonel who would shortly become Eisenhower's staff secretary, and who much later would become Supreme Commander of NATO forces, attended the NSC meeting on July 16. According to Goodpaster, all of the administration's top national security officials were present and heard him estimate the probabilities of success for each of the three strategic options and their implications. Goodpaster's judgment was that "roll-back sank, it was finished as of that day." Eisenhower's aim, Goodpaster thought, was to forge "a simple controlling idea that would dominate his administration." Thereafter, as Goodpaster said, Eisenhower expected "others to act within that broad, defined policy."[8] Drawing lines in the sand and rolling back Soviet gains won during World War II were rejected. Containment, in all its complexity, remained the conceptual model to guide the development of a national strategy.

Eisenhower's basic strategic policy was laid down in a document called NSC 162/2. It implied that the United States might initiate the use of nuclear weapons in any conflict in which it was engaged. One key sentence read: "In the event of hostilities the United States will consider nuclear weapons to be as available for use as other munitions" (paragraph 39.b). Creating the impression that war in Europe would be a nuclear war was one of the basic tenets of Eisenhower's deterrent strategy. NSC 162/2 stated that "the major deterrent to aggression against Western Europe is the manifest determination of the United States to use its atomic capability and massive retaliatory striking power if the area is attacked" (paragraph 15.b). As early as 1951–52, American military commanders in NATO had begun planning for the use of nuclear weapons in the European theater. General Lauris Norstad, a former Supreme Allied Commander, has said that Eisenhower, when NATO's first Supreme Commander, had personally approved Allied planning for the use of several nuclear weapons, each theoretically to be of a yield equivalent to the Hiroshima bomb.[9]

Eisenhower's secretary of state, John Foster Dulles, sought to sum up the administration's policy in a public speech on January 12, 1954. He spoke of the "deterrent of massive retaliatory power" and said that the free community should deter aggression by being "willing and able to respond vigorously at places and with means of its own choosing." His speech introduced the term "massive retaliation" into the historical lexicon, although Eisenhower's policy was considerably more nuanced than Dulles's speech suggested. Compounding the difficulties of under-standing what was really meant was the assertion that the United States had decided "to depend primarily upon a great capacity to retaliate, instantly." The speech, with its hair-trigger connotations, created a furor that haunted Dulles throughout his term of office.[10]

Eisenhower had reviewed the speech, and some of the draft is in his own hand. He was deeply aware, however, that in the nuclear age he was faced with a series of bad choices. He concluded that the least bad was a policy declaring that the United States would use nuclear weapons if war was ever forced upon the nation. Eisenhower emphasized the *deterrence of war* by nuclear weapons, and never talked lightly about their use, an outcome he described as "self-defeating." Perhaps for this reason Eisenhower was opposed to the idea of injecting American ground troops into local conflicts in the developing world. Pressed by key advisers to intervene in Indochina, Eisenhower refused, while assuring that responsibility for the decision would be shared with others. He thought that countries in the developing world should be assisted with arms and economic aid, and perhaps with U.S. air and naval forces, but he thought of the United States as a "keep" and opposed stationing "packets" of American troops around the world. Military solutions in those cases could only be a last resort.

Western Europe was different. It was the blue chip. He held his European connections in high esteem and carried into his peacetime relationships the same insistence on cooperation with America's Western allies that had distinguished his service as Supreme Allied Commander in World War II and as the first NATO commander. With the full support of the European Allies, he moved the American nuclear umbrella firmly over their heads. "General war" was defined as a war between the United States and the Soviet Union. A Soviet attack on Western Europe would be general war and would call forth the use of American nuclear weapons against the Soviet Union.

Eisenhower's nuclear deterrent doctrine penetrated very deeply in Western Europe, but Europeans themselves had prepared the ground. Marshal of the Royal Air Force Sir John Slessor had advocated a nuclear deterrent strategy while Eisenhower was at NATO headquarters; Eisenhower was familiar with Slessor's thinking before becoming president. Slessor's book *Strategy for the West*, published in 1954, could have been the basic treatise on Eisenhower's strategy.[11]

Eisenhower's views sometimes echoed and may have encouraged notions that Slessor had advocated and tried to popularize. In an NSC meeting on December 3, 1954, for example, Eisenhower remarked that there were some who believed that modern warfare imposes its own limitations.[12] Slessor had written that "war has abolished itself because the atomic and the hydrogen bombs have found their way into the armories of the world."[13]

Who Authorizes the Use of Nuclear Weapons?

The dispersal of nuclear weapons to the armed forces during Eisenhower's presidency raised command-and-control questions that rightly troubled succeeding administrations and should have troubled him. But Eisenhower did not intend to surrender his responsibility for deciding how nuclear weapons would be used short of a Soviet effort at a decapitating attack on U.S. national command authorities, not a serious scenario in his time.

The Korean armistice was signed on July 27, 1953, and in the fall of that year Eisenhower was determined to reduce his defense budget. He was being told by the Joint Chiefs of Staff (JCS), however, that they could not recommend cuts in force levels unless it was clear that the JCS could use nuclear weapons in future conflicts. Eisenhower was determined to keep the initial decision to use nuclear weapons in his own hands. He therefore wanted to retain some ambiguity concerning the conditions that would warrant use of these weapons. His principal advisers had a different objective. The Joint Chiefs of Staff knew they had a powerful card in their hands when they insisted that their support for budget cuts would depend on assured authority to use nuclear weapons. Secretary of State John Foster Dulles was intent upon stressing the credibility of the American threat to use nuclear weapons, hence his implicit support for the JCS. Adding to the pressure on the president was the formidable secretary of the treasury, George Humphrey. In an NSC discussion on October 7, 1953, Eisenhower was told that the JCS had strongly insisted on using nuclear weapons in Korea if necessary. The president replied that nothing would so upset the whole world as an announcement at this time by the United States of a decision to use these weapons. Secretary of Defense Charles Wilson pressed Eisenhower for a clearer position, remarking that the Defense Department needed to know whether or not to plan for the use of nuclear weapons. Eisenhower's response was that he was the one who had to make the ultimate decision on the use of these weapons; if their use was dictated by U.S. security interests, he would certainly decide to use them.

Not satisfied, the chairman of the JCS, Admiral Arthur Radford, asked whether the military could use nuclear weapons from bases where the permission from a foreign government was not required. Eisenhower repeated that no policy statement should be issued until officials had had a chance to convince U.S. friends of the desirability of using nuclear weapons. As far as war plans were concerned, however, the president thought that the JCS should count on making use of nuclear weapons in the event of *general war.* They should not, he said, plan to use them in minor affairs. He added that if the United States actually got into a global war we would certainly use nuclear weapons.[14]

The question of Eisenhower's position on use of nuclear weapons was raised again a week later, October 13, at an NSC meeting on the defense budget. Secretary of Defense Wilson reported that on October 2 the JCS had advised him that since Eisenhower had made no clear decision on the use of atomic weapons, they had not felt it possible to make significant changes in the levels of combat forces. George Humphrey, whose agenda was to cut the federal budget, jumped into the debate on the side of the JCS. It was absolutely essential, he said, to settle the issue of the use of atomic weapons. Only the authority to use nuclear weapons on a broad scale, in his view, could really change the programs of the Defense Department and cut the costs of the military budget. Admiral Radford added that unless the United States could use nuclear weapons in a blanket way, no possibility existed of significantly changing the present composition of the armed forces. The JCS believed that cost reductions could be achieved only by bringing home U.S. forces stationed overseas.[15] Humphrey indelicately pushed his president into a corner, asking Eisenhower why the Defense Department could not proceed on the assumption that they could make use of nuclear weapons. The president's famous temper flared up at this point, and the notes on the October 13 meeting solemnly recorded that "the President turned on Secretary Humphrey." The nub of Eisenhower's response was that savings could not be found in bringing U.S. troops home from Europe, first, because they were needed there and, second, because the costs of bringing them home would offset any savings.

Dulles, Humphrey, and Wilson had another day in court with the president on November 11, 1953. This time, they met in relative privacy, and without Radford. It was evident from the October 13 discussions that the political needs of all three secretaries would be met by an understanding that the threat to use nuclear weapons would substitute, in some way, for conventional forces. They knew by then, of course, that the president had no wish to give Radford everything he wanted. They proposed, therefore, a limited withdrawal of troops based overseas on the theory that this would provide a rationale for cutting the budget while avoiding an overly explicit commitment to grant the JCS authority to use nuclear weapons. Their plan was to begin the withdrawal of ground troops from Korea and to thin out support units in Europe. This would make it possible to reject the army's request for a force level of 1.5 million men and to reduce the defense budget for fiscal year 1955. As Humphrey and others had made clear at the October 13 NSC meeting, Eisenhower's defense budget and the composition of the forces looked embarrassingly similar to Truman's. The changes recommended would deal with this political problem.

Eisenhower bought the plan and noted in a memorandum for record that "it was agreed that the dependence that we are placing on new weapons would justify completely some reduction in conventional forces—that is, both ground troops and certain parts of the Navy."[16] Thus, all the civilian parties to the debate got something that they needed: the president retained the flexibility he needed on the question of whether nuclear weapons would be authorized for use; Dulles got an endorsement of air and naval strength as a means of offsetting communist ground force superiority; Humphrey received his budget cuts and a beginning of bringing troops home; Wilson, who would have to make his peace with the Joint Chiefs of Staff, could argue that Radford's question about the use of nuclear weapons in Korea was a little closer to being answered.

It was not until May 1956, in the midst of a debate between Radford and Army Chief of Staff Maxwell Taylor, that Eisenhower agreed, for the record, that the first use of nuclear weapons would be authorized in situations *short of general war* when required by military considerations. The reason for the decision was budgetary. Radford thought that financing the development of strategic nuclear forces should come out of savings to be realized from cutting the army's budget. Maxwell Taylor insisted on a doctrine permitting use of conventional forces, rather than nuclear weapons, even in the initial stages of a U.S.-Soviet conflict, for which strong conventional forces and a larger budget would be needed. Eisenhower accepted the thesis that even limited wars *not* involving the USSR would justify first American use of nuclear weapons, but still he reserved for himself the decision actually to use nuclear weapons. But when Radford tried to push the president's decision to its logical conclusion by proposing to cut the army to the size of a corporal's guard, including massive troop withdrawals from Europe, the admiral was thwarted by a timely "leak" to the *New York Times*. The resulting storm of protest in Europe forced Radford to back down under instruction from his superiors.[17]

Can Authorization to Use Nuclear Weapons Be Delegated?

The question of who would really authorize the use of a nuclear weapon was tied to unresolved questions of how the nation would go to war in the age of nuclear-armed missiles. Eisenhower wanted it to be believed without question that nuclear weapons would be used if the United States were attacked. Because of this policy and because he was concerned about the immediate effects of a Soviet nuclear attack on the nation's ability to respond, he dispersed nuclear weapons to major military commanders. This step required the development of elaborate procedures to ensure that weapons were not used without proper authority. Several analysts report that predelegation to use nuclear weapons under certain limited conditions, however, was granted to some senior military commanders by Eisenhower. Their evidence appears quite solid, especially regarding air defense operations.[18]

Eisenhower insisted on tight control over an *initial* U.S. strategic nuclear retaliatory attack. After that, he seemed to expect nothing but chaos. In the record of a meeting between Eisenhower and his senior military advisers on August 11, 1960, Eisenhower said that the initial military operations of the future would impose a requirement for greater rigidity in planning than in the past. He said he was very clear on this point: "for the first strike there must be rigid planning, and it must be obeyed to the letter."[19]

Military commanders accepted that the president, as commander-in-chief, was the ultimate authority for the use of nuclear weapons. Because surprise attack was considered a possible Soviet option, however, commanders were worried about delays in securing authorization from the president to use nuclear weapons. At the NSC meeting of October 13, 1953, Secretary Dulles proposed that the Department of State and the Joint Chiefs of Staff work together to define the areas in which the military could count on being able to use nuclear weapons.[20]

On December 22, 1953, President Eisenhower approved an interpretation of paragraph 39-6 of NSC 162/2. This was the famous paragraph that said that "the United States will consider nuclear weapons to be as available for use as other munitions." The purpose of the interpretation was to make clear that the paragraph was *not* a decision in advance that atomic weapons would be used in any type of hostilities.

The operative paragraphs of the interpretative memorandum are as follows:

1. The purpose of the paragraph is primarily to permit the military to make plans on the basis of the availability of nuclear weapons, and to permit transfer of the custody of such weapons, in large part, from the AEC [Atomic Energy Commission] to the Defense Department.
2. The paragraph is not a decision in advance that atomic weapons will in fact be used in the event of *any* hostilities. In certain cases the use of nuclear weapons by the United States would be automatic. For example, if there were an atomic attack on the United States or Western Europe, the United States would from the start use nuclear weapons.
3. Many situations, however, will involve political questions of the gravest importance which cannot be precisely foreseen. For example, in the event of limited hostilities, it will be essential to consider whether immediate use of atomic weapons by the United States would increase the danger of their strategic use by the enemy, lose the support of allies, expose them to devastation, or widen the hostilities.
4. The President should be in a position to consider such issues and make his decision as each case arises, in the light of the circumstances existing at the time. This is inherent in his role as Commander-in-Chief.
5. This position does not unduly enhance the uncertainty for planning purposes. Whenever the United States engages in hostilities, the President has to decide the nature and scope of the action to be undertaken. These decisions will inevitably involve questions of the manner and extent of the use of atomic weapons in any such hostilities. These questions are so intimately bound up with the political and other factors that they cannot be governed by hard and fast rules adopted in the abstract.[21]

An Accommodation or Preventive War?

Although he was more willing than Truman to threaten first use of the atomic bomb, Eisenhower had rejected the idea of a "critical date," a key element of Truman's NSC 68. The idea of a "critical date" was used in NSC 68 to emphasize the need for urgency in building military forces. It had other connotations, however. Many Americans, among them some of Eisenhower's top military advisers, believed that the Soviet Union would move aggressively against Western interests once a condition of mutual nuclear deterrence had been achieved. Included in this assessment was the expectation that a series of local aggressions sponsored by Moscow would ensue. The JCS thought that immediate operational consequences should flow from a conclusion that the Soviet Union could be in a position in the future to do severe damage to the U.S. homeland. They repeatedly drew Eisenhower's attention to a statement contained in NSC 162/2, paragraph 45:

> In the face of the developing Soviet threat, the broad aim of U.S. security policies must be to create, prior to the achievement of mutual atomic plenty, conditions under which the United States and the free world coalition are prepared to meet the Soviet-Communist threat with resolution and to negotiate for its alleviation under proper safeguards.[22]

The JCS never were clear in the records about what they wanted Eisenhower to do, but they called for a more aggressive diplomacy and a higher degree of risk-taking in relations with the Soviet Union. Eisenhower understood that a more aggressive policy, if followed to its logical extreme, raised the question of "preventive war," that is, an attack on the Soviet Union before the Soviets achieved the capability to strike back with nuclear arms. In a meeting of the NSC held on June 24, 1954, Secretary of State Dulles described the JCS policy as "press the Russians hard during the few years in which it would retain atomic superiority" and argued that not many American allies would go along with such a policy. According to the summary of the meeting, President Eisenhower remarked that "we should perhaps come back to the very grave question: Should the United States now get ready to fight the Soviet Union?" Eisenhower reminded his listeners that this was not the first time that he had raised the question in the NSC.[23]

The record shows that the idea of preventive war was discussed on several occasions during Eisenhower's meetings with his advisers. But everything Eisenhower said and did established quite clearly that he never entertained the idea of preventive war as a serious policy option. In this he was strongly supported by his three senior cabinet members, the secretaries of state, treasury, and defense. NSC 5440, Eisenhower's basic statement of national security policy, specifically rejected the concept of preventive war. In the NSC meeting of December 21, 1954, Dulles and Humphrey spoke of preventive war as ruled out, while Wilson spoke of containment and coexistence.[24]

Eisenhower always took the view that the U.S.-Soviet struggle was going to last a long time and that it had to be dealt with as a series of practical issues, not as a geopolitical problem that had some clear and perfect solution. This was illustrated in an NSC meeting on November 24, 1954, when Radford was pressed by Dulles to explain specifically how he would "forestall" communist actions instead of "reacting" to them. Radford came up with the idea of outright support of the Arabs against the French in North Africa. This effort to define in practical terms the more "dynamic" policy advocated by the Joint Chiefs of Staff quickly sank out of sight, and no better illustration of how to be "dynamic" was advanced by Radford.

The president was moved at the end of that meeting to remark wearily that he was tired of abstractions. They got him down, he said.[25]

The Tradition of Nonuse

Eisenhower's position on nuclear deterrence was all the more remarkable in light of his clear understanding of the terrific consequences of a nuclear war. He understood these well and spoke of them often. Eisenhower had not favored the use of the atomic bomb against Japan.[26] From his first months as president, Eisenhower repeatedly voiced his abhorrence of nuclear war.[27] Earlier than most, he foresaw the dilemmas that would come when living in the shadow of a surprise Soviet first strike. In a memorandum to Dulles, dated September 8, 1953, he wrote that

> our own preparation could no longer be geared to a policy that attempts only to avert disaster during the early "surprise" stages of a war, and so gain time for full mobilization. Rather, we would have to be constantly ready, on an instantaneous basis, to inflict greater loss upon the enemy than he could reasonably hope to inflict upon us.[28]

In March 1954, Eisenhower discussed with the National Security Council a paper on objectives in the event of war with the Soviet Union. The president obviously thought the whole exercise was ludicrous. The first national objective was "to achieve a victory which will ensure the survival of the United States as a free nation and the continuation of its free institutions in the post-war period." Eisenhower thought that the sentence should stop after "victory" and probably the rest of the paper could be scrapped.

In the later years of the Eisenhower administration, the meaning of "atomic plenty" became quantified in ways that convinced Eisenhower that his imagination was not "overdeveloped." A team of experts on military matters called the Net Evaluation Subcommittee of the NSC had been formed to assess the results of a U.S.-Soviet nuclear exchange. The president recorded in his diary the results that a briefing in January 1956 had revealed to him. "Casualties were enormous," Eisenhower wrote, whether there was a month's warning or only a few hours. "It was calculated that something on the order of 65 percent of the [U.S.] population would require some kind of medical care and, in most instances, no opportunity to get it." He described the postattack situation as "a business of digging ourselves out of ashes, starting again." Regarding the Soviet Union, the president wrote that "the damage inflicted by us against the Soviets was roughly three times greater. The picture of total destruction of the areas of lethal fallout, of serious fallout, and of at least some damage from fallout, was appalling."[29]

On February 10, 1956, Eisenhower met with the Joint Chiefs of Staff. The report he had heard the month before was still very much on his mind. He told the JCS that the report left him with an overall question—how would we fight a war after the amount of devastation shown in that report, or a small fraction of that amount?[30] On April 14, 1956, Eisenhower wrote about nuclear weapons in stark terms:

> We are rapidly coming to the point that war can no longer be won . . . When we get to the point, as some day we will, that both sides know that in any outbreak of general hostilities, regardless of the element of surprise, destruction will be both reciprocal and complete, possibly we will have sense enough to meet at the conference table with the understanding that the era of armaments has ended and the human race must conform its actions to this truth or die.[31]

Eisenhower's view of the dire consequences of nuclear war remained quite consistent over the years, although what he said depended, of course, on his audience. In a meeting with Chairman McCone of the U.S. Atomic Energy Commission in January 1959, Eisenhower erupted over the weapons requirements the Defense Department was requesting. He said the Defense Department wanted enough nuclear weapons to destroy every conceivable target all over the world, plus a threefold reserve. This he compared with an earlier determination that the destruction of seventy targets would be enough to defeat the Soviet Union. Eisenhower told McCone that he was worried about the unrealistic attitude of the top military men. McCone, no dove himself, agreed that they talked about megaton explosions as though these were almost nothing.[32]

Later that same year, on March 11, Eisenhower was asked in a press conference about the use of nuclear weapons in the context of Khrushchev's threat to the Western presence in Berlin. He replied with one of his most pessimistic public assessments of the results of recourse to nuclear war:

> And, I must say, to use that kind of a nuclear war as a general thing looks to me a self-defeating thing for all of us. After all, with that kind of release of nuclear explosions around this world, of the numbers of hundreds, I don't know what it would do to the world and particularly the Northern Hemisphere; and I don't think anybody else does. But I know it would be quite serious.[33]

Eisenhower left office in January 1961 and was succeeded by John F. Kennedy. Eisenhower's legacy was mixed: nuclear weapons had been "conventionalized" to an extraordinary degree and had been dispersed widely to the military. Command-and-control procedures were not as highly developed as the wide dispersal warranted. Taking advantage of Truman's expansion of nuclear production plants, the numbers of nuclear weapons had been increased dramatically—to eighteen thousand weapons. But Eisenhower had held the line on presidential authority to use nuclear weapons. His personal instincts were strongly inclined against the use of nuclear weapons as war-fighting weapons— he saw them as deterrent and, to a very limited extent, coercive instruments. He thoroughly understood, and conveyed to others, the true nature of any decision to use nuclear weapons. Despite the fears of his advisers that the increasing nuclear capabilities of the Soviet Union spelled disaster for the United States, Eisenhower refused to be panicked or stampeded into precipitate actions to deal with the Soviet threat. Preventive war was an action he refused to seriously contemplate.[34]

At the end of Eisenhower's term of office Professor Thomas Schelling was able to write of a "tradition" of nonuse of nuclear weapons.[35]

McGeorge Bundy has called this "the most important single legacy of the first half century of fission."[36]

The Kennedy Correctives: Second Thoughts about Strategies of Survival in the Nuclear Age

Kennedy narrowly won the election of 1960 and in his inaugural address spoke of nuclear weapons in words at least as apocalyptic as Eisenhower's: "man holds in his mortal hands the power to abolish . . . all forms of human life." Kennedy, however, did not share Eisenhower's hope that nuclear weapons might eliminate warfare among nations. He thought that the threat of nuclear retaliation would not indefinitely deter regional conflicts and that the United States would someday have to choose, as he put it, "between holocaust and humiliation." Furthermore, Kennedy wanted ironclad assurances that nuclear weapons could not be used without his permission. Eisenhower's dispersal of weapons to the armed forces and arrangements for their use in times of crisis caused Kennedy to have serious doubts that he would have absolute control.

Kennedy dealt with some of the same military problems faced by Eisenhower, but he responded with a much larger nuclear weapons program than Eisenhower had planned and with a greater capability for conducting a nuclear war. But, like Eisenhower, the idea of preventive wars was never a rational choice for him. By the time of his assassination, in November 1963, the Cuban missile crisis and the Limited Nuclear Test Ban Treaty had underscored the need for extreme prudence in dealing with nuclear weapons and pointed to a more cooperative method of dealing with them.

President Kennedy's decision to shift to a strategic concept of "flexible response" was announced early in his administration in a Special Message on the Defense Budget. This statement, transmitted to Congress on March 28, 1961, revised the image of instant nuclear retaliation that Eisenhower and Dulles had created. A key sentence in the message announced that "our weapons systems must be usable in a manner permitting deliberation and discrimination as to timing, scope and targets in response to civilian authority."[37] This policy led to several changes in U.S. doctrine and force posture. The whole saga is much more than an epilogue to Eisenhower's pioneering decisions, of course, but the present account will be limited to the steps Kennedy, with the strong support of Secretary of Defense Robert S. McNamara, took to correct what they perceived to be weaknesses in Eisenhower's application of the concept of nuclear deterrence.

Flexible Response and Nuclear War-Fighting Doctrines

The importance of controlling nuclear forces *before* and *during* a war was emphasized to a greater extent by Kennedy than Eisenhower ever had thought necessary. Two things were accomplished: tighter presidential controls over nuclear weapons but also the basis for a war-fighting strategy, not just a deterrent strategy. The latter emerged during later administrations, but the basis was laid in Kennedy's. Kennedy's vision of strategic nuclear war diverged from Eisenhower's image of an all-out "spasm" attack, but both he and his secretary of defense agreed in their budget reviews not to seek a first-strike capability, since they judged it to be infeasible.[38] Even considering the growing superiority of the United States over the Soviet Union, Kennedy's advisers told him in late 1962 that over the next few years "the prospect of real victors emerging from any major nuclear war diminishes further."[39] Those conclusions would have been supported by briefings he received from the NSC Net Evaluation Subcommittee, of the type that had moved Eisenhower to enter gloomy thoughts in his private diary. Ted Sorensen wrote that such a briefing in 1961 confirmed for Kennedy "the harsh facts he already knew: that a policy of pre-emptive first strike or preventive war was no longer open to either side."[40]

Kennedy and McNamara recognized that much of what they thought was wrong with Eisenhower's strategy—excessive reliance on nuclear weapons, inadequate conventional capabilities, inflexible doctrines, and loose command and control at the national level over nuclear forces—was epitomized by the NATO alliance as they found it in 1961. NATO—its strategy and forces—absorbed a large part of American defense resources and energies. There was considerable suspicion, both bureaucratic and political, in NATO about the defense policies of the Kennedy administration. Because of Eisenhower's insistence that any war in Europe would be a nuclear war, nuclear weapons policies—

regarding both deployment and use of nuclear arms—came to a focus in Europe more than anywhere else. Objectively, NATO strategy *was* too rigid and *was* losing credibility. The United States and its allies in Europe *could* do more to construct a more effective conventional defense. The Kennedy administration, therefore, began the process of revising NATO's force posture and agreed strategy, a process that turned out to be a wrenching struggle for many years and that in some respects continued on into the 1980s.

The specifics of much of the Kennedy policy toward Europe were developed in a study that Kennedy had asked former secretary of state Dean Acheson to undertake. Acheson handed over his report in March 1961. It advocated a stronger conventional defense for NATO, a tactical nuclear defense option, and a U.S. strategic targeting policy that would strike Soviet military targets rather than cities—a counterforce option. The latter policy was designed to strengthen the credibility of the U.S. nuclear deterrent in the face of growing Soviet nuclear capabilities. The report also took a stern line against independent Western European nuclear forces.[41]

Kennedy bluntly emphasized to NATO's military leaders his intense concern that the release of nuclear weapons should remain under his control at all times:

> We propose to see to it, for our part, that our military forces operate at all times under continuous, responsible command and control from the highest authorities all the way downward—and we mean to see that this control is exercised before, during, and after any initiation of hostilities against our forces, and at any level of escalation.[42]

This stance reflected not only Kennedy's wish to control a nuclear war to the extent he could, but also a concern in the Kennedy administration that nuclear weapons might be fired without proper authority. An illustration of this concern was McGeorge Bundy's January 30, 1961, memorandum to the president, in which Bundy remarked that "a subordinate commander faced with a substantial Russian military action would start the thermonuclear holocaust on his own initiative if he could not reach you."[43]

Kennedy and Khrushchev met for their first and only summit in Vienna on June 3 and 4, 1961. It was an inauspicious occasion, especially after the recent Bay of Pigs disaster. Khrushchev threatened to change the status of Berlin in a note he delivered to Kennedy directly. Eisenhower had met similar threats in the period after Sputnik, but had brushed Khrushchev's demands aside and held fast to his nuclear deterrent doctrine. Kennedy reacted very differently. Soon after his return to Washington, he dramatically appealed to Congress for more resources for American conventional forces, especially for the army. He requested increases in the size of the army from 875,000 to 1 million men and smaller increases in the size of the air force and the navy. Draft calls were to be doubled and tripled; reserve units were called to active duty. More money was to be spent on conventional weapons. These actions were to be seen as a sign of America's determination to defend its rights in Berlin. The Berlin crisis also offered Kennedy an opportunity to do what he wanted to do anyway—create a more balanced U.S. force structure.

The conventional buildup ordered by Kennedy in the United States was not matched by the allies in Europe. Faced with this resistance, Kennedy authorized McNamara to try the tactic of overwhelming the allies with rational argument, challenging long-held dogma on virtually every point. In May 1962, McNamara launched a full-scale attack on the status quo with a comprehensive speech at a meeting of NATO foreign and defense ministers in Athens.[44] Kennedy had read and approved the Athens speech. McNamara delivered a shorter public version of the speech at Ann Arbor, Michigan, on June 16, 1962.

McNamara's speech not only outlined the rationale for building a "flexible response" into NATO defense plans, but also addressed U.S. theories about the nature of strategic warfare. He argued that a strategy of attacking Soviet military forces while sparing Soviet cities would limit Soviet civilian casualties. Washington policymakers had hoped that this targeting doctrine would strengthen the credibility of the American promise to defend Europe by making a war-fighting strategy more credible. To accomplish this would require "unity of planning, executive authority, and central direction," McNamara maintained, and, hence, weak nuclear forces operating independently (read the United Kingdom and the incipient French) were undesirable. The secretary argued that stronger NATO conventional forces would be needed and that tactical nuclear weapons, while necessary, were likely to be of limited value rather than a panacea.

The Nuclear Paradox

European leaders did not conceive of nuclear weapons as war-fighting instruments but as the ultimate deterrent. The idea of their controlled use was not congenial to the Europeans, since they expected that their countries would be destroyed even in a limited nuclear engagement. Nor was the idea of making Europe safe for another conventional war appealing to them. Furthermore, preparing for conventional war was more expensive than relying on a nuclear deterrent. Europeans were not disposed to think in terms of the "worst plausible case," the form of analysis that McNamara had borrowed from the RAND Corporation. Rather, the Europeans tended to think in terms of the most likely situation and that, to them, was a situation in which the Soviet Union would be deterred by the prospect of what would happen if it chose war in Europe in the face of a strong American commitment. As the credibility of "trading New York for Hamburg" came to be questioned by the French, among others, the credibility of a nuclear retaliation began to fade, but even a doubtful nuclear deterrent was thought by the Europeans to be adequate.

Declaratory policy in the United States permitted the first use of nuclear weapons. In fact, a stated willingness to use nuclear weapons first under various circumstances was the official stance of the United States from the 1950s, and this idea exists even today in the defense doctrines of NATO and the United States. Although the Soviet Union declared a no-first-use policy, it was universally believed that Moscow would use nuclear weapons first, if needed. In training exercises on both sides, nuclear weapons were assumed to come into use. Russia's current defense doctrine makes it clear that nuclear weapons could be used first.

The United States tried hard to remove any ambiguity about the first use of nuclear weapons by NATO if Soviet troops invaded NATO territory. President Eisenhower, supported strongly by European governments and NATO commanders, insisted that nuclear weapons would automatically come into play in the event of a Soviet invasion of Western Europe. President Kennedy replaced this automaticity with a doctrine of flexible response, over the opposition of most European leaders, but the doctrine of first use remained. The fear of possible use of nuclear weapons lived on through the Cold War and took the form of "existential deterrence," to use the apt phrase of McGeorge Bundy, the idea that the very existence of nuclear weapons exerted a deterring influence on rash behavior.[45] NATO doctrine was updated at a summit meeting of the allies in London in 1990 to stipulate that nuclear weapons would be used only as a "last resort." This formula still permits the first use of nuclear weapons.

To give credibility to the doctrine of nuclear deterrence, the development, production, and deployment of weapons was required on a large scale, especially after the introduction of multiple, independently targeted reentry vehicles (MIRVs). A readiness for instant use was and is a part of the deterrent posture. In the face of this threat, both sides during the Cold War understood that it would be tempting fate to threaten the vital interest of either the United States or the Soviet Union. A doctrine that relied on first use of nuclear weapons was intertwined with a conviction that these weapons should never be used. The dilemma arose from a national interest in physical survival pitted against a national interest in a world congenial to basic American values. It led to certain tacit understandings designed to avoid situations where nuclear weapons might come into play.[46] And nuclear weapons were not used. A practice that has been sustained for a half-century is at least a "tradition," as Schelling described nuclear nonuse thirty-seven years ago, and it may fairly be called a "norm."[47]

In the 1980s, President Ronald Reagan said that "a nuclear war cannot be won and must never be fought." That was an important statement, but the truly remarkable phenomenon of the Cold War period was that American presidents—and whole generations of people everywhere—had learned that lesson long before President Reagan spoke those words. That wisdom seemed to come through divine grace with the first light from the blast at Alamogordo in 1945. It was not always easy in the early days to act on that principle. The rules of the game had not been locked in: they were still being invented in secret debates among American presidents and their advisers. The United States blazed the trail into the nuclear age and, therefore, decisions taken by American presidents were crucial in establishing the regime that affected so many aspects of East-West relations during the Cold War.

The next chapter will describe the rules that guided international behavior as these emerged in the early years of the Cold War. These rules—both tacit and explicit—had the effect of upholding the bipolar order of Europe during the Cold War, including the division of Germany and Europe into hostile camps. They were the rules by which nations lived, "facts of life" with which nations became intimately familiar. They were like navigational aids that told policymakers what the "logical" direction of policy was likely to be in given circumstances. They defined how these nations should conduct their relations with one another. And their starting point was the understanding that the use of nuclear weapons in war would represent a defeat for any state that possessed them. The rules of the road were well understood, as the next chapter will demonstrate, but they were not immutable. They could be—and they were—changed as history moved on. As the fear of nuclear war receded, the nations of Europe demanded and attained greater control over their own affairs. The device they used to accomplish this was an unlikely negotiation that awarded legitimacy to Cold War frontiers in return for legitimacy of the right to require governments to treat their own people with respect.

2

Challenging the Bipolar Order

The American Origins of the
West's Campaign for Human Rights

Nuclear weapons in the hands of the United States and the Soviet Union provided a powerful incentive for the two countries to settle their disputes without resorting to force. To enhance the prospects for that result, Moscow and Washington tacitly, and more by trial and error than by design, developed a set of rules that became the basis for a bipolar order in Europe. These rules will be described in this chapter. Their implicit purpose was to minimize the chances that either side could be pushed to the point where it would have to use nuclear weapons.[1]

In the late 1960s, a desire for change began to appear across the continent of Europe. It was reflected in the "Prague Spring" and in Willy Brandt's "Ostpolitik," and it found an echo in Richard Nixon's "Era of Negotiations." The U.S. government was faced with a situation it had not encountered before in the Cold War. The issue was whether to consolidate a not entirely satisfactory East-West status quo or to mount a political challenge to the Soviet Union, the outcome of which would be unpredictable. The U.S. foreign policy establishment was split on the question. Ultimately, the new thinking of that time led to changes in popular and governmental perceptions concerning a government's treatment of its own citizens that undermined the bipolar order in Europe.

The policy basis for this new thinking emerged in Washington earlier than is generally believed and was more consciously aimed at changing the status quo in Eastern Europe than is usually understood. And much of the leadership for this was provided by William Rogers's State Department. This chapter will describe the origins of this attack on the status quo. Three lessons emerge from this account: the importance of concepts in foreign policy during a time of change; the major role that international organizations—NATO, in this case—have played in the past, and could again, as an engine of change and as an instrument for imprinting an order on international relations; and the importance of shared values in Western diplomacy.

Norms for the behavior of nations had been established in the Charter of the United Nations before the Cold War began and, in theory, these should have provided guidelines for governmental decisionmaking. The major security crises of the Cold War revealed, however, that the real rules and expectations of behavior in Europe bore little resemblance to the abstract norms laid down in Articles 1 and 2 of the charter. Disputes were supposed to be settled "in such a manner that international peace and security, and justice, are not endangered." And, indeed, peace and security were rather well preserved between East and West, but it is hard to argue that all three of these goals were protected in the eastern part of Europe. The prohibition against "the threat or use of force against the territorial integrity of political independence of any state" was clearly not the norm observed in East Germany in 1953, in Hungary in 1956, or in Czechoslovakia in 1968.

Internationally accepted norms of good behavior were less influential than the self-interest of nations in surviving the era of thermonuclear weapons. Governments relied on precedents gained from experience or taboos encouraged by U.S. presidents and others, rather than on citations from the UN Charter. No master plan existed either in the West or in the East to point the way to the rules of behavior that gradually emerged during the Cold War years.[2]

Seven Rules of the U.S.-Soviet Relationship

Several scholars have tried their hand at codifying the implicit rules of U.S.-Soviet relations during the Cold War.[3] The following are seven basic rules that I believe guided U.S.-Soviet relations in Europe. Several of these rules also were applicable elsewhere in the world, of course.

1. *U.S. and Soviet forces should not engage in direct combat anywhere and especially not in Europe.* This rule was never violated. Only in Berlin did U.S. and Soviet troops ever come close to significant combat and that

only twice, once when Stalin blocked land access to Berlin and the other on the occasion of the building of the Berlin Wall. U.S. contingency planning envisaged the use of force in response to Khrushchev's threats to block all Western access to the city, but Khrushchev never put the issue to a test. The rule was tested much more severely in Korea, Vietnam, and the Middle East, where U.S. troops were actively engaged in operations that directly or indirectly affected Soviet allies and Soviet interests. There were breaches of the rule in Korea but no open official Soviet acknowledgment of its military participation in the war. Nor did the United States choose to publicize this. By and large the rule held even in cases where Moscow's commitments were being seriously tested.[4]

2. *The United States and the Soviet Union will conduct their affairs with allies in a way designed to avoid armed conflict between the two superpowers.* In Eastern Europe, Moscow had no problem in ensuring that satellite governments did not inadvertently trigger hostilities between the nuclear-armed superpowers except on the relatively rare occasions when those governments lost, or were perceived in Moscow to be in danger of losing, control of political life in their countries. Soviet relations with the government of the German Democratic Republic (GDR) were sensitive because Berlin and access to Berlin were under the jurisdiction of Great Britain, France, the United States, and the Soviet Union; Moscow's interests were not identical to those of the GDR. But the GDR owed its existence to Moscow and toed Moscow's line. Although the Soviets threatened to give the GDR responsibility for allowing access to Berlin from the West as a means of pressuring the West, it is clear that the Soviets had firm control of the situation. Western governments tended to follow the U.S. lead on critical security issues, and the United States almost invariably took a harder line on security issues than its allies. In the 1960s, President Kennedy worried about the potential of independent nuclear forces to trigger a U.S.-Soviet nuclear war, but as time went on this concern proved to be groundless. The major problems that both superpowers had with fractious allies were outside of Europe, in the Middle East on occasion, and in the Soviet Union's relations with China, Cuba, North Korea, and Vietnam.

3. *Nuclear weapons should be tightly controlled and their use authorized specifically by national command authorities.* Nuclear weapons were

recognized as different from other weapons of war from the very beginning. Military commanders, especially in the early years of the nuclear age, sometimes disputed this and sought advance assurances that nuclear weapons could be used. Successive U.S. presidents and, apparently, successive leaders of the Soviet Union resisted almost all efforts to allow decisions regarding use to be made at less than the highest levels. However, the dispersal of nuclear weapons and contingency arrangements made for release of nuclear weapons in the event of decapitation of the national command authority might have taken matters out of the hands of government chiefs in the event of major war.

4. *A "firebreak" should be maintained between conventional and nuclear warfare.* Because nuclear weapons were seen from the beginning as supremely threatening, distinctions were always made between the use of conventional forces and the use of nuclear forces. The logic of this distinction led to sometimes contradictory efforts to shore up conventional forces while maintaining a link to the potential use of nuclear weapons at the upper end of the escalation ladder. Toward the end of the Cold War period, efforts were being made in NATO and in the Warsaw Treaty Organization to strengthen conventional forces so as to make resort to nuclear weapons unlikely. The groundwork for the firebreak doctrine was prepared in the Truman and Eisenhower administrations, and from the Kennedy administration onward the conventional-nuclear firebreak was vigorously promoted by the U.S. government.[5]

5. *An American military presence in Western Europe is regarded as legitimate by both East and West if it is calibrated to the needs of stability in Europe.* Tacit agreement on this rule came at least by the early 1970s, when Brezhnev accepted the idea of negotiations with the United States on troop levels in Europe. His speech in Tbilisi on May 14, 1971, ensured the defeat of a U.S. Senate resolution calling for reductions of U.S. troop levels in Europe.[6] From the Soviet point of view the status quo in Europe had become quite comfortable. U.S. troops in Europe probably were perceived as preventing any German aspiration for a stronger military or for nuclear weapons.

The vision of nuclear weapons in the hands of the Germans had been a recurrent nightmare for the Soviets throughout the Cold War. The achievement of nuclear parity by the Soviet Union, more or less codified in the SALT I agreements of 1972, had given Moscow reason to feel that nuclear relations with the United States were manageable. This stable state of affairs was severely tested in the late 1970s by Soviet deployment of the SS-20 intermediate-range nuclear-armed ballistic missile targeted on Western Europe. NATO responded with deployment of its own intermediate-range nuclear missiles. The two actions resulted in overturning an unwritten rule regarding U.S. missiles in Europe in effect since the United States had withdrawn Jupiter missiles from Turkey following the Cuban missile crisis of 1962. The advent of the Gorbachev era made possible the 1987 treaty that eliminated all such missiles on both sides.

6. *The United States and the Soviet Union shall have "spheres of interest" in Western and Eastern Europe respectively, and neither side shall upset this arrangement by force.* Although the Yalta Conference is often blamed for this situation, the fact is that the Soviet army's occupation of eastern Germany and most other Eastern European nations could not be dislodged through any means the West was willing to use. Furthermore, as Winston Churchill records in his memoirs, the British government was satisfied with a spheres-of-interest policy in Eastern Europe, although Churchill did not have in mind the tight control exercised by Moscow over all aspects of life in Eastern Europe.[7] In the United States, spheres of interest were seen as immoral, and Soviet domination of Eastern Europe, as practiced by Moscow, was never accepted. It may be stretching a point even to suggest that the North Atlantic Treaty area was a U.S. "sphere of interest," but a sphere of interest need not embody tight repressive control by the dominant power.[8]

George Kennan and Charles Bohlen debated the desirability of a spheres-of-interest policy in Europe while ideas about U.S.-Soviet postwar relationships were still being formed.[9] Kennan thought at one point that an explicit agreement on spheres on interest would be the best way to guarantee peace and stability in Europe. Bohlen, closer to the prevailing sentiment in the State Department and in the country, pointed out that such a policy could never be endorsed by the United States.

Several fruitless foreign ministers' meetings confirmed that Moscow was determined to dominate Eastern Europe. Soviet suppression of uprisings and even of liberalizing tendencies in Eastern Europe made it clear that the Soviet Union would keep its sphere of domination under its thumb by any means necessary and would tolerate "liberalization," if at all, only in small steps carefully weighed and approved in Moscow. Western criticism of Soviet actions was sharp and unanimous in each case of suppression, and in Western Europe sympathy for the Soviet system declined precipitously with each Soviet display of brutality. But no military action was taken by the Western countries to reverse decisions imposed by Soviet military power. The result over time was an acceptance, in the West, of a *zone of hegemonic domination* for Moscow that went far beyond the usual concept of a sphere of interest. The contrast with the exercise by the United States of its influence in Western Europe was dramatic and ultimately self-defeating for the Soviet Union. This was the Soviet Union's Achilles' heel, and the West's human rights campaign struck hard at this vulnerability.

7. *Germany will be united, if at all, only on terms that effectively bring it into one camp or the other.* The Soviet leadership may have come close to adopting conditional unification as its policy in the early 1950s, when, it is said, Beria, then Soviet KGB chief, advanced the idea. It is a fact that on March 10, 1952, the Soviet government handed a note to the British, French, and U.S. governments proposing four-power talks on a united, independent, and neutral Germany. The talks were never held.[10] Despite Soviet overtures aimed at neutralizing Germany as part of the conditions for unification, however, it is likely that Soviet leaders never seriously considered negotiating a deal that would result in German unification.

The Austrian State Treaty of 1955 was seen by some Europeans and Americans as a model for how Germany might unite, but neither side in the Cold War took that very seriously. The U.S. position, more or less supported by other Western powers, was that Germany should be unified "in peace and freedom." In practice this meant that Germany should unite, but only as a member of the Western camp. This was Adenauer's position very clearly, and his successors as chancellor pursued the same policy. When Willy Brandt launched his policy of Ostpolitik he was criticized in West Germany and by some Western governments on grounds that the policy threatened to weaken the Federal Republic's ties with the West.[11] Brandt, of course, denied this and argued that he was trying to improve conditions for East Germans and strengthen ties between the two parts of divided Germany, but not at the price of German neutrality.[12] The standoff between East and

West over German unification became a normal part of the Cold War landscape, and the rule governed East-West relations in this area until the Soviet Union began to withdraw from Eastern Europe following the revolutions of 1989.

Explicit Rules of Behavior

In the late 1950s and thereafter a serious effort was made to codify rules of behavior explicitly through arms control. The Limited Nuclear Test Ban Treaty, the Treaty on the Nonproliferation of Nuclear Weapons, and the strategic nuclear arms agreements were examples of this. The period 1957 through 1968 was a decade of experimentation in arms control rules: what worked and what did not in formalizing coopera- tion between adversaries? One lesson learned was that first steps should not be too ambitious, but that first steps—for both sides—will blaze a trail that will lead to larger achievements. Another lesson was that progress in institutionalizing cooperation will produce safety nets and ratchets—safety nets, in the sense that when relations go badly there is something there to prevent the adversaries from falling into the abyss of war; ratchets, in the sense that relations never quite go back to the level of hostility that prevailed earlier. The two adversaries also found that there were limits to this process: arms control could not compensate for or overcome deep-seated antagonisms. Its importance was that it could create an infrastructure for cooperation when conditions permitted. These early experiences taught the lesson that leadership is essential. Eisenhower and Kennedy, so different in background and outlook, pur- sued strategies of cooperation frequently against the will of their advisers and supporters. Without them, the experiments in formal cooperation between adversaries might not have occurred.

U.S.-Soviet Cooperation in Consolidating the Status Quo

A remarkable fact about the whole Cold War period is the informality or even absence of procedures for making decisions about the establish- ment or revision of the most important rules of behavior. An inference might be drawn from this observation that national decisions were essentially independent rather than joint, but this would be only partly true. The creation of a bipolar Europe resulted from independent and parallel but not autonomous decisionmaking: there was a shared perception that war should be avoided. This perception derived from an agreed norm, in Reagan's words, that a nuclear war could not be won and should never be fought. The lesson learned from several experiences in the early years of the Cold War was that decisionmaking that was truly autonomous generally misjudged the interests of the other superpower, and led to results that no one liked. The Cuban missile crisis was a perfect example of this. So was the Soviet decision to deploy large numbers of SS-20 missiles targeted on Western Europe. In contrast to these misjudgments, the unwritten U.S. and Soviet decisions to maintain a sharp distinction—a firebreak, as it was called—between nuclear and conventional weapons resulted from a shared perception of danger and were jointly taken in the sense that the logic of peace required risk-avoidance when it came to using nuclear weapons. Both sides understood this.[13]

Some of the rules cited above were not only tacit but also deniable, that is, nothing passed between Moscow and Washington that could confirm their existence. In fact, some of these rules probably would have been formally rejected if the leaders and officials of the two sides had been asked to ratify them. But they were the unwritten constitution for the whole Cold War bipolar edifice in Europe. A shared logic—the logic of peace during the Cold War—was created in the calculations and judgments of the two superpowers by their shared perceptions of nuclear dangers and their experiences in dealing with one another in that environment.

The bipolar division of Europe was not what all of the major state actors wanted. As an equilibrium solution it could have been improved upon from the standpoint of almost any of the major players but only at the cost of destroying the equilibrium. In practice, therefore, the leading members of the two blocs—the United States and the Soviet Union—had the task of leading their respective alliances in courses of action that reinforced the status quo. Other desirable outcomes were seen as achievable only at the cost of war—very likely a nuclear holocaust.

Khrushchev's aggressive attempts to change the status quo in his favor, especially after acquiring thermonuclear weapons and an intercontinental ballistic missile capability in 1957, were steadfastly resisted by the United States. He personified the threat to the peace and stability of Europe that could result from decisions divorced from the tacit rules that had emerged in the aftermath of World War II. He dramatized the risks of truly autonomous decisionmaking. Especially after the Khrushchev interlude, Moscow and Washington came to believe strongly in the value of predictability and stability in Europe. Their rivalry was strong and frequently bitter, but the elements of restraint and cooperation in it offered political advantages for both sides. Recent assessments of the period suggest that Stalin saw his position in Central and Eastern Europe as adequate for security purposes.[14] The United States had no expansionist ambitions.

It seems fair to say that war was never seen by the major parties to the Cold War as an acceptable way of achieving national objectives in Europe. The major exception to nonuse of force, of course, was Soviet repression of uprisings or potential uprisings in Eastern Europe and Khrushchev's adventures in Berlin and Cuba. But the lesson learned from the Berlin and Cuba maneuvers was that such high risks should not be taken. As their behavior at the end of the Cold War demonstrated, Britain and France both supported the division of Germany, but they would never admit that.[15] The United States, the Soviet Union, and, of course, the Germans themselves preferred the logic of peace over the logic of war as a way of dealing with the German question. Many people in Europe had come to the conclusion that the arrangements established after World War II, while certainly unjust, nevertheless contributed to a stable order.[16]

Cooperation achieved under the threat of annihilation and under conditions of bipolar rivalry is difficult to accept as a system built around norms and rules. The elements of competition and the constant evocation of the nuclear threat naturally tended to conceal the restraint that was, in fact, practiced and expected. Kissinger's detente policy was consciously intended to give the Soviet Union a vested interest in the status quo on a global basis, but in Europe that condition already had been achieved by the late 1960s.[17] Restraint in military activities and restraint in political maneuvering had become the normal habit of both sides.

Challenge to the Cold War Order

In 1975, a document was signed in Helsinki by the leaders of thirty-five European and North American governments that had participated in the Conference on Security and Cooperation in Europe (CSCE, and since December 1994, the Organization on Security and Cooperation in Europe, or OSCE). It was called the Helsinki Final Act, and it enshrined ten principles designed to guide the behavior of states in Europe and North America. The Final Act also contained concrete and detailed provisions concerning the behavior of governments toward their own citizens, including freedom of movement of people, information, and ideas. In enacting these provisions and in conducting periodic meetings to review their implementation, the member-states of the CSCE ensured that actions *within* a state would be a legitimate and frequently discussed matter for comment and criticism by the international community.

The CSCE had an important role in creating and strengthening new norms for its participants. Even more important, it provided the beginnings of institutional structures and procedures for enhancing adherence to those norms. But by the time of the summit meeting in Helsinki when the Final Act was signed, the public attitude in the West toward formal and explicitly defined norms of behavior had become so skeptical, if not totally cynical, that the document was widely seen as nothing more than a gift to the Soviet Communist Party's general secretary, Leonid Brezhnev. The balance between the human rights provisions and the affirmation of the territorial status quo was seen, especially in the United States, as a false equation: the West was ceding Eastern Europe to the Soviet Union in return for promises Moscow would not keep. Ronald Reagan said, "I am against it, and I think all Americans should be against it."[18] Henry Kissinger had shown little enthusiasm for the CSCE while serving in the White House. Keeping U.S. troops in Europe with the help of an East-West negotiation on troop reductions was his main interest. His expectation was that the CSCE would be buried and forgotten as an irrelevancy amid the realities of balance-of-power politics. The allies were quite clear about his attitude.[19] But in the roughly fifteen years between the signing of the Helsinki Final Act and the collapse of Soviet power in Central and Eastern Europe, the

Final Act remained a living and operationally meaningful document for Eastern Europeans. The rise of the Cold War order can be traced to fear of nuclear weapons. Its fall can be credited to many factors, but one of the most important was the issue of human rights.

The Seeds of Change

The year 1969 was pivotal for East-West relations. Nixon took office in January, French president Pompidou in April, and German chancellor Brandt in October. The launching of Ostpolitik by Willy Brandt and the interest shown by Georges Pompidou in an East-West security conference were critical developments, without which the changes in the bipolar order would have been substantially delayed. Nixon's "era of negotiations," of course, seemed to give the American imprimatur to the resumption of a dialogue with Moscow that had been interrupted by Brezhnev's decision to crush the Prague Spring in August 1968.

Ostpolitik was the critical step in the process. Brandt saw his policies as ways to change the politics of Central and Eastern Europe, but he was counting on events in the long term to bear out his expectation that the change would open up those societies to Western influence. In the short term Bonn appeared to have given the Soviet Union and East Germany in a bilateral framework almost everything they could hope to get in an all-European security conference that Moscow had been advocating since the 1950s. The new element in the security conference, however, was that it might have the quality of a surrogate peace treaty ending World War II, and this was important to Brezhnev. Ostpolitik lifted restraints from the other European countries in their own dealings in the East. It prompted Europeans to act as though they had a hunting license to do what they could to advance their own interests in the East. This included, of course, taking a fresh look at the old Soviet idea of a European security conference.

The invasion of Czechoslovakia in August 1968 was a major moral defeat for Moscow. A peace offensive seemed to be a way to recover respectability, and so Moscow launched a renewed appeal for a European security conference with the Warsaw Pact's Budapest Appeal on March 17, 1969. An air of imminence and reality was given to this effort when in May 1969 Finland offered Helsinki as the site for such a conference. Between these two events, a NATO ministerial meeting in Washington in April heard the new American president, Richard Nixon, speak about negotiations with the East and decided to authorize a study of East-West negotiations. And on April 28, 1969, Charles de Gaulle resigned as president of France.

Pompidou's coming to power was another major factor in the gathering momentum behind the idea of a European security conference. De Gaulle had not been sympathetic to Soviet efforts to launch such a conference, apparently thinking that multilateral gatherings were the antithesis of state-to-state efforts to break down the division of Europe. Pompidou changed this policy and thereby gave his blessing to the idea of a European security conference. By July 1969, the French were passing the word to both East and West that they were prepared to consider a conference. Furthermore, Paris was interested in fostering contacts and exchanges between East and West, which it thought would have long-run political implications.[20]

Enter NATO

Consultations within the Atlantic Alliance were established on a permanent basis when the North Atlantic Council was created early in the life of the Alliance. Effectively used, the permanent representatives have the capacity to negotiate positions that bind each member of NATO. In the 1970s, NATO's internal negotiations played a very significant role in supporting the detente process. NATO consultations played a central role in defining the terms of the Helsinki Final Act and in rejecting the idea that the division of Europe should be legitimized through the process of detente.

In a political climate marked by a serious interest in Europe in East-West negotiations, the U.S. Department of State launched an effort to construct a NATO position for future negotiations. The idea at first was that the task of resolving specific negotiating issues would be assigned to a forum most appropriate for each subject. It was not assumed a priori that there would be a European security conference or that it would be the right forum for any of the issues under study. On April 21, 1969, the State Department's Bureau of European Affairs instructed the U.S. Mission to NATO to support a study of concrete issues for East-West negotiations by NATO's Senior Political Committee.[21] The spirit of the instructions matched closely what President Nixon had said to the North Atlantic Council in Washington on April 10, 1969:

> It is not enough to talk of European security in the abstract. We must know the elements of insecurity and how to remove them. Conferences are useful if they deal with concrete issues, which means they must, of course, be carefully prepared.[22]

The specifics of the U.S. approach were mentioned by the president in his *First Annual Report to the Congress on United States Foreign Policy for the 1970's* of February 18, 1970:

> The division of Europe gives rise to a number of interrelated issues— the division of Germany, access to Berlin, the level of military forces on both sides of the line, the barriers to economic and cultural relations, and other issues.[23]

Except as a part of cultural relations, the issue that became a central part of East-West relations in the 1970s—freer movement and human rights—was not what the Department of State was pursuing in its dialogue with NATO allies during 1969. Nor were these themes pressed by the White House or by the Europeans.

The North Atlantic Council tasked its Senior Political Committee to undertake the study of issues for possible negotiations with the East. The study was pursued during the summer and fall of 1969 and, in the usual manner, completed in good time for the December ministerial meeting. Human rights and freer movement of people, information, and ideas still were noticeable mainly for their absence at this point in alliance preparations for talks with the East. Freer movement ideas were mentioned in the context of intra-German discussions, and the expansion of tourism generally was cited as a matter ripe for early negotiation with the East. There was, in fact, real hesitation on the part of the allies about going beyond this and thereby arousing the suspicions of the Eastern European and Soviet governments about the effects of such contacts. The job of rebutting the Brezhnev doctrine, it was thought, could be handled by prohibitions on the use of force and codes of good conduct between states. Changing the way governments behave toward their own people was an idea that had not yet taken hold in NATO consultations.

French foreign minister Maurice Schumann visited Moscow in October 1969 and gave a further push to the idea of a European security conference. The French and the Soviets, interestingly, accepted jointly the principle that a European security conference should help put an end to the Europe of blocs. During the same month, another meeting of the Warsaw Pact foreign ministers held in Prague gave Moscow's blessings to Eastern European bilateral talks with Western governments on matters concerning an all-European conference. The notion that a European security conference would give more maneuver room to the Eastern European states became one of the Western European staple arguments in support of a conference.

U.S. Secretary of State William Rogers at this time, while critical of the Soviet proposal as it stood, was telling Europeans that the best way to handle a European security conference was to think of counterproposals. He thought there was some risk in being entirely critical of the idea.[24] Seeking to gain the high ground in the exchanges between East and West, Washington authorized its NATO Mission in Brussels to introduce a declaration on European security into the preparations for the December ministerial. This was done on November 25 and resulted in the issuance of a Declaration of the North Atlantic Council on December 5, 1969. Paragraph 11 of the declaration is as follows:

> Allied governments consider that not only economic and technical but also cultural exchanges between interested countries can bring mutual benefit and understanding. In these fields more could be achieved by freer movement of people, ideas, and information between the countries of East and West.

The last sentence of this paragraph provided the authorization for the U.S. Mission to NATO and the State Department from then on to urge a strong "freer movement" plank in the allied positions for multilateral East-West negotiations. While continuing to emphasize the idea of tailoring the means of negotiation to each individual subject, the declaration acknowledged the possibility of eventually holding a general conference. Criteria for judging the acceptability of a conference included

- progress on fundamental problems of European security in other forums;

- participation of North American members of the alliance;
- careful advance preparation and prospects of concrete results;
- assurance that a conference would not serve to ratify the division of Europe, but instead would represent an effort to tackle the problems that separated the nations.

These criteria, adopted by NATO at the end of 1969, were taken as serious guidance by Department of State officials during the next three years of preparation for what became the CSCE.[25]

A Different White House Judgment

In 1975, Henry Kissinger decisively and positively influenced the human rights outcome of CSCE by telling Gromyko that more Soviet concessions were necessary.[26] But during the runup to the East-West talks, the Nixon White House saw the CSCE essentially as a bargaining chip to secure Soviet concessions on European security issues like Berlin and troop levels. There were sharp differences of view in Washington on how much weight to give the CSCE. Much of the bargaining with Moscow was carried out secretly by Henry Kissinger, which had the inevitable effect, especially after the Moscow summit of May 1972, of creating two American policies toward the CSCE, one espoused by the White House staff, the other by the State Department, primarily officials of the Bureau of European Affairs. The situation was tolerated because the White House saw the negotiations at NATO headquarters as nothing more than diplomats playing in their sandbox. After May 1972, draining the CSCE of any prospects of concrete results became the White House approach, apparently in the hope that the political effect of a conference would be minimized. A strategy of neutering the conference might help to avoid ratifying the division of Europe, but it obviously could not help to overcome that division. Kissinger thought that overcoming the division of Europe could not be achieved through such a process in any event. This decision by Nixon and Kissinger in the end put them basically at odds with the NATO allies.

The White House approach as it developed during the Nixon period was not greatly at variance with Moscow's thinking about the conference. In the course of its renewed drive for a European security conference in the months after the Czechoslovak invasion, Moscow made it clear that a few simple declarations would suffice for its purposes. The Warsaw Pact foreign ministers meeting in Prague on October 30 and 31, 1969, identified two agenda items: nonuse of force and economic, technical, and scientific cooperation. While informing the State Department on November 19 that the United States could take part in an all-European conference if it wished, Soviet Ambassador Dobrynin also assured his listeners that "acute questions" would be outside the framework of an all-European conference.[27] Such a conference evidently would accomplish Soviet objectives as the State Department saw them at the time: recognition of the German Democratic Republic, acceptance of the status quo in Eastern Europe, and papering over the invasion of Czechoslovakia.[28] The Soviets were well aware from press reports that the North Atlantic Council was reviewing an extensive list of issues for negotiation with the East. Moscow's consistent response was that the work program for a European security conference should be kept simple. Furthermore, while some East Europeans talked about a series of conferences, the typical Soviet view was that one conference would suffice.

The State Department Attacks the Status Quo in Europe

By the spring of 1970, the Department of State had become worried that the NATO allies were drifting toward a European security conference without, in effect, waiting for the criteria of the December declaration to be met. On April 18, 1970, the department provided U.S. ambassador to NATO Robert Ellsworth with initial views on East-West issues to be addressed at the May ministerial meeting. The State Department believed that "strong and early U.S. substantive and procedural leadership" would be needed to offset the drift it perceived. Among the goals for the alliance should be that of breaking down obstacles against "freer movement of people, ideas, and information." The State Department saw value in "underlining Western desire to move toward gradual normalization of relations with Eastern Europe—in line with the president's February 18 statement—and also thereby undercutting Soviet efforts to solidify their political, economic, and ideological authority in Eastern Europe."[29] Here we find a clear expression of the aim of changing the status quo in Eastern Europe, using the issue of human rights as a means of challenging Soviet dominion over that area. At that time, the State Department was toying with the idea of a conference on cooperation in Europe, an idea that it thought might be an effective counter to the Soviets' European security conference. The idea never caught on but the substance of it was embedded in NATO studies of an agenda for a security conference.

The State Department's concerns about drifting into a conference without adequate preparation were well taken, considering the limited progress that had been made in defining what "freer movement" really meant after the bold declaration of that objective in December 1969. The substance of the NATO studies up to the May ministerial meeting of 1970 was still focused on countering the Brezhnev doctrine. The value of a conference was seen to be the maneuver room it would give Eastern European states and the reinforcing of principles of sovereignty and territorial integrity. The idea of a standing commission was attractive to some allies because of the relief it might offer Eastern European governments from total Soviet domination. The French had some ideas about "human contacts," but these were limited to vague concepts about political exchanges and tourism.

The spring NATO ministerial meeting on May 27 issued a declaration that strengthened the allies' posture on freer movement by giving it more status as a desirable goal quite apart from other forms of cooperation:

> 16.(b) the development of international relations with a view to contributing to the freer movement of people, ideas and information.

But there was no substance behind this noble thought and little in the way of strategic purpose except for American ideas about undercutting the status quo in Eastern Europe and French ideas about ending the Europe of blocs. Coming at the problem from quite different premises, the Americans and the French came to some remarkably similar conclusions about human rights.

The Soviets, of course, were not about to embrace freer movement in order to get a European security conference. Meeting at Budapest on June 21 and 22, the Warsaw Pact ministers issued another appeal for the convening of a conference but ignored freer movement. The Soviet response to this allied issue was cultural exchanges, a carefully controlled feature of relations between East and West that hardly corresponded to the more sweeping goal of freer movement of people, ideas, and information. The Budapest meeting showed, however, that freer movement was making some impression in Moscow.

Returning to the charge on October 29, the State Department told the U.S. Mission to NATO that

> substantially freer movement between East and West of people, ideas and information would tend to increase pressure for liberalization upon Warsaw Pact regimes and therefore dilute ideological rigidities . . . we believe that NATO allies should insist that this topic be among those explored for discussion in context of preparation for an eventual CES.[30]

This idea, in almost exactly those terms, found its way into the NATO studies that were moving toward completion for the December ministerial meeting. Thus an important change in allied thinking about the role of an East-West conference can be traced to the fall of 1970. The concept that a conference should uphold the principles of state sovereignty and noninterference in internal affairs had been central to the aim of negating the Brezhnev doctrine of limited sovereignty. This had been the only strategic aim of NATO as it considered a European security conference in 1969 and through most of 1970. It had been a limited aim, in that it sought only to inhibit Moscow's ability to coerce its own allies, using military force if necessary. The nature of the Eastern European regimes themselves had not been the primary consideration in this strategy, but it had to be in a strategy designed to break down walls in Europe.

Beginning in the fall of 1970 after repeated prodding from the State Department, the NATO allies began to consider how to go beyond state-to-state relations and into the domain of a state's relation to its own people. The follow-through was feeble at first, but a seed had been planted that led to the beginning of a profound change in European thinking about the possible uses of a security conference. It marked the beginning of the CSCE as it finally emerged in 1975. All of the subsequent reviews of compliance with human rights provisions of the Helsinki Final Act owe something to the shift in Western European thinking that began in late 1970. Even though the crusading zeal of the State Department disappeared as a major factor through much of the subsequent East-West negotiations that produced the Final Act, its work had been well done. The NATO allies continued to press for freer movement as a necessary part of the Final Act even in the face of stiff Soviet resistance and at times when American support was difficult to discern.

The first freer movement specifics stemmed from the late-1970 activities. They included

- ending restrictions on the rights of individuals to travel abroad;
- stopping the jamming of radio broadcasts;
- freer circulation of books, newspapers, and periodicals and improved conditions for foreign journalists; and
- free access to foreign diplomatic missions.

Family reunification and the abolition of closed zones in the USSR appeared later in the NATO consultations. The latter idea did not survive the negotiations, but the others, in one form or another, all became part of the Helsinki Final Act.

Defining the East-West Bargain

The NATO consultations in the fall of 1970 also foreshadowed the general character of the Helsinki Final Act as it emerged five years later. The allies discussed the possibility of a declaration that would define improved cooperation in several specific areas of human contacts. Other models considered were a more general declaration and a binding convention.

Again, on December 4, 1970, the NATO ministerial meeting addressed freer movement in its communiqué, this time picking up the State Department's theme that the topic was key to the development of international cooperation:

> Ministers reaffirmed that the freer movement of people, ideas and information is an essential element for the development of such [international] cooperation.

In the late winter and early spring of 1971 the six members of the European Community (EC) began their own consultations on the European security conference. This was the beginning of the political consultations within the EC that some members hoped—and still hope—would lead to a common EC foreign policy. The first meeting of the EC working group on the European security conference took place in Paris on March 1, 1971. The development was of prime importance for the later development of the CSCE. The solidarity, shaky at times, engendered by the effort to harmonize their policies on the security conference strengthened the ability of the EC members to pursue a vigorous human rights policy once the CSCE negotiations got under way in Helsinki and Geneva. Procedures for the conference, however, occupied most of their time in the early stages of their work.

At about the same time, the U.S. Mission to NATO began to move into a leadership position in shaping U.S. policies regarding the CSCE. The mission had shared many of the misgivings of the Nixon White House as the conference idea began to gain support during 1969–70. But in March 1971 Ambassador Robert Ellsworth cabled Washington to express his concern about widespread support for a hortatory conference largely devoid of substance. The U.S. government, he thought, should mount a study of the type that had supported arms control preparations and negotiations. Unless the United States provided the focus for discussion among the allies by submitting carefully drawn papers, he thought, the vacuum would not be filled by others.[31] The mission then proceeded to draft and cable to Washington a series of papers outlining the substance of proposed U.S. and allied positions on each major item for discussion in a conference on European security. The last of these papers was sent to Washington on March 26, 1971, and it dealt with freer movement of people, ideas, and information.[32]

The general objective of the study exercise would be to identify real and substantial measures that would be an inseparable part of any declaration of principles.[33] The specific objective of freer movement provisions would be to obtain Soviet and Eastern European acceptance of the fact that any durable order of peace and cooperation in Europe must include the normalization of human contacts and fundamental respect for the rights of individuals to enjoy freedom of movement and information. Concrete proposals should therefore be developed to give meaning to the propositions that

- everyone in Europe has the right to leave any country, including his own, and to return to his country
- each individual in Europe has the right to seek, receive and impart information and ideas through any media regardless of frontiers.[34]

During the spring of 1971 studies by NATO's Political Committee consolidated the progress that had been made in identifying a NATO position. Substantively, however, matters remained about where they were at the end of 1970 except for the additional impetus given to the topic by Ambassador Ellsworth's March initiatives. Nonetheless, the ministerial communiqué of June 4, 1971, strengthened the allied commitment to the freer movement topic by referring to the internal NATO studies:

> The report also reviewed in detail the essential elements on which agreement would be desirable in order to promote the freer movement of people, ideas and information so necessary to the development of international cooperation in all fields.

Later in the summer, the State Department identified the priority NATO objectives in the freer movement issue in a cable to the U.S. Mission to NATO:

- reduction of restrictions on the exit of Warsaw Pact nationals;
- cessation of radio jamming;
- freer circulation of books, newspapers, and periodicals;
- better working conditions for journalists.[35]

These initiatives were of special interest also to the U.S. Information Agency. On July 2, 1971, Director Frank Shakespeare wrote to the Department of State to urge a resolute NATO position on freer movement of the type defined in the report of the Political Committee. Under Secretary John Irwin replied on August 4 that he agreed that any conference on European security should indeed take a resolute position on freer movement of people, ideas, and information.[36]

By this time, NATO members were in broad agreement on the agenda for a conference. This agenda later became the basis for the three "baskets" of the Helsinki Final Act. As identified by the chairman of the Senior Political Committee, the main topics for further alliance study would be:

- principles governing relations between states;
- freer movement of people, ideas, and information and cultural relations;

- economic, scientific, and technical cooperation;
- environment.[37]

Differences with the Germans

During September, as NATO's Political Committee continued its work on freer movement, a breach developed between the U.S. and German positions. The U.S. Mission reported that the German representative in the Political Committee had introduced a paper on "freer movement" that argued for limiting the allies' proposals in this field to enhancing cultural relations. The U.S. Mission reported that this was a "specific rebuttal" of the U.S. approach.[38] The rebuttal was all the more pointed since the State Department earlier had instructed the American embassy in Bonn to argue the case for a strong freer movement position directly with the German Foreign Ministry. The case was put in terms of leverage the West might have on this issue because of strong Soviet interest in renunciation of force and respect for existing frontiers. The department argued that "if allies merely seek limited goal of expanding traditional cultural exchanges, they might forego opportunity for more significant improvements."[39] The Germans, and some other allies, were worried that the freer movement proposals sponsored by the State Department would be too much for the Soviets to accept. Prospects for a successful conference on European security would therefore be damaged. The Germans thought that such measures should come later in the détente process. This approach—postponing difficult subjects for a later stage—in the view of the State Department would be a serious tactical error.[40] The issue was not immediately resolved and, in fact, remained a sore point within the alliance for several months.

Questions from the White House

While the NATO consultations were proceeding with the drafting of position papers for use by allied negotiators, Henry Kissinger issued National Security Study Memorandum (NSSM) 138 on October 2, 1971. It asked for a discussion of differing concepts of a conference on

European security. The short deadline—November 1, 1971—did not allow much time for an in-depth study, even though the memorandum invited the Interdepartmental Group for Europe to consider matters not yet agreed within NATO.

The Bureau of European Affairs took the lead in drafting the study, and it sought to emphasize the potential importance of a conference on European security in achieving long-term U.S. objectives:[41]

> To the extent the influence of the Western community can be extended eastward, common Western purposes are served. . . . Within the longer perspective of an emerging trans-Atlantic order, involving not only Western but Eastern Europe, CES [conference on European security] assumes heightened potential relevance.

Caution, and even a touch of opportunism, were expressed regarding the prospects for freer movement. But the conclusion was clear that Soviet concessions might be obtainable:

> The Soviets would resist any concrete concessions in this area though there are tactical and propaganda advantages in keeping the issue in play and there might be some significant Soviet concessions if the Allies press firmly.

The interagency report described U.S. policy as "damage limiting" in its approach to the conference on European security. Even so, its authors thought that a compromise might result:

> the Soviets make some concrete concessions on freer movement and accept a declaration on principles that would apply regardless of political or social systems, while the allies agree to a formulation pledging "respect" for existing European frontiers.

The report discussed general concepts for the conference on European security, as requested by NSSM 138. It gave favorable notice to a new approach that would place more emphasis on permanent machinery to perpetuate and reinforce the U.S. presence in Europe. It tended to dismiss the concept of a "conference for the sake of detente." No discernible change in U.S. policy resulted from this study. To work for an outcome of the kind sketched out in the report remained the policy followed by the State Department and the U.S. Mission to NATO.

The Final Phase of Preparations for East-West Talks

The main issue at the December 1971 NATO ministerial meeting related to whether enough progress had been made in the Berlin Quadripartite Talks to permit the alliance to announce its readiness to begin multilateral talks in Helsinki. The secretary of state thought not, and the NATO ministerial communiqué was a compromise between this position and that of French foreign minister Schumann and others, who were ready to begin the Helsinki talks. Freer movement was not a major issue at that time. The agenda item was described as "freer movement, of people, information and ideas and cultural relations" in the NATO ministerial communiqué of December 10, 1971. The chief substantive disagreement concerned the paucity of security-related proposals in the report of the Senior Political Committee. In a series of meetings of the Permanent Representatives in the North Atlantic Council on November 23, 25, and 26, 1971, several allies said that the report was weighted much too heavily toward cooperation and that more work was needed on security.[42] From the meeting of November 23 onward, however, the conference was entitled the Conference on Security and Cooperation in Europe, the name by which it was known until December 1994.[43]

Historic events far transcending the U.S. and NATO efforts to define a satisfactory outcome of a CSCE provided the impulse necessary to enter the final phase of maneuvering toward Helsinki. Germany's Eastern Treaties and conclusion of the Quadripartite Agreement on Berlin marked the end of the first phase of Willy Brandt's Ostpolitik. The only remaining obstacle standing in the way of multilateral preparatory talks on the CSCE was Soviet refusal to enter into negotiations on mutual and balanced force reductions (MBFR). This was an obstacle for the Americans and a few of their allies, but the intensity of Kissinger's interest was not widely shared in NATO. The French wanted CSCE but not MBFR. London thought MBFR was more dangerous than CSCE. The Germans preferred MBFR as an included item within CSCE. Most of the smaller NATO allies were ready to go to Helsinki once the Berlin agreement was out of the way. Kissinger saw MBFR as necessary to maintaining the U.S. military presence in Europe and, therefore, far more consequential than CSCE. Furthermore, the feeling was widespread in Washington that serious negotiations on sensitive security matters could not be given over to a forum as large and unpredictable as CSCE.

Given this situation it was not surprising that Kissinger resorted to bilateral U.S.-Soviet diplomacy to solve the problem. At the Nixon-Brezhnev summit in Moscow in May 1972, the United States agreed to the convening of a CSCE. Nixon and Kissinger refused to commit the United States, however, to any particular date for beginning the CSCE talks until the issue of beginning MBFR negotiations was settled. The Soviets, who thought of CSCE as a very short and essentially declaratory event, wanted to proceed to the CSCE before committing themselves to MBFR. This issue was not resolved until the fall of 1972. NATO's ministerial meeting of May 30 and 31 was able to agree without difficulty, however, to enter into the CSCE multilateral preparatory talks in Helsinki by omitting a date for beginning those talks. The ministers concerned with MBFR (France was not represented, Paris having opted out of the military institutions of NATO) proposed that "multilateral explorations on mutual and balanced force reductions be undertaken as soon as practicable, either before or in parallel with multilateral preparatory talks on a Conference on Security and Cooperation in Europe."

So matters stood until Kissinger visited Moscow in September 1972 and returned with a compromise that CSCE would formally begin in June 1973 and MBFR in September or October 1973. Although many —probably most—of the allies took umbrage at the method by which Kissinger had worked out this solution and some worried that they would be under pressure to finish CSCE before MBFR began, the deal was approved by NATO and final preparations for the CSCE began. Summing up the three years of discussions on freer movement, in November 1972 the Bureau of European Affairs was able to report the following, with evident satisfaction:

> The U.S. has taken the lead, during NATO consultations on CSCE issues to develop the freer movement topic as a major Allied proposal. . . . In the West . . . the general belief is that European security will be enhanced by the gradual bridging of the divisions of Europe. Moreover, the West cannot accept the "legitimacy" of the political status quo in Eastern Europe. The freer movement proposal thus reasserts the Western interest in constructive, peaceful and liberalizing change, in

contradistinction to Soviet emphasis on legitimizing the status quo at the level of state-to-state relations.[44]

The Europeans Pick Up the Torch

When the multilateral preparatory talks began in Helsinki on November 22, 1972, the high-profile American posture on freer movement abruptly switched to a behind-the-scenes role. The U.S. delegation understood from Washington that it was to adopt a positive and non-polemical attitude toward the work of the preparatory meeting and also toward the Soviet delegation. But George Vest, the senior American representative in the talks, also believed strongly in Atlantic solidarity, and he hoped to work within the framework of NATO positions as they developed at Helsinki. This was also the understanding in the State Department, which gave the delegation much latitude and much responsibility. John Maresca has commented on this in his classic book on the CSCE, *To Helsinki:*

> While there was a vivid desire in the delegation and at the working level of the State Department to support the Western side, the officials concerned were afraid that if they attempted to put instructions in writing, Kissinger would not agree to a strong U.S. position.[45]

When the chief Soviet representative at Helsinki, Ambassador Lev Mendelevich, observed what was happening, he complained to Vest about the American attitude. The Soviets, he said, had a clear understanding with the United States that the CSCE would without question take place in June 1973. The debate over terms of reference was casting doubt on this. Mendelevich asked that the United States pass word through official channels in Moscow or Washington that it remained committed to the CSCE in June.[46] On December 20, Secretary Rogers wrote to President Nixon that he had instructed the U.S. delegation to avoid polemical exchanges at Helsinki. He also guilelessly told the president that the U.S. delegation had succeeded in "sidestepping several Soviet suggestions for stage-managing the proceedings through private understandings with us."[47]

On June 8, 1973, the participants in the Helsinki talks gave their collective agreement to the Final Recommendations of the Helsinki

Consultations. A committee on questions relating to security in Europe was charged with the drafting of a declaration of principles, including "respect for human rights and fundamental freedoms, including the freedom of thought, conscience, religion or belief." A committee on co-operation in humanitarian and other fields was established with several responsibilities for human contacts, information, and culture. Among them was the duty of preparing "proposals to facilitate freer movement and contacts individually or collectively, privately or officially, among persons, institutions and organizations of the participating States." And another was to "prepare proposals to facilitate the freer and wider dissemination of information of all kinds."[48]

A long and difficult negotiation lay between that agreement and the signing of the Helsinki Final Act on August 1, 1975. Even more distant in time and in the cause-and-effect sense are the tenuous beginnings of NATO's consultations on East-West negotiations in 1969 and the revolutions of 1989 in Eastern Europe and of 1991 in Russia. But there was a connection. The inability of the communist system to deliver adequate levels of goods, services, and technology under conditions as they emerged in the late twentieth century had become quite clear by the 1970s. Gorbachev's failed efforts in the 1980s to reform the Soviet system were aimed at correcting this basic defect, not only in the interests of the Soviet peoples, but also in the interest of strengthening the ability of the Soviet state to compete with the West. Contributing to this systemic failure was the communications revolution and the resulting inability of communist governments to control access to information. Diplomacy and public activities legitimized by the Helsinki Final Act added to the instabilities that already were undermining the structures created during the Cold War. The Helsinki Final Act resonated in Eastern Europe until this dimension could no longer be repressed or ignored.

The revolutions of the late 1980s would eventually have occurred anyway, given the systemic failures that generated them, but diplomacy and, more important, active resistance by citizen groups in Eastern Europe accelerated the developments that led to the revolutions.[49] And once again, a powerful concept motivating U.S. foreign policy had become an agent for change and for imprinting an order on the international system. The remarkable feature of this particular episode is that an alliance organized by the Americans to prevent the Soviets from dominating Western Europe provided the essential mechanism for concerting Western policies in an enterprise that helped to end the bipolar order. And equally remarkable is the fact that the West, so divided on so many things, found unity at last in insisting on tough human rights provisions in the Helsinki Final Act. In the end, it was this consensus on values, even more than top-level leadership, that produced this charter for human rights.[50]

3

Testing the Utility of Nuclear Restraints after the Cold War

*The Bases for Ukraine's Adherence
to the Nonproliferation Treaty*

The end of the Cold War brought new strategic circumstances.[1] By 1992 the bipolar global order no longer existed, signs of a turn to quasi isolationism in the United States had appeared, and the independence of Ukraine had become a key element in calculations about European security. Nearly all of the seven rules cited in the last chapter had become irrelevant as Germany had reunited and the military confrontation in Europe disappeared.

Would the nuclear restraint regime created during the Cold War endure, or had its utility, too, come to an end? A test case began to press for the attention of Washington's senior decisionmakers in 1991. The order imprinted on the international system by the United States and other nations during the Cold War included a set of understandings aimed at limiting the number of nuclear weapons states. The strategic judgment underlying the 1970 nuclear nonproliferation treaty (the NPT, or, to give it its full name, the Treaty on the Nonproliferation of Nuclear Weapons) was that *any* increase in the number of nuclear weapons states would threaten international peace and security.

Inherent in the disintegration of the USSR was a fundamental threat to the Cold War's nuclear restraint regime. The crisis posed three potential dangers: (1) loss of state control over the possession and use of nuclear weapons and fissile material; (2) an increase in the number of declared nuclear weapons states; and (3) rising tensions between

Ukraine and Russia, caused in part by disputes over possession of nuclear weapons. With more than 30,000 warheads, the Soviet Union had deployed short-range (tactical) weapons in most of its fifteen republics. Four of the republics that became the independent states of Belarus, Kazakstan, Russia, and Ukraine had long-range (strategic) weapons. How should the United States respond to this new challenge to international peace and security?

The Bush administration was the first U.S. administration to face the Soviet nuclear succession crisis, and it did so by revalidating the Cold War's nuclear nonproliferation regime in the strongest possible terms. In this and in his handling of German reunification, Bush began the process of defining the post–Cold War order in Europe. He retained old rules in the nuclear area and established new ones in the political field. But even in the political field, Bush's judgments were influenced by a well-understood way of doing things through NATO.[2] In the case of the nuclear restraint regime, Bush conducted an effective diplomatic campaign to uphold that regime, using a mix of coercion and incentives to deal with the situation that developed as the Soviet Union collapsed. A second phase of the nuclear succession crisis began to unfold, however, even while actions were under way to deal with the first signs of trouble. The second phase was clearly discernible by the summer of 1992, and was focused mainly on Ukraine, potentially the world's third-largest nuclear weapons state, with over 1,900 strategic nuclear warheads. The crisis reached its peak intensity during 1993.

The dispute, in the context of other differences between Ukraine and Russia, was generating a high level of tension between Kiev and Moscow. Ukrainian politicians spoke of the status accorded nuclear weapons states in the international community and of the potential threat posed by Russia. But from Moscow's perspective, Ukraine did not own the nuclear warheads and was making unreasonable demands on Russia, the true owner of the weapons.

Ukrainian fears of a confrontation with Russia were heightened by the spectacle of President Yeltsin's struggle with the Russian Congress of People's Deputies, where claims to the territory of Ukraine were publicly voiced. At the same time, the president of Ukraine, Leonid Kravchuk, was losing his authority over the Ukrainian parliament. His ability to fulfill promises made to the United States and Russia was increasingly cast in doubt as his own power ebbed and the situation in Russia looked more ominous.

After a short period in which the United States deferred to Russian assurances that Russia and Ukraine could work out the nuclear problems, the Clinton administration recognized the validity of Ukrainian desires for a more active U.S. role. From its self-described role as catalyst, Washington moved from mediator to active participant in the negotiations. This shift to fully engaged U.S. diplomacy was essential to resolving the nuclear succession crisis. It was an example of U.S. diplomacy imprinting an order on an international system in flux. In the fall of 1993 a very active period of diplomacy began that included the highest levels in all three of the governments concerned, using channels that sometimes included all three nations simultaneously, at other times only two of them. The results were of truly historic significance: on February 3, 1994, the Ukrainian parliament gave its approval to ratification of the START I treaty and its protocol. In Budapest, on December 5, 1994, the United States, Russia, Belarus, Kazakstan, and Ukraine completed the last step in the ratification of START I, and on the same day Ukraine acceded to the nuclear nonproliferation treaty. On June 1, 1996, pursuant to these agreements, the last nuclear warhead crossed the Ukrainian border for dismantling in Russia.

Neorealist theory predicts that a new nation like Ukraine would insist on being a nuclear power if it had the capacity to become one. Ukraine did not make its choice this way, despite a strong presumption that if it chose to keep the nuclear weapons within its borders it could have done so. There were two major ingredients in the recipe for success: first, active and persistent U.S. diplomacy; second, an order already imprinted on the international system, one of whose aims was preventing an increase in the numbers of nuclear weapons states. This order and the rules that went with it defined for the principal actors, including Ukraine, a general course of action.[3] With the help afforded by these rules, order-building diplomacy, using a combination of steady pressure and incentives, was skillfully conducted by the Bush and Clinton administrations. The success of this diplomacy meant that the nuclear restraints developed during the Cold War had survived the passage to a different era.

Challenge to Nuclear Restraints

The rise of Mikhail Gorbachev to leadership of the Communist Party of the Soviet Union made possible a series of dramatic negotiations on nuclear arms reduction with Presidents Ronald Reagan and George Bush. Gorbachev's recognition of the need for a fundamental change in Moscow's relations with the United States and Reagan's determination to achieve deep reductions in nuclear weapons created an opening for serious negotiations. A first dramatic success came with the exchange on June 1, 1988, by Reagan and Gorbachev of ratification instruments bringing into force the Treaty on the Elimination of Intermediate Range and Shorter-Range Missiles (INF). The United States and the Soviet Union agreed to eliminate intermediate-range nuclear weapons, principally U.S. Pershing II ballistic missiles and ground-launched cruise missiles and Soviet SS-20 ballistic missiles.

The next step was the START I treaty, signed by Bush and Gorbachev on July 31, 1991, which limited the United States and the Soviet Union to 6,000 accountable strategic nuclear warheads and 1,600 nuclear delivery vehicles on each side. After that came a framework agreement for a second strategic arms reduction treaty (START II), approved by President Bush and President Boris Yeltsin of the Russian Federation on June 17, 1992. Bush and Yeltsin signed the START II treaty on January 3, 1993. This agreement was intended to reduce the number of warheads to 3,000–3,500 on each side and correct the failure of the earlier Nixon and Brezhnev negotiations to ban land-based MIRVed missiles in the SALT I agreement of 1972. Thus, the greatest disarmament program in the history of the world began during Reagan's second term and Bush's single term, measured in terms of destructive potential removed from deployment. It was made possible by the end of the Cold War and the new relationship between the United States and the Soviet Union, and later the Russian Federation, inaugurated by Gorbachev and carried forward by Yeltsin.

But, ironically, the very changes that made possible these remarkable agreements presented a fundamental challenge to the nuclear restraints that had been constructed over more than four decades.[4] The collapse of the Soviet Union in 1991 had three immediate consequences: first, fifteen newly independent states emerged, in many of which nuclear weapons had been deployed; second, a once highly structured society with a well-defined sense of identity and values began a disorderly and economically difficult transition to an unknown future; and third, relations between Russia and the other newly independent states became at best unsettled and at worst antagonistic. These developments threatened to undermine the rules of nuclear restraint. "Yugoslavia with nukes" was the image Secretary of State James Baker used to describe the nightmare that could result from a loss of central authority and control over these nuclear weapons.

The possession of nuclear weapons by additional states would automatically weaken the nuclear nonproliferation treaty, not only by increasing the number of countries in the category of nuclear weapons states, but also by placing pressure on neighboring countries to acquire nuclear weapons. Newly independent states bordering on a nuclear weapons state with imperialistic traditions were bound to consider—and they did—how nuclear weapons might help them in their struggle to remain free and independent. The transition from authoritarianism to nascent democracy was accompanied by outbreaks of violence, considerable disruption in the machinery of government, and a breakdown in social discipline with consequent rise in criminal activities. The situation seemed likely to present opportunities for theft and smuggling of nuclear materials. The lack of suitable employment for scientists and technicians skilled in Soviet nuclear weapons research and development presented a "brain drain" problem with ominous implications. All of these factors added up to a potential nuclear proliferation catastrophe. Leakage of nuclear weapons or materials from government control to criminal or terrorist organizations, rogue military units, or purchasing agents representing other governments became a real possibility. This problem was seen in the United States by people in and out of government as a major potential threat to the security and stability of all nations, including those emerging from the collapse of the Soviet Union.[5]

As Ukraine and other republics of the Soviet Union moved toward independence, the Bush administration realized that START I and, perhaps, the nuclear nonproliferation treaty as well might become unintended victims of the collapse of the Soviet state. The dominant factor in the equation, for the Bush administration and later the Clinton administration, and for the U.S. Congress, was that if Ukraine failed to ratify START I, the treaty would be dead. Russia's Congress of People's Deputies resolved in November 1992 that START I should be ratified but that the instruments of ratification should not be exchanged until Ukraine had acceded to the nonproliferation treaty. The situation that seemed to be shaping up, as the Bush administration saw it, would challenge the nonproliferation restraints at a particularly inopportune time, with the treaty's global review conference scheduled for 1995. Nor did they believe that Ukraine's possession of nuclear weapons was either necessary or even useful to its security interests.[6]

Testing the Utility of the Rules of Restraint

As it became increasingly apparent that the Soviet Union was in the process of disintegration, the National Security Council's interagency committees took under consideration the problem of control of nuclear weapons in the Soviet Union. Secretary of State Baker, aided by Under Secretary Reginald Bartholomew, took a leading role in shaping policy and conducting preventive diplomacy from 1991 through the end of the Bush administration. A remarkable feature of this period is that U.S. government officials never seriously considered any alternative to a nonproliferation policy, a vivid foreign policy example of Herbert Simon's theory about how decisionmakers "satisfice" (see note 3) as they look for acceptable courses of action. The U.S. government was prepared to support a transition from a Soviet to a Commonwealth of Independent States (CIS) nuclear force if such a force were centrally controlled, as Moscow had proclaimed. This would have meant little practical change since the Russian military would still have controlled the force, perhaps with a veto of uncertain value exercised by other members of the CIS.

The Bush administration reacted promptly to indications that mounting disorder within the Soviet Union might jeopardize centralized control of nuclear weapons in that country and create additional nuclear weapons states. Several preventive steps were taken in rapid succession. The first was announced by President Bush on September 27, 1991, little more than a month after the attempted coup against Gorbachev, which, although a failure, precipitated the breakup of the Soviet Union. The initial Bush strategy was summarized as follows:

The United States would withdraw all its nuclear artillery shells and all nuclear warheads for short-range ballistic missiles to the United States. These and any similar warheads currently stored in the United States would be dismantled and destroyed. All tactical nuclear weapons, including nuclear-armed cruise missiles, would be withdrawn from U.S. surface ships and attack submarines. Nuclear weapons associated with land-based naval aircraft also would be removed. Many of these weapons would be dismantled and destroyed and the remainder placed in secure central storage areas. All strategic bombers would be removed from day-to-day alert status and their weapons returned to storage areas. All ICBMs scheduled for deactivation under START I would be taken off alert status. The single warhead ICBM would be the sole remaining U.S. ICBM modernization program; certain other nuclear weapons programs would be terminated. President Bush called on the Soviet Union to take comparable, although not identical measures.[7]

On October 5, 1991, Gorbachev announced that the Soviet Union would take reciprocal actions. The most important were the following:

All nuclear artillery ammunition and nuclear warheads for tactical missiles would be destroyed. Nuclear warheads of anti-aircraft missiles would be removed from the army and stored in central bases; part of them would be destroyed. All nuclear mines would be eliminated. All tactical nuclear weapons would be removed from surface ships and multipurpose submarines. These weapons, as well as weapons from ground-based naval aviation would be stored, with part being destroyed.[8]

The Bush initiative provided political cover to Gorbachev and then to Yeltsin for withdrawing Soviet tactical nuclear weapons from republics that were suddenly no longer securely a part of the Soviet Union and in some of which ethnic conflict already had broken out. One of the best examples of foresighted decisionmaking in recent years, it was key to saving the rules of nuclear restraint.

Another act of historic importance was taken by the U.S. Senate during the same period. Legislation sponsored by Senator Sam Nunn (D-Ga.) and Senator Richard Lugar (R-Ind.) in 1991 provided for $400 million to be reprogrammed within the Department of Defense fiscal year (FY) 1992 budget and another $400 million from the FY 1993 budget to provide assistance to Russia, Ukraine, Belarus, and Kazakstan to expedite dismantling of nuclear weapons systems called for under START I and to strengthen nonproliferation programs.[9] The

Nunn-Lugar program gave the Bush and Clinton administrations a powerful new economic tool to strengthen nuclear restraints. The support this unusual legislation commanded was solid proof of the consensus that the rules of nonproliferation enjoyed.

The Bush-Gorbachev decision did not affect the long-range, strategic nuclear weapons that were still deployed in large numbers outside Russia, over 1,900 in Ukraine alone. On December 8, 1991, the chiefs of state of Belarus, Ukraine, and Russia issued a declaration that created the CIS and placed military affairs under joint command of these three states. Kazakstan joined the CIS a short time later. Responding to these developments, on December 12, 1991, Secretary of State James Baker gave a crystal-clear statement of the Bush administration's views in an address at Princeton University:

> We do not want to see new nuclear weapons states emerge as a result of the transformation of the Soviet Union. Of course, we want to see the START treaty ratified and implemented. But we also want to see Soviet nuclear weapons remain under safe, responsible, and reliable control with a single unified authority. The precise nature of that authority is for Russia, Ukraine, Kazakstan, Belarus, and any common entity to determine. A single authority could, of course, be based on collective decision-making on the use of nuclear weapons. We are, however, opposed to the proliferation of any additional independent command authority or control over nuclear weapons.
>
> For those republics who seek complete independence, we expect them to adhere to the non-proliferation treaty as non-nuclear weapons states, to agree to full-scope IAEA [International Atomic Energy Agency] safeguards, and to implement effective export controls on nuclear materials and related technologies. As long as any such independent states retain nuclear weapons on their territory, those states should take part in unified command arrangements that exclude the possibility of independent control. In this connection, we strongly welcome Ukraine's determination to become nuclear-free by eliminating all nuclear weapons from its soil and its commitment, pending such elimination, to remain part of a single, unified command authority.[10]

A few days later, on December 17, 1991, President Gorbachev announced that the Soviet Union would cease to exist as a unified state by the end of the year; he resigned on December 25. On December 18, 1991, Russia, Ukraine, Belarus, and Kazakstan declared that they would abide by the provisions of the START I treaty. On December 30, 1991,

CIS members signed an agreement specifying that joint command of strategic forces would be implemented under the unified control of the CIS commander, a Russian, and of the Russian president in agreement with the heads of state of the CIS nuclear states. The Ukrainian government, however, refused to acquiesce in Moscow's demand that the Russian CIS commander have administrative as well as operational control over strategic offensive arms that were deployed in Ukraine.

Washington's first reaction to these developments was that Moscow should take the responsibility for working out the relationship of Belarus, Kazakstan, and Ukraine to the provisions of the START I treaty. The four governments quickly showed that this would not be easy to do. Russia viewed itself as the only successor state to the Soviet Union in terms of being a possessor of nuclear weapons and therefore entitled to a privileged position in arms control negotiations. Ukraine disagreed. On February 20, 1992, President Kravchuk declared that Ukraine must be an equal partner with Russia in these negotiations. The Bush administration decided that U.S. bilateral negotiations directly with the newly independent republics would be necessary.

Another big decision was made by the Bush administration late in 1992: an offer to purchase 500 metric tons of highly enriched uranium (HEU) derived from dismantled Soviet warheads. The United States was to guarantee that the material would be used only as fuel for civilian nuclear reactors, and Russia was required to agree with Belarus, Kazakstan, and Ukraine on an equitable sharing of the proceeds ($11–$12 billion). The amount due each country would depend on the amount of uranium extracted from warheads deployed in each of the three republics and the expense borne by Russia in preparing the HEU for civilian use. On-site inspection measures were to be put in place in Russia to ensure that the uranium came from dismantled warheads. Initially, U.S. officials presumed that blending HEU down to low-enriched levels for use in fuel rods would take place in the United States, but the Russian government preferred that this process be carried out in Russia and this was accepted by the United States.

New conditions had brought forth new thinking. This innovative offer had no parallels during the Cold War. The plan had several advantages. It would not cost the U.S. government anything; money spent on the HEU would be recouped from sales of the blended-down fuel through the commercial nuclear fuel market. It provided an incentive to the new republics to return warheads to Russia since they would not be paid until they did. It provided badly needed economic assistance to each of the states participating in the program. Since the HEU would no longer be available for refabrication into weapons, the deal would make the dismantling of warheads irreversible and, to some extent, transparent. The HEU decision was one of the key elements in the effort to save and strengthen nuclear restraints. The Clinton administration ultimately relied heavily on the HEU offer to broker the agreement that led to Ukrainian acceptance of the START I treaty and the nuclear nonproliferation treaty.[11]

A Temporary Resolution

As a result of the Bush-Gorbachev initiatives, all Soviet short-range nuclear weapons systems had been relocated to sites within the Russian Federation by June 1992, leaving only long-range strategic nuclear systems with associated warheads still deployed in the territories of Belarus, Kazakstan, and Ukraine. The United States kept in touch with all four states on the question of strategic systems through several channels that included both Secretary of State Baker and Secretary of Defense Richard Cheney. The issue became urgent in the spring of 1992. The United States and Russia had made some headway toward a framework for negotiating START II, and the Bush administration wanted to complete START I. Moreover, START I was showing some signs of unraveling. Ukraine had briefly halted the shipment of tactical nuclear warheads to Russia. Although the transfer of these warheads was completed in May 1992, strategic warheads still remained. Furthermore, Kazakstani president Nursultan Nazarbayev said on May 5 that he wanted security guarantees from China, Russia, and the United States before fully giving up nuclear weapons. And, of course, 1992 was an election year in the United States, with one major international event being a Yeltsin visit to Washington planned for the summer.

The negotiations on START I obligations and the successor state question were successfully concluded in Lisbon, Portugal, on May 23, 1992, when a protocol to the START I treaty was signed. The Lisbon Protocol, signed by the foreign ministers of Belarus, Kazakstan, Ukraine,

Russia, and the United States, committed the first four of these countries to assume the obligations of the former USSR under the START treaty. They therefore became successor states for the purposes of the START I treaty. But in the case of Belarus, Kazakstan, and Ukraine, an obligation to adhere to the nuclear nonproliferation treaty as nonnuclear weapons states in the shortest possible time, as stated in Article V, meant that they would not be successors to the Soviet Union as nuclear weapons states. Article V was later challenged by the Ukrainian parliament. Each of the chiefs of state of these three countries also appended letters to President Bush. President Kravchuk wrote: "Ukraine shall guarantee the elimination of all nuclear weapons, including strategic offensive arms, located in its territory in accordance with the relevant agreements and during the seven-year period as provided by the START treaty."[12]

Although the contract and details pertaining to the HEU purchase were not completed for many months, the deal was immediately of great interest to Russia's Ministry of Atomic Energy (MINATOM). Naturally, this interest was shared by Belarus, Kazakstan, and Ukraine in view of the financial incentives offered. Russian-Ukrainian negotiations on sharing proceeds began late in 1992 and almost immediately ran into problems concerning the timing of compensating Ukraine. In addition, political pressure from the Ukrainian parliament required the Kravchuk government to ask for compensation for the tactical nuclear warheads that already had been shipped to Russia.

Three key decisions taken by the Bush administration were not only timely but also absolutely indispensable to subsequent diplomatic moves. First, the tactical nuclear initiative resulted in the removal to the relative safety of Russia of tens of thousands of nuclear warheads that might otherwise have been in harm's way. Because of this, the state-level proliferation problem was limited to three new republics instead of several. Second, the Lisbon Protocol committed Belarus, Kazakstan, and Ukraine to becoming nonnuclear weapons states and provided the legal basis for subsequent negotiations related to the denuclearization process. Third, purchasing 500 metric tons of HEU provided significant leverage for the United States, besides offering substantial economic relief to the four new independent states.

To sum up the situation at the end of the Bush administration, President Kravchuk had made quite clear to American officials what Ukraine would need politically and financially to proceed with the transfer of nuclear warheads to Russia and to complete the elimination of strategic offensive arms in Ukraine. There were three conditions: security assurances from at least Russia and the United States; compensation for the nuclear materials contained in the warheads transferred to Russia, including the tactical nuclear warheads already transferred to Russia in the spring of 1992; and tangible economic and technical support to offset the cost of eliminating strategic offensive delivery systems on Ukrainian soil.

The Bush administration had responses on the negotiating table to each Ukrainian condition by January 1993 when the Clinton administration took over. U.S. suggestions for security assurances were offered to Ukraine in January 1993 and discussed even earlier than that. Senators Nunn and Lugar, during a visit to Kiev in November 1992, had told President Kravchuk that between $100 and $150 million could be made available to Ukraine from the Nunn-Lugar program for dismantling nuclear delivery systems. President Bush wrote to President Kravchuk on December 5, 1992, promising up to $175 million for assistance to Ukraine from Nunn-Lugar funds. And the HEU deal was already under negotiation between Ukrainian and Russian officials by that time.

These three conditions were the same three that were at the heart of the U.S.-Russian-Ukrainian trilateral accord later concluded by Presidents Clinton, Yeltsin, and Kravchuk in Moscow on January 14, 1994. But second thoughts in Ukraine and political upheavals in Moscow and Kiev almost torpedoed the effort to save the rules of nuclear restraint.

The Backlash

President Kravchuk had dominated the Ukrainian political scene from the days when he led Ukraine to independence in December 1991, but his authority began to be challenged by the parliament in the summer of 1992. Kravchuk's decision to sign the Lisbon Protocol and to transfer over 2,000 tactical nuclear warheads to Russia without compensation in May 1992 was the last time that he could take such important actions without much hindrance from the parliament.

By the end of 1992, Kravchuk was insisting on the three conditions that would have to be met if Ukraine was to proceed with its obligations to surrender nuclear weapons on its territory. The Ukrainian parliament also declared that Ukraine was the owner of all nuclear weapons on its soil and a successor to the Soviet Union in this respect. This prompted rage in Moscow and heated exchanges between officials of the two governments. The Russian government declared that the Ukrainian position was completely unacceptable, and the Congress of People's Deputies resolved that the START I treaty could not come into effect until Ukraine had ratified it, including its protocol, and had acceded to the nuclear nonproliferation treaty.

Kravchuk continued to speak publicly of "an unchanging commitment to becoming the first nation in history to destroy voluntarily all its nuclear weapons and become a non-nuclear state," but this view did not go unchallenged in Ukraine. Although it was a small minority, a faction in parliament had come to favor retaining some nuclear weapons, focusing particularly on the modern, made-in-Ukraine SS-24 ICBMs. One of the most influential spokesmen for this view was General Volodymyr Tolubko, a respected deputy in the parliament, a former division commander in the Soviet Strategic Rocket Forces (SRF), and nephew of a former SRF senior commander. For him, security alone justified Ukraine's retention of modern nuclear forces. Deputy Yuri Kostenko, later minister of the environment, also stressed Ukraine's security and the possible role of nuclear weapons. Other deputies believed that Kravchuk had erred in letting the tactical nuclear warheads be transferred to Russia without compensation. They argued that this must not be repeated in the case of the more than 1,900 strategic warheads located in Ukraine. Later, in April 1993, 162 deputies signed a letter to this effect.

These attitudes were gaining strength partly in response to a growing worry about developments in Russia. As seen from Kiev, President Yeltsin's struggles with the Congress of People's Deputies displayed a Russian political scene increasingly more nationalistic and hard-line, with a weakened Yeltsin fighting a desperate rear-guard action against neo-Sovietism. Difficulties had arisen over use of the port of Sevastopol by the Russian navy and over division of the Black Sea fleet between Russia and Ukraine. In December 1992, the Russian Congress resolved to reexamine the status of Sevastopol. Russian vice president Alexander Rutskoy angered Ukrainians by extravagant pronouncements about Russia's rights in Crimea and with respect to the Black Sea fleet. The Russian Congress also insisted that the U.S.-Russian umbrella agreement for Nunn-Lugar assistance, signed by Bush and Yeltsin in June 1992, should be subject to its approval; the deputies' skepticism about American intentions called into question the whole basis for Nunn-Lugar cooperation.[13] This reflected conservative and nationalist suspicions that the Americans were gaining unfair advantages, including access to state secrets, through cooperation in the nuclear field.

Ukrainian hopes that independence would automatically bring economic support and security assurances from the West also had not been met by the summer of 1992. This, too, caused a feeling of disillusionment and some despair in a society where economic distress was serious and strikes were being called in protest. Nor were the political rumblings heard only in Ukraine. Kazakstani officials also were having second thoughts. Hearing the speeches being made by politicians in Kiev and Moscow, they reconsidered their own readiness to renounce nuclear weapons. Only in Belarus, where 70 percent of the fallout from Chernobyl had been deposited, and where nationalist feelings were not strong, the Lisbon Protocol and the nonproliferation treaty continued to enjoy strong support.

The policy of the Bush administration in its last weeks in office was to insist that agreements had been signed, and the United States expected they would be carried out. The Congress strongly supported this policy. Nunn-Lugar legislation, in fact, required that the administration certify that recipients of assistance were committed to compliance with arms control agreements into which they had entered. A strategy to ensure that this would happen would have to be developed by the incoming Clinton administration.

Clinton Policy: Reaffirmation and a Midcourse Correction

The starting point for the Clinton administration's review of policy toward Ukraine was the Lisbon Protocol, which required that Ukraine, Belarus, and Kazakstan eliminate all the nuclear weapons located on their territories. Clinton had campaigned on a strong nuclear nonproliferation platform, and he understood that START I would not be ratified if Ukraine retained nuclear arms. Congressional leaders like Senators Nunn and Lugar were insistent that Ukraine live up to its Lisbon Protocol obligations. In March 1993, therefore, President Clinton decided to maintain the policy of denuclearization that he had inherited from George Bush, and he issued instructions to that effect. Very little help would be given to Ukraine until it had fulfilled its promises to ratify START I, including the Lisbon Protocol, and had acceded to the nuclear nonproliferation treaty. For an administration that regarded nonproliferation as one of its highest foreign policy priorities, this was an almost automatic outcome. As was the case with the Bush administration, at no time was there any consideration given to the view that Ukraine should become a nuclear weapons state. Ukraine's basic security problems were seen as economic and social, not matters that could be cured by acquiring a nuclear deterrent.

It quickly became apparent that the Clinton administration's hard line toward Ukraine was not working. The perceived lack of support from the United States caused a political climate in Ukraine in which a U.S.-Russian agreement on the details of the HEU purchase in February 1993 was seen as a form of betrayal. Ukrainian officials felt that the United States was making deals with Russia that significantly affected Ukrainian interests without adequately consulting them, even though it had been made quite clear that the contract would not be signed by the United States until a revenue-sharing formula had been worked out. Similarly, the Clinton-Yeltsin summit meeting in Vancouver on April 3 and 4, 1993, was seen in Kiev as a U.S. tilt toward Moscow that rankled in an already touchy environment. Particularly noticeable in Kiev was a sentence in the Vancouver Declaration that said "the Presidents stressed their expectation that all countries of the former USSR which are not already NPT members will promptly confirm their adherence to the treaty as non-nuclear states." Yeltsin's government added to the Ukrainian concern when it issued a declaration on the day after the Vancouver meeting saying that "recently the situation around nuclear weapons stationed on the territory of Ukraine has sharply deteriorated . . . the position of Ukraine . . . is fraught with extremely dangerous consequences . . . nuclear weapons cannot and must not be an object of political games."[14]

Other Russian-Ukrainian disputes added to the tension. Nationalists in Russia voiced concern about ethnic Russians stranded in the newly independent states. Other major irritants were the long connection of the Russian navy with Sevastopol, disagreements over how to divide the Soviet Black Sea fleet between Russia and Ukraine, and anger among Russians over the way Khrushchev's "gift" of Crimea to Ukraine had backfired. Arguments over Russian supplies of oil and gas to Ukraine also figured in the equation periodically. Recognizing that its hard-line strategy toward Ukraine was not working, the Clinton administration initiated a major review of U.S. policy with one of the ablest of the National Security Council staffers, Rose Gottemoeller, in the lead. Changes were recommended that included more sensitivity to Ukraine's own problems, greater willingness to offer Ukraine incentives, and a broadening of the U.S.-Ukrainian dialogue. Support for these changes was found throughout the administration. This review led to a revised Clinton administration strategy toward Ukraine that included a more assertive U.S. role in direct talks with Ukraine. The goal remained the same, but from May 1993 onward the U.S. position changed significantly in ways that made it easier for the Ukrainian government to engage in serious talks with the United States.

U.S.-Ukraine Negotiations Are Joined

The U.S. decision to broaden the U.S.-Ukrainian dialogue to embrace economic, political, and other types of cooperation led to a visit by Ambassador-at-Large Strobe Talbott to Kiev in May. The visit and its message were seen in Kiev as a turning point in U.S.-Ukrainian relations. In June, the specifics of the U.S. position on START ratification and NPT accession as a condition for Nunn-Lugar assistance also began to change. Secretary of Defense Les Aspin conveyed to Russian defense minister Grachev and then to Ukrainian defense minister Morozov a proposal that Ukraine proceed immediately to deactivate the strategic offensive arms on its territory by separating the warheads from their delivery vehicles. The idea was not appealing to Grachev, who was concerned about storing warheads in facilities in Ukraine, even temporarily and even under Russian guard. Morozov, on the other hand, responded positively.

The U.S. proposal, provided to the Russians and the Ukrainians through several high-level channels, was fine-tuned over time to meet Ukrainian and Russian concerns. Basically, the proposal called for deactivation by removal of the warheads and temporarily storing them in Ukraine under joint Russian and Ukrainian supervision, perhaps with some international observers, pending their removal to Russia for prompt dismantlement. Ukraine would then be compensated for the value of the HEU in the warheads. The United States saw what it called "early deactivation" as a step on the way to Ukrainian compliance with START and the nuclear nonproliferation treaty, not a substitute. All three nuclear weapons systems on Ukraine's territory would be included— weapons associated with heavy bombers, SS-19s, and SS-24s.[15]

In June 1993 the United States changed its position on the conditions that Ukraine would have to meet to receive Nunn-Lugar assistance. Until then, Nunn-Lugar assistance was withheld because of Ukraine's reluctance to ratify the Lisbon Protocol and accede to the nonproliferation treaty. Henceforward, Ukrainian ratification of START and accession to the nonproliferation treaty would not be an absolute requirement to receive assistance for dismantlement. If the Ukrainians would agree to begin early deactivation by removing warheads from one regiment each of the SS-19s, SS-24s, and heavy bombers, the United States would agree to begin providing Nunn-Lugar assistance for dismantlement when removal of these warheads had begun. A pilot project to dismantle SS-24 missile systems would also be started.

Events then began to move more rapidly. Ukraine decided to begin in July the dismantling of SS-19 missiles, initially two regiments in agreement with the Russians. Many of the SS-19s were approaching the end of their service life and could not be deployed much longer without major refurbishment in any event.

Ukraine also decided to accept a visit by the U.S. delegation on Safe and Secure Dismantlement of Nuclear Weapons (SSD) at the end of August to discuss the Nunn-Lugar umbrella and implementing agreements. The most important of the implementing agreements was one that would provide up to $135 million for dismantling assistance. Even while Nunn-Lugar assistance had been withheld, technical talks had proceeded and had achieved some initial understandings on lists of equipment and financial offset measures. To this point, however, the unilateral SS-19 dismantling was taking place essentially at the expense of the Ukrainian government.

Simultaneously, the Ukrainian-Russian negotiations on disposition of nuclear warheads were coming to a head. These talks had been under way since November 1992 but had failed to make progress. The subjects under negotiation were schedules and methods for removing warheads from Ukraine, compensation to Ukraine for the value of the nuclear materials in the warheads, including compensation for tactical nuclear warheads removed in 1992, and security assurances. Problems had arisen over when compensation would be provided to Ukraine, whether tactical nuclear warheads should be eligible for compensation, and whether security assurances should refer only to the Commonwealth of Independent States and the reciprocal obligations contained in the charter.

By August 1993 the talks had been so successful that three papers were ready for signature at a meeting of the Russian and Ukrainian presidents, prime ministers, and other high officials. These included understandings regarding removal of nuclear weapons, revenue sharing, and ideas about compensation for tactical nuclear weapons. The accords had been readied for signature, and that process was under way at Massandra, in Crimea, when a Ukrainian official sought to leave open in the documents the question of which agreement was governing, the original START treaty or the Kravchuk letter included in the Lisbon Protocol. The difference was that a Ukrainian interpretation of START required only partial elimination by Ukraine of its strategic offensive arms. The Kravchuk letter, with the Lisbon Protocol, required Ukraine to eliminate all strategic offensive systems. The reasoning of this senior official was that the Ukrainian government should not preempt the decision of the parliament. Injecting this issue into the discussions resulted in immediate derailment of the accords.

This was not the end of the Massandra accords. The negotiations between the Ukrainians and the Russians continued after Massandra and were based on the agreements reached up to that point. Indeed, the Massandra agreements would be contributing elements in the final January 1994 trilateral accord. They were an essential part of the implementation of the trilateral accord and a main reason why a trilateral follow-on negotiation was not required. The Ukrainians and Russians had already prepared the ground for agreements on compensation and a timetable for withdrawal.

The Ukrainians remained convinced, however, that compensation agreements and security assurances should include the United States in some fashion. Agreements that included only Russia and Ukraine would not be acceptable.[16] This was probably another reason for Kiev's conclusion that the time had come for U.S.-Ukrainian negotiations on deactivation and dismantlement of strategic offensive arms. The first U.S.-Ukrainian meeting on Nunn-Lugar cooperation took place from August 30 through September 1, 1993. The second followed on October 21 to 26, 1993, and the third took place from December 2 to 6, 1993. The results of these meetings included the Nunn-Lugar umbrella agreement, the implementing agreement on dismantlement of strategic offensive arms, and the first notice from the Ukrainian government that it intended to deactivate all of its SS-24s in fairly short order by removing their warheads.

In the August meeting, the United States welcomed the agreement between Russia and Ukraine to start deactivating two regiments of SS-19s and asked that the process be continued beyond that. Noting that Washington also wanted to include heavy bombers and SS-24s, the U.S. delegation suggested alternative methods for deactivating missiles and proposed talks on methods of eliminating the SS-24s. Nunn-Lugar resources would be available for this. The Ukrainians were assured that the United States would not sign the HEU contract until a revenue-sharing agreement had been worked out with Ukraine, Belarus, and Kazakstan. As regards timing of compensation for Ukraine, it was the U.S. view that Ukraine should be compensated when the nuclear warheads located in Ukraine had been dismantled in Russia, and that warheads from Ukraine should go to the head of the dismantling queue. Discussions on the Nunn-Lugar umbrella agreement and the dismantling assistance agreement revealed some problems concerning audits and the status of American citizens working on these programs, as well as a desire that Ukrainian enterprises provide some of the necessary equipment.

The October meeting took place just prior to and during the visit of Secretary of State Warren Christopher to Kiev. The United States wanted progress on the SS-24s and hoped that Ukraine could decide on what deactivation option it would like to pursue. However, the

Ukrainian government was not ready to define exactly what deactivation or dismantling procedure Ukraine would be prepared to accept. Obviously, Ukraine had not reached a satisfactory conclusion at that point in its negotiations with Russia over compensation and security assurances. At the last moment, Kravchuk and Christopher agreed that an effort should be made to overcome the remaining problems in the Nunn-Lugar umbrella agreement, and they instructed their negotiators to do so on the spot. At one point in the evening, Kravchuk, Christopher, and Under Secretary of State Lynn Davis joined the negotiators to emphasize in no uncertain terms what was expected. This had the desired result. The remaining issues were resolved by 6 A.M. on October 26, and the umbrella agreement was concluded. Although the deactivation of SS-24s was left as an open question when Christopher left Kiev, it was clear that this issue now demanded a solution urgently. Christopher stressed this in a subsequent message to Foreign Minister Zlenko. The next visit of the U.S. delegation in early December would be an occasion to discuss it, he wrote. His suggestion, in the event, was accepted.

The End Game

It is likely that Kravchuk's decisions in this period were encouraged by Yeltsin's success in eliminating for a time the threat posed to his authority by the Russian legislature. Yeltsin was seen as at least tolerant of Ukranian opinions, while the Congress of People's Deputies was seen as hostile to Ukraine at a very fundamental level, including the issue of Ukraine's territorial integrity. Yeltsin's dissolution of the Congress of People's Deputies, with the help of the Russian army on October 4, relieved Kravchuk of one source of concern and assured him that his Russian negotiating partner would be around for a while.

These same considerations may have played a part in the next major development in the negotiation. On November 19, 1993, the Ukrainian parliament adopted a resolution ratifying with reservations the START I treaty and the Lisbon Protocol. However, the ratification resolution also had what many observers feared was a "poison pill" in a provision that declared inter alia that Article V of the Lisbon Protocol, which committed Ukraine to adhere to the nuclear nonproliferation treaty as a nonnuclear weapons state, was not binding for Ukraine and that this issue would be left to be addressed later by the parliament. The Russians were highly offended by the parliament's action, seeing it as a reversal of the denuclearization process. The resolution affirmed that START required Ukraine to reduce only 36 percent of the nuclear delivery vehicles and 42 percent of the warheads in Ukraine, but also stated that "this does not preclude Ukraine from eliminating additional delivery vehicles and warheads on the basis of procedures stipulated by Ukraine." Other reservations related to long-standing Ukrainian requests for security guarantees, financial and technical assistance, verification of warhead dismantlement in Russia, and compensation.

However, the resolution gave President Kravchuk the authority to proceed with SS-24 deactivation and a settlement of other issues. The American ambassador in Kiev, Bill Miller, saw it as a positive step—and he was right. Shortly after passage of the parliament's resolution, Kravchuk was able to inform the United States that warheads were being removed from some SS-24s. Senior Ukrainian officials informed the visiting U.S. Safe and Secure Dismantlement delegation early in December that by early 1994 all 46 SS-24s would be deactivated, a very positive response to the Christopher letter.

Several questions needed to be resolved before Russia, Ukraine, and the United States could agree on the fate of the warheads removed from the SS-24s. First, the HEU compensation issue had to be settled. Second, Russia had to help maintain and secure the warheads removed from the SS-24s. Third, the United States had to help Ukraine obtain security assurances from Russia. A meeting between Clinton and Kravchuk, which had been under discussion for some months, had to be scheduled. Regarding the necessary Nunn-Lugar agreements, the U.S. delegation was informed that the umbrella agreement could enter into force shortly. The implementing agreement on strategic systems dismantlement was signed, which made available up to $135 million for deactivation and dismantling assistance.

The next step was to inform the Russians of this breakthrough and seek their cooperation. As head of the U.S. SSD delegation, I met with Russian Ministry of Defense officials in Moscow on December 6 for this purpose. U.S. Ambassador to Russia Thomas Pickering discussed the report from Kiev with the Ministry of Foreign Affairs. Although surprised by the news, the Russians agreed with an American high-level suggestion that the opportunity should be seized to resolve the outstanding issues. Of prime importance was the long-stalled revenue-sharing agreement in connection with the HEU purchase. Russian-Ukrainian negotiations on the safety and security of the nuclear warheads and a schedule for transferring the warheads to Russia for dismantlement also had taken on new urgency. The Massandra agreements had paved the way for what, at least in Washington, was seen as the last stage of the negotiations.

The Trilateral Accord

To move the process forward decisively, the United States proposed that U.S. vice president Al Gore and Russian prime minister Viktor Chernomyrdin and their experts become directly involved. This was accepted by Moscow. Gore and Chernomyrdin met in Moscow on December 15 and 16, 1993, in the framework of a U.S.-Russian commission on technological cooperation in the fields of energy and space that had been created at the Vancouver summit. Ambassador-at-Large Strobe Talbott and other senior U.S. officials conducted fruitful discussions during the Gore-Chernomyrdin Commission meetings with Russian counterparts concerning a possible trilateral statement, particularly with respect to the HEU deal. Under Secretary of State Lynn Davis, a key adviser to Secretary Christopher, and a senior member of her staff, Dr. James Timbie, were major actors in these talks. Jim Timbie was the source of much of the creative energy behind the major decisions concerning Ukraine throughout the period discussed in this chapter. Their talks were followed immediately by a meeting with senior Ukrainian officials in Kiev, taking advantage of a visit by Secretary of Defense William Perry. The same U.S. interagency group accompanied Secretary Perry and, again, the conversations were promising and fully in line with the decisions President Kravchuk had made in late November. Ukrainian officials continued to view the Massandra agreements as part of a Ukrainian-Russian settlement.

The outlines of the trilateral agreement that was beginning to emerge left important matters to be resolved, mainly by the Ukrainians and Russians, but they also seemed to put Ukraine firmly on the track to ratifying START and acceding to the nonproliferation treaty. In late December, President Clinton approved the approach that his negotiators proposed to reach closure. A trilateral meeting, chaired on the U.S. side by Ambassador Talbott, was held in Washington on January 3 and 4, 1994. Considerable progress was made, so much so that issues like presidential visits and the timing of the Ukrainian parliament's ratification of START became ripe for discussion. A key element became a U.S. offer of a $60 million advance payment to Russia on the HEU purchase so that Russia would have the funds available to begin fabricating fuel elements to transfer to Ukraine. This allowed President Kravchuk to claim a tangible, short-term benefit for Ukraine's precarious energy problem.

A meeting between Clinton and Yeltsin had been scheduled for January 13 and 14, 1994, in Moscow. The final details now essentially in place, it was possible to plan for a trilateral meeting with Kravchuk and Yeltsin to settle on an arrangement that would satisfy all parties. Clinton approved the package deal and during a visit to NATO headquarters on his way to the Moscow meeting, the Americans preemptively announced that an agreement had been reached and that the president would meet with Kravchuk in Kiev before traveling on to Moscow. The final stage of summit diplomacy was successful, and the trilateral accord, including all the elements that had been under discussion since 1992, was issued in Moscow on January 14, 1994. The agreement included the following elements:

> The Presidents look forward to the entry into force of the START I Treaty, including the Lisbon Protocol and associated documents, and President Kravchuk reiterated his commitment that Ukraine accede to the Nuclear Non-proliferation Treaty as a non-nuclear-weapon state in the shortest possible time.
>
> Presidents Clinton and Yeltsin expressed satisfaction with the completion of the highly-enriched uranium contract, which was signed by appropriate authorities of the United States and Russia.
>
> The three Presidents decided on simultaneous actions on transfer of nuclear warheads from Ukraine and delivery of compensation to Ukraine in the form of fuel assemblies for nuclear power stations.
>
> Presidents Clinton and Yeltsin informed President Kravchuk that the United States and Russia are prepared to provide security assurances to Ukraine . . . once the START I Treaty enters into force and Ukraine

becomes a non-nuclear-weapon state party to the Nuclear Non-Proliferation Treaty (NPT).

President Clinton reaffirmed the United States commitment to provide technical and financial assistance for the safe and secure dismantling of nuclear forces and storage of fissile materials . . . including a minimum of USD 175 million to Ukraine.

Nailing Down the Agreement

This was not the end of the story. Several steps had to be taken to implement the trilateral accord, and a failure to agree on the details of those steps could negate the whole agreement. First, the Ukrainian parliament ratified the START treaty, including the Lisbon Protocol, on February 3, 1994, thereby endorsing the proposition that the trilateral accord met the conditions that the parliament had laid down in November 1993. Second, the Ukrainians and Russians reached an agreement a few days later on compensation, on maintenance and security for nuclear warheads, and on a schedule for the transfer of the warheads to Russia for monitored dismantlement. This agreement resolved the outstanding issues between Ukraine and Russia and made unnecessary a further trilateral meeting.

Not everything went so smoothly. The Ukrainian government hoped for security guarantees in the form of a treaty, and this went well beyond the assurances that the United States was prepared to offer. From the first discussions with Ukrainian officials in 1992 Washington had made it clear that a treaty commitment was not possible. The assurances that the U.S. government was prepared to offer were drawn from the principles of the Helsinki Final Act and assurances given by the United States in connection with the nonproliferation treaty. The trilateral agreement also recorded the fact that the United Kingdom, the third depositary state of the nonproliferation treaty, was prepared to offer the same security assurances to Ukraine once Kiev acceded to the treaty as a non-nuclear weapons state.

One other element played a part in the order-building diplomacy of 1993–94. The Ukrainian government, and Kravchuk personally, had expressed a serious interest in an international fund to support dismantlement. Working with its NATO allies, other interested European governments, and Japan, the United States assembled a package of assistance programs to offer Ukraine prior to the convening of the new parliament in March 1994. On February 21, 1994, the ambassadors of fourteen countries met with Kravchuk in Kiev to present a statement endorsing Ukraine's intentions to become a nonnuclear weapons state and offering pledges of tangible support. The countries represented in this international effort were Belgium, Canada, Denmark, Finland, France, Germany, Italy, Japan, the Netherlands, Norway, Sweden, Spain, the United Kingdom, and the United States. This show of international solidarity with Ukraine and its decision to renounce nuclear weapons was very welcome in Kiev and helped to reinforce the Ukrainian government's determination to proceed. An official visit to Washington by Kravchuk also had been part of the negotiating equation for months. The invitation now was issued and the visit took place on March 3 to 5, 1994.

The Last Act

Leonid Kravchuk was defeated in the Ukrainian presidential elections of June 1994 in a campaign fought primarily over economic issues. His successor as president was Leonid Kuchma, former director of a missile production complex in Ukraine. On nuclear dismantlement the new president adopted the same position as his predecessor, and the first fruits of his stewardship became the last act in the negotiating drama, which was played in November and December 1994. Finally reconciled to the reality that a treaty was impossible, Ukraine settled for the type of political document that had been foreshadowed in the trilateral accord and discussed with the Ukrainians long before that. And on November 16, 1994, the Ukrainian parliament voted overwhelmingly (301 to 8) to endorse Ukraine's accession to the nonproliferation treaty. The instrument of accession was deposited on December 5, 1994. On that same day the parties to the Lisbon Protocol—Belarus, Kazakstan, Russia, Ukraine, and the United States—exchanged instruments of ratification of the START I treaty at a ceremony in Budapest. The security assurances document was signed at the same time by Russia, Ukraine, the United Kingdom, and the United States.

The agreements that in various ways involved Russia, Ukraine, and the United States in HEU sales, in revenue sharing, and in protection, maintenance, and transfer of warheads for monitored dismantlement in Russia were effectively implemented despite occasional "bumps in the road." Secretary of Defense William Perry deserves great credit for his persistent and forceful oversight, from the American side, of the process of implementation. On June 1, 1996, the last nuclear warhead crossed the border of Ukraine for dismantlement in Russia. In a White House statement issued on the same day, President Clinton remarked: "In 1991 there were more than 4,000 strategic and tactical nuclear warheads in Ukraine. Today there are none. I applaud the Ukrainian government for its historic contribution in reducing the nuclear threat."

How Rules Simplify Governmental Decisionmaking

Skillful statecraft by two U.S. administrations was essential to the success of this venture, but another requirement for success in these negotiations should not be overlooked: two U.S. presidents and their administrations made quick and effective decisions according to the logic of an international order based on nuclear restraint. Explanations justifying this course of action to the public were readily available. No lengthy and agonizing debate was necessary to decide what should be done. The facts associated with the end of the Cold War—and of the bipolar order—could have pointed to a different solution. No longer essential as a prop to the bipolar order, the policy of blocking *any* increase in the number of nuclear weapons states might have given way to a toleration for some limited increase, especially in the cases of nations whose sovereignty and independence were important to the United States. In fact, no attention was given to alternative strategies because policymakers, operating under conditions of bounded rationality, tend to find that their interests can be served perfectly well under a regime where the risks and benefits are well known. They "satisfice," to use Herbert Simon's term.

Diplomacy was successful in the situation described in this chapter because the conceptual thinking and the rules flowing from this thinking had been established years before. While many other familiar guideposts of the Cold War had been washed away by the revolutions of 1989–91, the logical framework for decisions provided by the rules of nuclear restraint remained useful in confronting new problems. The logic of the nonproliferation model was understood by the U.S. political leadership and supported by public opinion. A principal lesson of the experience is that strategic concepts and rules of behavior that enjoy similar widespread support can be a crucial contributing factor in building a consensus behind U.S. foreign policy in the new world. As we shall see in the next chapter, however, there are situations where existing rules are inadequate and where new ideas must be developed to deal with these situations.

The rules of nuclear restraints encouraged Russia and the United States to cooperate because, in general, they had been acting according to these rules for many years. And in Ukraine the underlying assumptions of the rules of nuclear restraint also had broad public support, even amid the nationalist politics of the Supreme Rada, the parliament of Ukraine. The tangible and intangible benefits given to Ukraine during the course of the negotiations were important, of course, but concepts that Ukrainians shared with other nations also were important and are what prompted Ukrainian leaders to keep coming back to the theme of Ukraine's place in history.

Rules become irrelevant if the situation they address—the division of Europe, in this case—no longer exists. Others can emerge because of changed political perceptions and values—human rights as a legitimate subject for international review. Rules that encourage nations to act according to a logic of peace persist if they help governments make coherent decisions that respond well to foreign policy questions. The rules of an international system are, in historical terms, constantly in flux. When a great many of them collapse simultaneously as they did at the end of the Cold War, we think of it as a turning point in history. Those events are extremely rare, although we are living through such a period now. More typically, the process of change is incremental, piecemeal, and experimental. Much time must pass before old rules die and new rules become accepted. As the actions of recent U.S. presidents clearly show, national leaders prefer to hang onto some familiar reference points while new rules are being created elsewhere in the system. In a world of bounded rationality this is a classically conservative approach: it permits leaders to limit the number of issues they must address, and it helps to prevent out-of-control situations.

4

Bringing Order Out of Chaos

U.S.-Russian Cooperation in Blocking Nuclear Terrorism

D uring the Cold War, the Soviet Union built tens of thousands of nuclear weapons derived from the hundreds of tons of plutonium and highly enriched uranium that it produced in its "atomic archipelago," a vast complex of closed cities barred to outsiders. The Soviet system for protecting fissile materials relied chiefly on police-state methods; inventories of plutonium and highly enriched uranium were not precisely tracked and technical means of preventing theft were not well developed. In the chaos that accompanied Russia's transition from authoritarianism to democracy it was almost inevitable that conditions would encourage and permit pilfering of poorly guarded fissile materials that might conceivably fetch a good price in a black market. And indeed, several cases of theft soon surfaced, including thefts of naval reactor fuel and plutonium and enriched uranium from Russian research centers. All known cases of theft and attempted smuggling were intercepted by Russian authorities and by police in European countries. As the director of the Central Intelligence Agency observed in 1996, however, "we do not know what we are not seeing: significant quantities of fissile materials can be hypothetically as few as four kilograms— quantities easily smuggled with normal commercial transactions."[1] Nuclear weapons were well accounted for in Russia as in the Soviet Union and rather well guarded, but the "insider threat" had to be taken seriously in a country where salaries routinely were not paid for months. The elimination of strategic offensive arms mandated by U.S.-Russian arms reduction treaties meant that many warheads were being moved by rail over long distances in Russia and placed in scattered facilities originally not intended for long-term storage.

In parallel with these developments, a new challenge to international peace and security emerged during the 1990s. The New York World Trade Center bombing, the destruction of the Oklahoma City federal building, and the Aum Shinrikyo sect's nerve gas attack in Tokyo did not quite fit the pattern of terrorism seen in the past. Close observers of this scene detected a trend toward new types of terrorists who aimed at retribution or eradication of what they defined as evil rather than the achievement of a specific political goal.[2] Such people are not constrained by concerns about losing popular sympathy for their cause. The net result of this development is that weapons of indiscriminate destruction—chemical, biological, and nuclear weapons—may become more interesting to groups interested in mass violence.

In the last chapter we saw that old Cold War rules of behavior were skillfully applied to a quite unprecedented situation—the potential acquisition of ready-made nuclear arsenals by newly independent states. In this chapter, we shall examine another quite unprecedented situation —acquisition of nuclear materials by criminals and terrorist groups. But in this case, new rules had to be developed. This was a case, too, where globalization of technology and the threat of international crime required close cooperation among governments in areas that traditionally were regarded as domestic affairs: police work, for example.

International norms and the restraints that flow from them and, indeed, all the patterns of behavior associated with an international system concern the actions of governments. How relevant are international norms and rules to the problem of dealing with substate entities that act outside the law? The argument made in this chapter is that international norms not only facilitate interstate cooperation but also galvanize domestic actions. Governments have repeatedly pledged cooperation at the international level in dealing with terrorism, but the main instruments they use to combat terrorism are essentially domestic. Outside "interference" is frequently resented and resisted. And yet, a measure of international cooperation and of internal accommodation to this cooperation has been achieved. It is one of the most important results of the new U.S.-Russian relationship.

International Norms and the Fight against Terrorism

The initial U.S.-Russian experiments in trying to meet the challenge of securing nuclear materials in an age of turbulent transition call to mind the first U.S.-Soviet experiments in cooperation in the 1950s and 1960s. Survival was the issue then. In the 1990s the question was whether wary partners in global security could cooperate in ways that would have a direct impact on the conduct of their own domestic affairs. A reluctance to adapt time-honored ways of managing internal affairs is, at this writing (fall 1997), still preventing a full-scale assault on nuclear theft and nuclear terrorism. But it is possible to discern changes in behavioral patterns in response to international rules of behavior, and these have occurred in a much shorter period of time than comparable changes during the Cold War.

Noninterference in internal affairs is a cardinal principle of interstate relations. But in a world where borders are easily crossed by information, trade, and people, the principle no longer enjoys the sanctity it once did. In fact, the principle has been challenged repeatedly and increasingly in the last quarter century. In the 1970s, as we saw in chapter 2, the behavior of governments toward their own citizens was legitimized as a topic for international review. Decisions of the UN Security Council in the post–Cold War period have established the principle that international peace and security can be affected by the internal behavior of states. Examples of this are Saddam Hussein's treatment of the Kurds of Iraq and the refusal of Mu'ammar Qadhafi to hand over Libyan citizens accused of terrorism. As we shall see in the next chapter, the breakup of Yugoslavia and the accompanying violence prompted international intervention in what arguably was a civil war in Bosnia.

In the decade of the 1990s, citizens of many nations have become potential targets of terrorism on a vast scale. Formal norms and rules of behavior such as the nuclear nonproliferation treaty, the biological weapons convention, and the chemical weapons convention do not directly address substate entities with access to weapons of indiscriminate destruction. But neither are they completely irrelevant. They provide a basis for domestic legislation for parties to the conventions. Controlling proliferation and making the threatened use of weapons of indiscriminate destruction less salient in state-to-state relations are likely to have an indirect effect in discouraging nuclear terrorism—but only if the norms are upheld by the leading powers. Iraqi forces used mustard gas and nerve agents in the 1983–88 Gulf War and against Kurdish villagers in Iraq itself in 1987–88. In retrospect, Saddam's use of poison gas should have made his government the subject of international sanctions at the time. Failure of the key actors in the international community to punish governments for using weapons of indiscriminate destruction encourages a general disregard for international norms, and that affects the climate in which even terrorists work.

The record of cooperation between Washington and Moscow in upholding norms of interstate behavior regarding the control and the proliferation of weapons of indiscriminate destruction is mixed. The two governments worked together well in securing the indefinite extension in 1995 of the nuclear nonproliferation treaty. They have supported the programs of the International Atomic Energy Agency. Differences have arisen over Russian exports: assistance to Iran in building civil nuclear reactors, for example.

Cooperation between the two countries in eliminating biological and chemical weapons has been a disappointment. A 1992 U.S.-U.K.-Russian agreement that would have engaged the United States, Russia, and the United Kingdom in confidence building in the biological weapons field has not been fully implemented, owing to obstructive tactics by Russian government agencies. Reports persist that an offensive biological weapons program is still under way clandestinely in Russia. Bilateral cooperation in destroying chemical weapons stocks in Russia has been bogged down, again due to an inability to settle disagreements between the two sides. U.S. assistance in building a plant to destroy Russian chemical agents may lead to a breakthrough. In the United States, the debate on the ratification of the chemical weapons convention had to be taken off the Senate's calendar because of a sudden spurt of opposition to the treaty in the midst of the 1996 presidential election campaign. The convention was finally approved by the Senate, but it was a close call.

These shortcomings are bound to damage efforts to deal with terrorists. In a world where government-sponsored biological and chemical weapons programs still exist, it will be more difficult to control the acquisition of such weapons by terrorists, who are not deterred by the threat of retaliation. Nations have manufactured chemical and biological agents and weaponized them, ready for use. Some nations have actually used chemical weapons, and have suffered no punitive sanctions. Nuclear weapons are stockpiled in great numbers, and the right of using them first is explicitly upheld by the United States and other nuclear weapons states. This situation is not a disincentive to terrorism.

New Forms of U.S.-Russian Cooperation

Russia and the United States share a special responsibility for combating the global threat of terrorists using weapons of indiscriminate destruction. They are permanent members of the UN Security Council, possessors of advanced technologies and powerful military forces, and supporters of global arms control and technology supplier regimes. They are not the only countries responsible for meeting this new security challenge, but leadership exercised jointly by the United States and Russia could mobilize a global response to new substate challenges. U.S.-Russian cooperation, or lack of it, on such global issues tests the thesis that U.S.-Russian partnership is a key element in the building of a stable peace and of an international system based on accepted norms and rules.

Through trial-and-error methods, Russia and the United States have been experimenting with a type of international cooperation that is creating new norms and rules for protecting nuclear weapons and fissile materials against theft. This type of cooperation goes to the roots of national behavior.[3] When Russian officials react with wounded pride to suggestions that their protection of nuclear materials could be improved, the voice of Russia is being heard. When Russia insists that nuclear smuggling is an international problem, not just a Russian problem, the way that Russians think about things is coming to the fore. In fact, this particular reaction is helpful in rule-building diplomacy, for Russians are suggesting that international norms offer some help to them in organizing their own actions. The United States and Russia have struggled to overcome many obstacles to realize even a limited degree of cooperation in this area. The following description of Russia's stake in nuclear energy and of Russia's struggles to create a new legal order shows why this has been so.

The Ministry of Atomic Energy of the Russian Federation (MINATOM) presides over a significant sector of the Russian economy.

Ten closed cities with a total population of about 700,000 people are at the heart of it. MINATOM provides jobs for close to a million people. Like other sectors in the Russian economy it has seen hard times. The suicide, in October 1996, of Vladimir Nechai, head of one of the most prestigious weapons laboratories, Chelyabinsk-70, portrayed the problem in human terms. He was letting down his team, he thought, because funds from Moscow were not available to pay them. The atomic energy complex has been underfunded by the Russian state, and yet it has, by and large, survived intact.[4] It is also a successful hard-currency earner for Russia. All of these factors have made MINATOM a major player in Boris Yeltsin's Moscow.

Not surprisingly, MINATOM's leaders see themselves as stewards of Russia's crown jewels, an image that is justified in many respects. Criticism of MINATOM's protection of fissile materials is resented, and cooperation with the West is not an easy thing. Frequently encountered is the attitude that the good name of Russian technology is being blackened to create advantages for the West. One observer wrote that

> many foreign countries prefer, as they did during the years of nuclear confrontation, to see Russia and the other former Soviet republics as the main source of this new threat. . . . Certain political and financial circles in the West that do not balk at blatant provocation in order to discredit the new Russia in the eyes of the entire world have been trying to exploit these entirely legitimate public fears.[5]

The official view of MINATOM is that "there are forces abroad attempting to keep Russia out of this [advanced technologies] market." Since Russia is deprived, furthermore, of financial resources it might otherwise have by the difficulties it has in selling uranium and enrichment services on the world market, the government is limited in what it can do to account for and control fissile materials.[6]

The fact that cooperation with the United States has gone as far as it has in this area shows that Russia has succeeded in partially overcoming its tradition of secrecy. This has been extremely difficult for Russian government agencies to do; opposition has been strong, and threats of punishment for those crossing an ill-defined line have been made and carried out. A document prepared by the Russian Federal Counter-intelligence Service in late 1994 spoke of "the U.S. foreign policy course aimed at deterring Russia as a state potentially capable of competing with the "only superpower."

This assessment was contained in a report that described U.S. private research organizations with interests in Russia as essentially agents of U.S. intelligence. The report saw an "urgent need to take a range of measures to prevent the interference of foreign states, particularly the United States, in Russia's internal affairs and to protect and reinforce its scientific and intellectual potential."[7]

Furthermore, the Russians had to re-create a legal basis for protecting classified information under the new conditions of their state. On January 20, 1996, President Yeltsin signed an edict announcing the formation of the Interdepartmental Commission for the Protection of State Secrets.[8] Among its duties were "to prepare expert conclusions on documents containing information classed as a state secret with a view to resolving the question of the possible handover of the said information to other states." Russia's Interdepartmental Commission for the Protection of State Secrets was instructed to examine treaties, when requested by the Russian government, on the joint use and protection of information and to participate in international cooperation in that area. In short, Russia is moving to overcome the practices of the past, but it takes time and the process is cumbersome. International agreements and norms will help this process.

On November 21, 1995, not long before Yeltsin signed the edict on state secrets, he signed a federal law on utilization of nuclear energy that had been passed by the State Duma. The law makes the Russian government responsible for authorizing its agencies to establish a unified system of accounting and control of nuclear materials. Physical protection of nuclear installations is to be supervised by the agency responsible for safety regulation. Special units of the Ministry of Interior or the Federal Counterintelligence Service may be used.

In another recognition of the value of international norms and rules, the law requires that "the level of physical protection will be in compliance with Russia's international obligations." Imports and exports related to nuclear energy are to be executed "in accordance with the nuclear nonproliferation treaty and other international agreements signed by Russia."[9] The following section describes the first U.S.-Russian interactions in this area. It is a case study in the problems both governments have in coming to grips with new issues.

Initial Experience with New Forms of U.S.-Russian Cooperation

The international community has an interest in preventing the proliferation of weapons expertise, even that held in the brains of individual scientists. Fearing that the lure of high salaries and generous perquisites might entice Russian and Ukranian nuclear weapons experts to accept positions in the laboratories of aspiring nuclear weapons states, the United States and several other nations worked with the Ukranian and Russian governments to establish centers in Moscow and Kiev that could provide grants to weapons scientists for projects having civilian applications. The Moscow center became known as the International Science and Technology Center; Ukraine's was called the Ukrainian Science and Technology Center. Initially, the United States contributed $25 million to the Moscow center, the European Union provided an equal amount, and Japan gave $17 million. In the case of the Ukrainian center, the United States gave $10 million, Canada $2 million, and Sweden $1.5 million. After difficult startups, both centers became quite effective at what they set out to do. For example, by the end of 1995 the Moscow Center had received over 450 proposals from Russian scientists, according to MINATOM. So far as is known, no weapons scientists from the republics of the former Soviet Union became employed in the weapons development programs of the so-called rogue states: Libya, North Korea, or Iran, for example.

It was not easy to establish this arrangement, especially since it involved the domestic affairs of Russia and Ukraine. Although President Yeltsin and President Bush signed the U.S.-Russian umbrella agreement that provided the overall legal basis for Nunn-Lugar cooperation on June 17,1992, it was not until March 1994—after Yeltsin had forcibly dissolved the Congress of People's Deputies in October 1993— that the Russian government was able, finally, to allow the International Science and Technology Center to open for business. Many Russian deputies saw the International Scientific and Technological Center as a foreign plot to subvert the Russian state and steal its most vital secrets. Probably a similar reaction would have occurred in Washington had the situation been reversed.

From the beginning of the Clinton administration, U.S.-Russian cooperation in nuclear materials protection, control, and accountability was a high priority. The first visit to Moscow of the Clinton administration's delegation for Safe and Secure Dismantlement of Nuclear Weapons (SSD) took place March 22 to 26, 1993. Among other agreements, the U.S. and Russian delegations discussed and finalized "an Agreement Between the Ministry of the Russian Federation for Atomic Energy and the Department of Defense of the United States of America Concerning Control, Accounting, and Physical Protection of Nuclear Material." That agreement entered into force on September 2, 1993. It provided assistance not to exceed $10 million. In the Vancouver Declaration of April 4, 1993, Presidents Clinton and Yeltsin affirmed that the United States and Russia intended to cooperate "in the controlling, accounting, and physical protection of nuclear materials." From the beginning, the Russians wanted a cautious, step-by-step approach. Accordingly, they proposed, and the U.S. experts accepted, a test project for the low-enriched fuel production line at Elektrostal. A training center in protection and accounting techniques was jointly developed by the two countries at Obninsk.

It was apparent that this deliberate approach would not speedily enhance the safety and security of weapons-usable materials (so-called direct use materials), and the U.S. government offered a new proposal. Twenty million dollars would be added to the initial agreement, and the terms of the agreement would be broadened to address not only "civilian nuclear material" but also material that might be usable by the Russian military. The Russians had trouble with the inclusion of military material from the outset, partly because of the limits of MINATOM's authority and partly because of worries about opening up sensitive facilities. Some weeks of interagency debate in Washington resulted in a recognition that there was plenty of weapons-usable material in the civilian sector that needed protection. Accordingly, the U.S. delegation was authorized to propose an amendment (which we had suggested some weeks earlier) that referred to "civilian unirradiated, direct-use materials"—a term that refers to weapons-usable materials—and the Russians quickly accepted it. The amendment, which also raised the ceiling on U.S. support to $30 million, was signed and entered into force on January 20, 1995. At the time of the signing, the U.S. delegation suggested five open-city facilities where cooperation on a priority basis would be useful; the initial Russian reaction was positive.

At about the same time, the United States offered another conceptual approach to the Russians. This was called the "quick fix" approach in Washington and was modeled on a program of improvements that the United States itself had carried out in the mid-1980s called "Operation Cerberus." That operation had begun with a crash survey of every major site in the Department of Energy complex to identify vulnerabilities in the protection and accounting system. Improvements were then carried out in a matter of months. Recalling this experience, the United States offered to help Russia do the same thing and to finance the improvements that might be required. The Russians politely brushed this aside, but the process of stepping up the pace had the effect of engaging the top levels of the U.S. government in the policymaking and diplomatic efforts to cooperate with Russia.

Just before a scheduled meeting in Moscow between Presidents Yeltsin and Clinton in early May, a report of the President's Committee of Scientific and Technical Advisers was completed that addressed the Russian protection and accountability system. Several things happened as a result of that report. First, at their summit meeting in Moscow on May 10, 1995, the two presidents issued a joint statement, in which "they directed that the Gore-Chernomyrdin Commission prepare a joint report on steps that have been accomplished and additional steps that should be taken to ensure the security of nuclear materials." The purpose was to ensure that the subject of nuclear security would be on the agenda of U.S. and Russian leaders in future meetings.

Second, Vice President Gore met with Prime Minister Chernomyrdin on June 29 and 30 in Moscow and discussed the idea of a "quick fix." Gore explained why this was an urgent problem and asked for Chernomyrdin's personal attention to it. During that meeting of the Gore-Chernomyrdin Commission, Russian minister of atomic energy Mikhailov agreed with U.S. secretary of energy O'Leary that site surveys would be conducted in August at the five sites that the United States and Russia had identified as priority locations for cooperation.

Third, since the two presidents were scheduled to meet in October 1995, the United States suggested that an action plan be prepared for them to approve at that time. The idea would be to have a specific, practical listing of steps to be taken during 1996 to improve protection and accountability of nuclear materials in Russia. To back up this offer, the U.S. administration had asked for $70 million in appropriations.

At the Hyde Park meeting of Presidents Yeltsin and Clinton on October 23, 1995, the two presidents acknowledged receipt of the Gore-Chernomyrdin report, which had been completed a few days earlier and which described plans for improvements in the security of fissile materials during 1996. The presidents issued a joint statement saying they had "endorsed speedy implementation of these plans and directed that they be expanded and accelerated to the greatest extent possible." A White House fact sheet reported that cooperation during 1995 had expanded "from a handful of facilities to more than a dozen, enhancing the safety and security of tons of nuclear material."[10] During 1996, the program of intergovernmental cooperation would expand "to five of the largest civilian sites handling weapons-usable material in Russia, located in Dmitrovgrad, Obninsk, Podolsk, Mayak and Elektrostal." Several other important developments also were noted, including improvements in the security of nuclear materials at the national level and the acceleration of direct cooperation between U.S. and Russian nuclear laboratories.

The effort to engage Yeltsin and Chernomyrdin was a success, and the commitment of Russia's highest authorities to this project would have seemed to augur well for budgetary support from the Russian government. Nonetheless, worries were voiced in Washington that the report mechanism damaged programs being managed by the Departments of Energy and Defense by shining a spotlight on U.S.-Russian cooperation that might have a better chance of success if it were not so visible. The devolution of budgeting and of management responsibility in the U.S. government to several operating agencies weakened the ability of the White House to control the U.S.-Russian agenda. And so support vanished for continuing a top-down method of developing and reinforcing new norms and rules of behavior aimed at protecting fissile materials.

Evaluating the Methodology of Imprinting New Rules

This experience raises an important question for policymakers. Which is the better approach to imprinting norms and developing rules of behavior? Should they press for high-level, high-visibility agreements and statements, should they try to "change the culture" at the working level, or should they do both? If a particular issue is vital to international security, should it be handled at the top, by the president and the vice president? Or are technical issues better left to technical people to manage? The issue is much the same as the question of how best to deal with human rights—through quiet diplomacy or high-visibility public debate.

There is a place for both approaches, but norms are most likely to become entrenched and long-lived if sooner or later they become well known by receiving extensive publicity. This does not necessarily mean that heads of government or even any government officials have to take the lead in this, and it does not mean that the "bottom-up" approach does not work. Many issues have been successfully promoted by nongovernmental organizations and forced to the attention of governments.[11] Much indispensable work has been accomplished through quiet technical contacts.

The importance of the "top-down" approach was emphasized by Senators Lugar, Nunn, and Domenici, who were successful in 1996 in pressing for legislation calling for the appointment of a national non-proliferation/counterproliferation coordinator. The reason, as Senator Lugar explained, was that the U.S. response to the problem was "scattered and unfocused . . . a patchwork effort [that] suffers from lack of coordination, overlap, and duplication."[12] In a speech delivered on August 12, 1995, Senator Lugar argued that "the president must be willing to move nuclear-material security to the top of the Russian-American agenda. This will require the President of the United States and the President of Russia to raise the level of public awareness of the threat of nuclear leakage and potential destruction in both countries."[13]

International Norms as Prods to Organizing Action

Despite the difficulties in deciding how best to conduct a cooperative program that must, in the end, involve both high-level officials and technical experts in their laboratories, the process described above is strengthening the principle that the international community has a serious security interest in the effectiveness of state controls over weapons of indiscriminate destruction, including the fissile materials from which nuclear weapons are made. This principle was established earlier through cooperation in the framework of the International Atomic Energy Agency, but it did not really apply to the nuclear weapons states. Formal declarations such as that issued by the two presidents and, of course, the detailed Hyde Park report itself acknowledged that there was a mutual U.S.-Russian interest in guarding against illegal diversions of fissile materials.

Despite the widespread feelings in Russia that the nation had not been dealt with fairly on a range of other issues, President Yeltsin accepted the need for a modern nuclear control and accountability system in Russia and acknowledged the help of the United States in making this happen. For example, in a speech on April 10, 1996, President Yeltsin said,

> a priority task for our state is the creation of a modern system of physical protection, registration, and monitoring of nuclear materials. There are examples of fruitful cooperation between Russian and U.S. specialists in this sensitive sphere too. Eleven nuclear industry facilities in Russia are already being fitted with equipment developed as a result of this cooperation.[14]

In addition to cooperation with the MINATOM complex, several very important programs were created with the Russian Ministry of Defense, of which the following are a few examples:

- To enhance security at nuclear weapons sites, the United States and Russia cooperated by installing physical security equipment and training rapid reaction forces.
- To enhance security of nuclear weapons in transit, the United States and Russia cooperated in modifying Russian rail cars. Supercontainers to protect nuclear weapons while in transit also were provided by the United States, as was mobile emergency response equipment to deal with the consequences of accidents.
- To enhance Russia's ability to account for and track nuclear warheads in transit or storage, the United States and Russia cooper-

ated in establishing an automated inventory control and management system.

These programs were arranged in accordance with the proposition that controlling nuclear smuggling and nuclear terrorism is a matter for international cooperation. That Russia should not be blamed for all the problems and that the problem cannot be solved except by international cooperation are themes congenial to the Russians. The model the Russians like to depict downplays the magnitude of the problems that exist at Russia's nuclear facilities while endorsing the relevance of international norms requiring more effective control over nuclear materials.

It was President Yeltsin, after all, who proposed a Moscow summit of the Group of Seven plus Russia (Political 8, or P-8) to discuss nuclear safety. At their meeting in Moscow in April 1996, the heads of states or governments of the P-8 agreed to coordinate their efforts to fight illegal transactions in fissile materials. By this act, the leaders recognized that smuggling, international organized crime, and terrorism—even that carried out by indigenous groups—are major threats to international peace and security in an age when weapons of indiscriminate destruction have become available to private groups. The program they endorsed emphasized measures that each government should be taking independently to deal with the problem, but it also called for expanded international cooperation. Two key elements were

- the sharing of information on nuclear theft and smuggling incidents and establishing national points of contact for this purpose; and
- enhanced cooperation among national intelligence, customs, and law enforcement agencies.

Shortfalls in Responding to International Norms

Exchanging information as called for in that statement is a beginning, but only that. Just as the Partnership for Peace in the NATO context encourages joint training for peacekeeping missions, there is a need for joint exercises in dealing with terrorists and criminal gangs armed with weapons of indiscriminate destruction. Since the Group of Seven is not and does not intend to become an international organization, "points of contact" was the best the group could do to institutionalize cooperation, but the job needs doing on a full-time basis. Some other regional or global organization could take it on, perhaps under the UN Security Council's aegis.

Acts of terrorism are crimes against humanity, and if terrorists cannot be prosecuted vigorously by national law enforcement and judicial systems, other recourses should be available, as was the case in the destruction of PanAm 103. Governments should be able to refer cases to the United Nations or to an international tribunal, perhaps one that is an extension of the court established by the United Nations to try war criminals in the former Yugoslavia.

Russia and the United States could take the lead in tightening the enforcement of norms and rules governing weapons of indiscriminate destruction. They could do this by encouraging an exchange of texts of domestic legislation concerning implementation of the relevant treaties affecting weapons of indiscriminate destruction. Beyond that, the two governments could establish a standing committee of law enforcement officials and technical experts to review experiences and consider methods of further tightening enforcement of laws prohibiting private groups from engaging in the development, production, or use of nuclear, chemical, and biological weapons. This could subsequently be adopted on a broader international basis within the framework of the United Nations.

In the United States, the roles of the FBI and CIA in dealing with terrorism are still imperfectly meshed. New priorities for intelligence are not yet in place to focus on groups that are engaged in terrorism, foreign or domestic. Responding to attacks needs vast improvement. Funds for more positions and more equipment are available, but how best to use these resources is unresolved. The Nunn-Lugar-Domenici legislation of 1996 is intended to help local authorities in the United States respond to terrorist attacks that use weapons of indiscriminate destruction. Pursuing the same goal at the international level is beyond the capacity of the United States or other governments. It is predictable that federal funds being spent for counterterrorism will be limited in their effectiveness in the absence of better meshing of domestic and international agencies. A national coordinator is needed for this purpose, as the Congress and a number of observers have recommended.

Perhaps the time has come to consider a joint statement of the UN Security Council that the use of weapons of mass destruction by any nation or subnational group is a serious violation of international norms and that such use would require the council to consult immediately regarding action against the transgressor. The dilemma here is that while the use of biological and chemical weapons already is prohibited by international agreements, the use of nuclear weapons is not. Nuclear deterrence during the Cold War depended on a perception that the United States might be the first to use these weapons if necessary, and that remains the situation today. However, the logic of a policy of joint sanctions against a nation or substate group that used weapons of mass destruction would lead inexorably to a policy among the five declared nuclear weapons states that they would not be the first to use *any* weapons of mass destruction, including nuclear weapons. This would leave open the right of "belligerent reprisal," a legal doctrine that broadly speaking entitles a country to respond to another country's violation of an agreement.

A nuclear non-first-use policy would be a major departure from long-standing U.S. policy, supported also by our British and French allies. It could be considered only if, after serious reflection, it appeared that joint sanctions against terrorists or rogue states would help to deter a threat that is now much more likely than any attack by one of the current nuclear powers against another. It would be a flimsy barrier against terrorists and criminals. But we need to erect all the barriers we can find, even flimsy ones, to deter the threat that most experts think is the most serious we face and against which, under the best of circumstances, we will have very little real defense.

So the question remains of how well national governments are doing in building international and domestic defenses against terrorists or criminal gangs armed with nuclear, biological, or chemical weapons. The response has not been equal to the potential threat. Applying international norms in situations that have a high domestic component requires an integration of foreign and domestic policies and of government agencies that deal with foreign and domestic programs.

Now Russia and the United States are working their way through a learning period similar to their first experiments with cooperation during the Cold War. They have conducted the first experiments in dealing with terrorism and illicit trafficking in nuclear materials. They are learning over again the value of first steps, of ultimate goals, and of institutionalizing cooperation. They are dealing with a phenomenon that could be called a new medievalism. New forms of cooperation among states are required, based on for a firm connection between international norms and domestic actions and policies. The wall between the "foreign" and the "domestic" realms will have to be broken down if the fight against the new medievalism is to succeed.[15]

Leadership from the top is needed to overcome inertia and entrenched resistance from the upholders of old ways of managing the nation's affairs. Without leadership from the top, the funding to deal with problems of nuclear theft, nuclear smuggling, and nuclear terrorism will not be available, either in the United States or in Russia. Without top-level commitment in Russia, the barons of MINATOM and the Federal Counterintelligence Service will continue their feuds with one another and with the United States, while essential improvements in protecting fissile materials lag. It is evident from Russian government statements and decrees that international norms and international cooperation provide a legitimacy and a requirement for Russian efforts to prevent nuclear smuggling. Top-level U.S.-Russian dialogues, such as those very effectively carried out in the Gore-Chernomyrdin framework, need to continue despite the temptation to move on to other issues. And finally, it is only from the top level in the U.S. government that the true nature of the threat can be explained and the management of foreign and domestic concerns be effectively conducted to combat it.

5

Principles, Leaders, and the Use of Force

The Case of Yugoslavia

Moving beyond the norms and rules associated with a conditional peace in Europe, a peace where war is still thinkable, requires a vision that both the Bush and the Clinton administrations have declared and embraced as their own: "Europe whole and free," in the words of President Bush, and "a peaceful, undivided, and democratic continent," in the words of President Clinton. Achieving this goal is almost synonymous with achieving a stable peace between Russia and the United States. Achieving a stable peace in Europe, built on democratic norms and rules, requires the governments that espouse this goal to devise a strategy to deal with conflicts arising from tendencies toward internal fragmentation. Leaders must respond to ethnic or communal conflicts that threaten to vitiate the norms and rules that support international peace and security. The sobering lesson of repeated wars in Europe, as elsewhere, is that rules are not self-enforcing.

Norms and rules of behavior require enforcement, either by direct countervailing action, in the cases of the major powers, or by collective action. Sometimes enforcement requires the threat or use of armed force. Without that possibility, order-building diplomacy will be fatally ineffective. But if no major power believes its interests are seriously affected, if the cost of enforcement is high, or the circumstances ambiguous, any action, whether unilateral or collective, inevitably becomes difficult and perhaps impossible. Such was the case in the former Yugoslavia, the tragic source of many lessons concerning the relationship between norms and the use of force.

Marshal Tito, the undisputed leader of Yugoslavia, died in 1980, a success in having prevented ethnic conflict during his long reign but a failure in preparing the way for a peaceful breakup of the country or, alternatively, in creating an enduring sense of Yugoslav nationhood. The result of this failure was a slow fragmentation of the country, marked by devolution of authority to the republics and a disavowal by the leaderships of those republics of a real sense of responsibility for the future of Yugoslavia as a whole. Those leaders found that nationalism was an effective device for justifying their hold on power after the collapse of communist ideology. They felt no responsibility to the outside world for settling their growing disputes over the nature of the Yugoslav federation and the sanctity of internal boundaries imposed by Tito. There were standards that the international community had a right to ask these men to consider as they moved toward their bloody confrontation, but hardly any pressure was exerted on them. The principles and practices of the Helsinki Final Act of the Conference on Security and Cooperation in Europe provided ample grounds for expecting the leaders of the disintegrating federation to settle their differences peacefully, if not amicably. Neither the Yugoslav politicians nor the leaders of other countries saw fit to insist that these norms be observed—until it was too late.

The Western Europeans had turned their backs on the problem in the fall of 1990 when the United States had raised the issue. The United States gratefully and quickly passed the buck to the ill-prepared Europeans in 1991.[1] As the crisis was building, there was no leader, no organizing agent that could galvanize the international community, or that part of it most affected by the crisis in Yugoslavia. Consequently, norms and rules of behavior were discredited. Since the war in Bosnia may be the archetypical threat to Europe's peace and security in the coming decades, we should learn well the lessons of that tragedy. That is the purpose of this chapter.

The Political Dilemmas of Defending International Order

As the war escalated, the costs of a successful military intervention to impose a settlement were seen to be progressively higher. Arguments were made in the United States that the war was a European affair and in Europe that American proposals to help the Bosnian government would be self-defeating. Ideas about how nations should behave were themselves in conflict in Bosnia: the principles of self-determination, territorial integrity, and rights of minorities served each of the parties to the dispute, making it hard for people outside the area to weigh the merits of the case. The readiness of the Bosnian Serb military and militias to slaughter innocent civilians on a scale that suggested genocide was the clearest distinction for outsiders to see.

Because of these circumstances, the leaders of the European and North American countries faced real dilemmas. All of them had public opinion problems. Each of them had qualms about the casualties their military forces would take if they intervened. At the same time, probably most of them were concerned by the prospect that prohibitions against changing frontiers by force would be weakened—a dangerous development in a continent where most frontiers are arbitrary. And so they dithered, while thousands of people lost their lives and other thousands all their worldly belongings.

At the heart of the debate over Bosnia's future was the problem of reconciling the principles of self-determination and territorial integrity. How could ethnic minorities be guaranteed their legitimate rights without massive population shifts? How could Bosnia survive as a single state with internal arrangements acceptable to the three constituent nations? Through most of 1991 to 1995 the governments whose decisions would be most influential in shaping a diplomatic approach to a settlement could not define, collectively or individually, how or why these issues mattered to them. The question of whether a conflict in the Balkans presented a direct threat to the interests of outside powers found governments and the public in the West deeply divided. If the Bosnian disaster was a civil war, it was easy to say that outsiders should not intervene. If the war was a blatant act of aggression, everything would be different. Naturally, this ambivalence had an effect on the commitment to the peace process of senior Western leaders even though the need for a settlement was unquestioned. The images of Munich and Vietnam and Lebanon were evoked in the Yugoslav crisis as reminders of appeasement, quagmires, and a failure to identify clear political objectives to be achieved by military force. Some Western officials found it difficult to accept that Bosnia-Herzegovina was a real state, given the paucity of convincing history on that score.

Earlier and firmer action by external actors could have headed off the Yugoslav conflict or at least limited its scale, in the view of most commentators on the Yugoslav disaster. Circumstances almost always make early intervention difficult especially in cases that can plausibly be labeled as civil war. The basic dilemma is a familiar one: it is indeed obvious that as events move from a minor dispute to a major crisis greater efforts will be required to deal with the situation. But at the earliest stage of a diplomatic dispute, the case for external intervention cannot be convincingly made.[2] In fact, concerted action faces a series of hurdles that routinely appear in every crisis:

- There is no clearly definable point at which outside forces—great powers, neighboring states, or international organizations—should begin to concert their policies to deal with a conflict that is only potential.
- It is difficult to identify a threshold beyond which lies the possibility of violence on a major scale.
- Nations are usually unwilling to use coercive measures before violence has occurred and then only if the level of violence shocks the international community into action.
- The international community is not well organized for crisis prevention activities that involve less than crystal-clear state-on-state aggression.
- There is no method by which the international community can gauge the ultimate impact on international peace and security of a slowly developing crisis.
- There are few criteria to determine whether the better course would be to contain and isolate a dispute or to attempt to settle it.

Diplomacy in a Disintegrating Order

The West, and the United States in particular, had hoped that the able Yugoslav prime minister Ante Markovic could lead the Yugoslav federation through its crisis in 1991. Washington's support for Markovic, however, was insufficient to overcome the rise of the nationalists in

Serbia and in the other republics, all of whom worked to undermine him. The process of disintegration gathered momentum rapidly, and Markovic resigned in December 1991. As the federation began to split apart, the Western powers began to consider their interests in a new Yugoslav constitution based on loose ties among the republics. For Serbia, in the absence of border changes, this meant that very substantial parts of the Serb nation would live in states not under Belgrade's control.

The last of the prewar efforts to save Yugoslavia from disintegration was announced on June 6, 1991, after a meeting of the Yugoslav Collective State Presidency. Put forward by President Izetbegovic of Bosnia-Herzegovina and President Gligorov of Macedonia, the idea essentially was to convert Yugoslavia into a loose confederation. It was too little and too late. As the last U.S. ambassador to Yugoslavia, Warren Zimmermann, has reported: "When Croatia opted for independence in mid-1991, Bosnian President Izetbegovic saw the writing on the wall for his republic. . . . He pushed, without success, the dying Izetbegovic-Gligorov plan for a loosely connected Yugoslavia."[3] Slovenia and Croatia announced their independence from the Yugoslav federation on June 25, 1991. The first stage of the war began immediately thereafter.

The Brioni Declaration of July 7, 1991, brokered by the European Community (later "Union"), recognized that the principle of a Yugoslavia federated as it had been under Tito had to be revised.[4] By that time nationalism and the drive for separation had assumed such emotional force in Serbia and Croatia that a constitutional connection between them was an impossibility. The fate of Bosnia-Herzegovina had to be resolved in the context of a disintegrating Yugoslavia in which that republic's frontiers were challenged by its neighbors, for whom many borders were invalid after the end of the federation. When the idea of a loosely confederated Yugoslavia was discarded, other approaches to the status of Bosnia-Herzegovina had to be devised. They all faced the same problems of norms and rules guiding minority rights, self-determination, and territorial integrity.

On September 7, 1991, the European Community (EC) convened a peace conference in The Hague. It included the leaders of the six republics of Yugoslavia and EC ministers and was chaired by Lord Carrington. Among the proposals advanced by the EC was one to replace the Yugoslav federal structure with a "free association of republics with an international personality." Guarantees for the rights of minorities would be provided, ethnic enclaves would be disarmed, and programs for economic cooperation would be established. There would be no uni-lateral changes in borders. Serbia, Montenegro, and Slovenia refused to accept this restructuring plan. On October 7, 1991, after an EC-brokered three-month delay in implementing their declarations of independence, Slovenia and Croatia proceeded to nullify their legal connections with the Yugoslav federal government.[5] Lord Carrington persisted a bit longer. On October 18, 1991, he issued a document entitled "Arrange-ments for a General Settlement." It mentioned the option of "sovereign and independent republics with international personality for those who wish it."[6] But by the end of October, President Milosevic of Serbia was dismissing the EC plan as a violation of Yugoslavia's federal constitu-tion. The hope that a loose confederation might replace the old order had ended.

At the EC foreign ministers' meeting in Brussels on December 16, 1991, prodded forcefully by Germany, the ministers agreed unani-mously that they would extend recognition by January 15, 1992, to any Yugoslav republics that asked for it by December 23, but they tied this to certain norms and rules:

- respect for human rights, the rights of ethnic minorities, and the democratic process;
- acceptance of border changes only by peaceful means; and
- agreement to submit territorial disputes to binding arbitration.[7]

The decision, however, would permit EC members to extend recog-nition even if the order that these standards would imprint had not been met.[8] Thus, as the new year of 1992 dawned, the conflict in Yugoslavia would cease being a civil war and become an international European war. The media speculated that fighting would soon spread to Bosnia-Herzegovina. Just at this point, the first phase of the war of the Yugoslav succession ended with an agreement on the fifteenth cease-fire on January 3, 1992, and the subsequent stationing of UN peacekeeping troops in Croatia. The instability of the military and political situation in the former Yugoslavia was not altered by this development. In fact, the position in which the UN peacekeepers were placed when they were deployed was quite ambiguous and left the UN vulnerable to the criticism that was not slow in coming.

Failure to Reconcile Conflicting Norms

For several months in 1991–92 it had seemed possible that the war in the former Yugoslavia could be contained. The fighting had been essentially limited to border areas between Serbia/Montenegro and Croatia. Slovenia ceased to be a war zone after a few days of limited combat when the Yugoslav People's Army pulled out to focus its attention on Croatia. The other republics, Macedonia and Bosnia-Herzegovina, maintained neutrality between the combatants and remained at peace. Kosovo and Vojvodina, which had been autonomous administrative units under Tito, lost their autonomy between the fall of 1988 and spring 1990. Vojvodina fell first with Milosevic taking control of the political apparatus in the region. Milosevic dissolved the Kosovo assembly and government on July 5, 1990. These areas remained quiescent during the fighting in 1991, the latter under harsh repressive control by Belgrade.

The period between July 1991 through April 1992 was a critical juncture for crisis prevention. Diplomacy had failed to deal effectively with events in Yugoslavia prior to July 1991, but there was still a chance to prevent war in those parts of Yugoslavia not affected by the dispute between Croatia and Serbia. Bosnia-Herzegovina was a microcosm of the Yugoslav federation. In the November 1990 elections in Bosnia-Herzegovina the following resulted: Muslims, 86 seats; Serbs, 72 seats; and Croats, 44 seats—a near-perfect representation of their relative percentages of the population. The Bosnian Muslims watched the conflict between Serbia and Croatia with considerable alarm. As 1991 wore on, the three nations of Bosnia-Herzegovina—Serbs, Croats, and Muslims—began to split apart. The Serbs opposed independence, Croatia armed the Croats in western Herzegovina, and while the Muslims still entertained the idea of ethnic pluralism they expected to be the dominant group.[9]

What might have been expected of the three communities in Bosnia-Herzegovina in this period, and how could the international community have encouraged that outcome? Immense caution regarding the governance of the republic and a maximum commitment to intensive dialogue among the communities was what was required. It cannot be said that this obligation was met by any of the parties, and the external parties intervened in a manner that made dialogue impossible. Both the European Community and the United States insisted that a referendum should be conducted in Bosnia in order to determine whether the citizens really wanted to opt for a status outside the Yugoslav federation. Only thereafter would Bosnia and Herzegovina be given recognition.[10] This exerted irresistible pressure on the Muslims and Croats in Bosnia-Herzegovina to seek independence before working out any understandings about interethnic rights and responsibilities. It can be argued that understandings would have been impossible to achieve, and there is much merit in that argument. On the other hand, forcing the pace of events served little purpose. The Bosnian government's decision to conduct a referendum on independence predictably led to a refusal of the minority Serbs to take part in the voting.

The question of whether minorities could safely live in republics dominated by another ethnic group had been at the heart of the question of whether alternatives to a federated Yugoslavia could be created without bloodshed. By the time the voting took place in Bosnia-Herzegovina, the Serbian-Croatian conflict foretold without a doubt that disintegration of the federation could not proceed without violent conflict. The Bosnian Serbs rejected the results of the referendum, and fighting began in April 1992. As the fighting began, former U.S. secretary of state Cyrus Vance, now the representative of the UN Secretary-General, went to Sarajevo to try to prevent the conflict from escalating. But the United Nations lacked the resources to mount a second massive peacekeeping operation in the former Yugoslavia. Secretary Vance was driven to say in April 1992, "We are not going to put in any additional forces. We simply do not have any resources to do it."[11]

The horrific consequences of a war in Bosnia-Herzegovina were predicted, but some terrible aspects of it were not. Serbs, Croatians, and Bosnian Muslims continued to live peaceably among themselves in Bosnian government–controlled Sarajevo during the siege. Not all Bosnian Serbs held the extreme nationalist views that Karadzic championed, nor did all Serbs support the extreme positions of Milosevic. But all Serbian members of the Bosnian parliament followed Karadzic to the Bosnian Serb capital of Pale, and all but two Croatians went with the Croatian separatist Mate Boban. Predictions of a bloodbath were understated, if anything. It was almost unimaginable that the Nazi-like "ethnic cleansing" strategy of the Serbs and later of the Croatians could occur in the 1990s, yet Vukovar, a largely Croat city in Croatia, had been subjected to exactly this treatment by Serbia in the first phase of the Balkan war. More was to come in Bosnia. Three major effects of the war were given scant attention in prewar analysis: the precedent of state-sponsored racism in post–Cold War Europe, the destabilizing effect of refugees, and the propensity for the dynamics of the situation to involve other Balkan states.

The Diplomacy of Reconstruction

During the years 1991–95 several different approaches to the question of how to organize Bosnia-Herzegovina and end the fighting were explored. Each approach faced the problem of reconciling conflicting principles: territorial integrity, self-determination, and rights of individuals and of minority groups. The use of force was an element in each approach. And underlying each approach was a tension between the United States and the Europeans. This section recounts the experience of trying to reconstruct a political entity that was never well constituted in the first place.

Alternative 1: Partition Bosnia

Without external intervention a settlement in Bosnia would almost certainly have been achieved by force majeure. The strongest parties— Serbia and Croatia—would have agreed on partition and imposed it on Bosnia. Probably this was discussed seriously between Serbs and Croats as early as 1990. It is known that on May 7, 1992, the Serbs and the Croats met at Graz, Austria, to discuss the future of Bosnia-Herzegovina. The map that resulted from that meeting granted large tracts of land in the north, east, and southeast to the Bosnian Serbs, most of Herzegovina to the Bosnian Croats, and the central portion of Bosnia and the Bihac pocket to the Muslims.[12] Under this plan the central government of Bosnia-Herzegovina would lose control over most of its territory. The Bosnian Serbs and the Bosnian Croats would have a right to and would expect to merge with their brethren across the borders.

The plan in its various forms was consistently rejected by the Western powers. Condoning the territorial conquests of the Serbs was not possible for the United States and the European Community. The Bosnian government, of course, rejected anything like a solution that would deprive it of control of most of its territory. Only during the desperate summer of 1993 were the Bosnians encouraged to acquiesce in the short-lived Owen-Stoltenberg plan, a concept that would have led in short order to a merger of the Croatian- and Serbian-dominated areas of Bosnia with Croatia and Serbia.[13] It was never seriously discussed.

The outside powers were critically important in determining the outcome of the partition alternative: they stood in the way. It is doubtful that the Bosnian government could have successfully resisted partition if the Western powers had been completely neutral on the question. Some in the West did hold the opinion that the sides should simply battle it out and let partition be the result. For those who doubted that Bosnia ever could be a viable state, this was a logical position to hold. But most governments were influenced, and strongly so, by the lessons of Munich (namely, that condoning acts of aggression only feeds the ambitions of the aggressor) and by the principle that frontiers should not be changed by force. Had matters been otherwise, and Western governments had actively supported partition on the best terms available, Bosnia almost certainly would have succumbed. Certainly, it was within the power of Croatia and Serbia to produce this result through military means. Western pressure helped to prevent that, thus leaving the door open to a negotiated political settlement.

Alternative 2: Cantonize Bosnia-Herzegovina

The spring of 1992 witnessed the first attempt at political settlement specifically directed at Bosnia-Herzegovina by the outside powers: the European Community, continuing to take the lead in finding a solution to the fighting, empowered its negotiator, Ambassador José Cutileiro of Portugal, to propose separate districts for each of the three ethnic groups with power-sharing arrangements at the central government level. Ambassador Cutileiro established the goal of "cantonization" as the basis for the negotiations. Ten rounds of talks with senior representatives of the three Bosnian nations took place under his chairmanship. The high-water mark was reached on March 18, 1992, when agreement was reached in Sarajevo among the three parties on a Statement of Principles for New Constitutional Arrangements for Bosnia and Herzegovina, and on a map appended to the principles.[14] The Bosnian Serbs had accepted the idea that Bosnia-Herzegovina would be divided into three ethnically defined regions but that the country would remain intact and not be divided between Serbia and Croatia.[15]

President Izetbegovic repudiated his agreement to the plan almost immediately, which undermined whatever prospects the plan had of being applied. Ethnic partition was not possible because of Bosnia's mixed composition, he argued, adding that he had signed because the EC had made his agreement a precondition for diplomatic recognition. The official U.S. position at the time was neutral: whatever the EC and the parties to the conflict could work out would be acceptable to Washington.[16]

Additional principles on human rights were agreed to on March 31, but at the same time the Croats reneged on the map. The entire agreement was repudiated soon after.[17] War on a large scale was guaranteed when, on May 19, 1992, the Yugoslav People's Army pulled out of Bosnia-Herzegovina, leaving weapons and Bosnian Serb members of the army to augment Bosnian Serb militia forces. By August 1992 the United States was firmly on record as opposed to cantonization. A statement released by the State Department on August 19, 1992, recorded that Acting Secretary Eagleburger "agreed with the [Bosnian] Foreign Minister that 'cantonization' of Bosnia-Herzegovina contradicts CSCE principles, sets a bad precedent for future conflicts, and could well lead to partition of Bosnia-Herzegovina—thus rewarding the use of force."[18]

The coolness of the United States toward the Cutileiro plan made it impossible for a negotiation aimed at cantonization to succeed. The Bosnian government hoped for U.S. support for a better deal, and so long as that could be held out as a possibility by hard-line Bosnian Muslim politicians, rejection of peace plans based on cantonization was inevitable. Given the serious objections of many top Bosnian Muslim officials to the Cutileiro plan, sustained backing from the European Community and at least tacit support from other nations would have been required to make it work.

The situation in the early part of 1992 was highly unstable, and a military input much greater than any external power was prepared to offer would have been necessary to help the Cutileiro plan succeed. Some argue that a limited military intervention would have deterred the Bosnian Serbs. A Western response to the Serb attack on Dubrovnik was a course urged by many in the West for that reason. But a military response of that type almost certainly would not have been followed by any other military action by the Western European Union or NATO. The Serbs could draw their own conclusions from that.[19]

The massive population shifts that took place in Bosnia-Herzegovina later in the war had not yet taken place in 1992. The only questions are whether under the Cutileiro plan these might have been prevented or if they might have occurred with less bloodshed and suffering than was actually the case in later years. It is very likely that there would have been violent efforts to effect "ethnic cleansing" and that forced population shifts would have occurred.

Alternative 3: Divide Bosnia into Small, Self-Administered Units

A third approach to a political settlement, and the most elaborate, came from the Geneva International Conference on the Former Yugoslavia (ICFY), which replaced the EC Conference on Yugoslavia in August 1992. Cyrus Vance and David Owen were named cochairs of the Steering Committee. Ambassador Martti Ahtisaari, a distinguished Finnish diplomat, later to become president of Finland, was named chairman of a Working Group on Bosnia-Herzegovina. The problem they faced as they began work in Geneva on September 3, 1992, was that the Bosnian government and the Bosnian Serbs had opposite ideas about the future of Bosnia-Herzegovina.[20] The Sarajevo government advocated a centralized, unitary state arranged for administrative reasons into a number of regions. The Bosnian Serbs wanted Bosnia-Herzegovina divided into three independent states, one each for the Muslim, Serb, and Croat populations.

The cochairmen, Vance and Owen, concluded that the intermingling of the population meant that three separate sovereign territories based on ethnicity could be achieved only through enforced population transfer. Furthermore, the Serb and Croat states could be expected to form ties with Serbia and Croatia, rather than with the Muslim-dominated state. One answer to the problem, a centralized state, would not be accepted by the Bosnian Serbs and Croats, who would fear that it would not protect their interests. From this reasoning, Vance and Owen came to the conclusion that the answer to the dilemma lay in *two* cardinal features. One was that Bosnia would have to be a decentralized state. The central government, in the words of the Vance-Owen report, "would have only those minimal responsibilities that are necessary for a state to function as such."[21] The other feature was division of the country into several administrative units. Seven to ten (ten, in the final version) autonomous provinces would be established that would independently handle most of the affairs of the republic. Ethnic considerations would not be the only factor determining the boundaries of the provinces. Geographical, historical, economic, and other factors also should be taken into account. Their report of October 25, 1992, however, could not avoid noting that "a high percentage of each group would be living in a province in which it constitutes a numerical majority, although most of the provinces would also have significant numerical minorities."[22]

By January 30, 1993, Vance and Owen had succeeded in securing the agreement of the three groups to nine principles that reflected the concept of a decentralized state with most governmental functions carried out by the provinces. Other features of the proposed political settlement were not accepted. The Croats accepted the constitutional principles and the map drawn up by the Vance-Owen team defining the boundaries of the ten provinces. The Bosnian government and the Bosnian Serbs, however, held out against the proposed boundaries for the provinces.[23] The Bosnian government also would not sign the agreement on Military and Related Issues, believing that UN provisions for the internment and monitoring of Serb heavy weapons were inadequate.[24]

Another document was presented to the three Bosnian parties on January 29, 1993, entitled "Interim Arrangements for Bosnia and Herzegovina." This was a proposal for establishing an interim central government through a procedure that envisaged each of the parties nominating three representatives who would be subject to the approval of cochairs Vance and Owen. The existing presidency of Bosnia-Herzegovina would then transfer its powers and authority to the interim central government that would remain in power until elections could be held. There would also be interim governments in each of the provinces. A governor would be nominated by one of the three parties, depending on the ethnic composition of the particular province. The allocation to ethnic groups was designated in the document. This document, too, was rejected by the Bosnian government's representatives.

The cochairs had decided that the Geneva negotiations should be suspended after January 1993 and the negotiation shifted to the United Nations in New York. There, the cochairs hoped, pressure could be brought to bear on the parties by the Security Council to accept the proposals worked out by the Vance-Owen team. Owen stated at the time, "I hope that by the time we get to the Security Council we will have all the parties signed up. That is why we brought it deliberately to a crunch. We have the feeling it can be resolved in New York."[25] According to aides to Vance and Owen, the negotiators hoped to isolate the Bosnian Serbs and to get Belgrade and the Russians to press the Bosnian Serbs to settle the conflict.[26]

The hope entertained by Vance and Owen was dashed in fairly short order, in part by a February 10 declaration by U.S. secretary of state Warren Christopher.[27] His statement made it clear that the Clinton administration found serious flaws in the Vance-Owen plan and thought it could be improved. The administration would not pressure the Bosnian Muslims to accept it. Shortly after, President Clinton sent his secretary of state to Europe to inquire whether the Europeans would support a "lift and strike" strategy of lifting the arms embargo and using air power to strike at the Bosnian Serbs. They would not, and the strategy was shelved.

Despite these events, on March 3, 1993, President Izetbegovic signed the document on separation of forces and cessation of hostilities, and on March 25, 1993, the Bosnian government signed the agreement on interim governmental arrangements and accepted a revised map of the provincial boundaries.[28] The Bosnian Serb representatives kept their distance from the map and the interim arrangements, asserting that these proposals would have to be sent to their assembly for consideration and decision. To keep up the pressure, the Bosnian government announced that its signature would be invalidated if the other parties did not sign within a reasonable time period, if the international community did not undertake to enforce the agreement, and if the aggression continued.[29] The Bosnian Serbs signed the interim arrangements and the map on May 2, 1993, in a meeting in Athens, Greece, but

Bosnian Serb leader Karadzic stated that his signature would be void if the Bosnian Serb assembly failed to support the decision in a vote that would take place on May 5, 1993.[30] This was as close as the Vance-Owen plan came to becoming the basis for a political settlement. The Bosnian Serb assembly rejected the accord, as did a "popular referendum" among the Bosnian Serb population two weeks later. The Vance-Owen plan expired at that point for all practical purposes. Lord Owen declared the plan officially dead on June 16, 1993, and shifted his support to what amounted to a delayed partition solution.[31]

Critics of the Vance-Owen plan believed that the proposed political settlement awarded too much to the aggressors and that there was much that was unclear about enforcing it. But the plan clearly would have done more to preserve the multiethnic character of Bosnia than any of the alternatives. The fundamental question that each of the proposed political settlements tried to address was how ethnic groups should be governed, protected, and guaranteed their basic human rights within a single state.

In the Vance-Owen plan, ethnic groups were given constitutional recognition and the central government was to be organized along ethnic lines, with power sharing among the three groups. The constitution would regulate all matters of vital concern to any of the constituent parties and could be amended in these respects only by consensus among the three groups. The leading official of each of the individual provinces would be a member of an ethnic group designated according to the composition of the population. Critics of the plan argued with much evidence on their side that the dominant ethnic group in each province would probably indulge in ethnic cleansing. The deliberately weak powers of the central government suggested that, at the least, the provinces would develop stronger ties with Serbia and Croatia than with each other or with the central government.

Some supporters of the plan pointed out that Bosnia-Herzegovina had never been an independent, sovereign state and that Vance and Owen were essentially creating a state where none had existed before.[32] The plan certainly could not be self-enforcing, and tens of thousands of outside troops would be required, probably for years, to police the settlement. At the time, the Bosnian Serbs had reached a commanding position militarily within Bosnia-Herzegovina. The United States would provide up to twenty thousand troops to help monitor a peace settlement, the Clinton administration pledged. A civilian-run administrative structure also would have to be put in place by the UN to parallel the tripartite central government structure created by the Vance-Owen plan. Bosnia-Herzegovina would be virtually a UN trust territory for many years to come.

Alternative 4: Cantonization Revisited

The fourth alternative proposal for a political settlement was offered up on a take-it-or-leave-it basis by the "Contact Group," formed on April 25, 1994, among the United States, Russia, and the European Union, represented by Britain, France, and Germany. From April through early July 1994, the Contact Group worked out a plan for a political settlement that focused on allocation of territory to the three nations of Bosnia-Herzegovina within the current boundaries of Bosnia-Herzegovina. A map devised by this group would give 51 percent of the territory to a federation of Bosnian Muslims and Bosnian Croats, and 49 percent to Bosnian Serbs; the Serbs would be required to hand back areas around Srebrenica, Gorazde, and Zepa—the Muslim enclaves in Eastern Bosnia—and lands in the north that would shrink the size of the corridor linking Serb-controlled lands to the west and the east. Details regarding constitutional arrangements would be offered once the parties had agreed on the map. The five powers agreed that economic sanctions would be the punishment of first resort if their take-it-or-leave-it plan was rejected. The map was accepted by the Bosnian government and the Croats, but was effectively rejected by the Bosnian Serbs.[33]

Russia's Appearance on the Bosnian Stage

The impetus for a more active and direct U.S. participation in the search for a political settlement was a mortar attack on a marketplace in Sarajevo on February 5, 1994, that left sixty-eight dead and hundreds wounded. This completely changed the political context. The United States and the European Union quickly agreed to set a deadline for Serb withdrawal of artillery and mortars, NATO air strikes being the punishment for noncompliance.[34] Before the collapse of the Soviet Union, Moscow had made it very clear that the Soviet government opposed Western intervention in Yugoslavia and that it leaned toward Serbia's cause. A Soviet statement in August 1991 warned that "to enter . . . on one side of the conflict would mean to come into conflict automatically with others inside and outside Yugoslavia. And the conflict would grow into an all-European one."[35] Moscow also opposed NATO's intervention in 1994, saying there should be an investigation into the February 5 attack. Russian foreign minister Kozyrev's first statements were ominous. He was quoted as saying that air strikes would "cast a very dark shadow over our relationship" with the West.[36] The Russians seemed particularly incensed that the forum for discussing the issue had been NATO and not the UN. The Russians finally conceded that NATO had the authority under existing UN resolutions to carry out the air strikes, but nevertheless insisted on a Security Council meeting. The Security Council met on February 14, and Russia settled for no change in the previous UN resolution.

Russia had consistently supported UN Security Council resolutions on the former Yugoslavia but had remained aloof from the efforts to settle the conflict. Serbia's cause was popular in Russia, and while the Bosnian Serbs were doing well, there was no need to intervene. Faced with the unappealing prospect of NATO's use of force in the Balkans, the Russians now became more actively engaged in the negotiations. Special Russian envoy Vitali Churkin played a major role in the compromise for a Bosnian Serb withdrawal of heavy weapons around Sarajevo with all that this implied for future involvement. This was managed by Churkin's proposal to place some eight hundred Russian peacekeepers in Sarajevo for unspecified duties and was worked out between Churkin and Bosnian Serb leader Karadzic.[37] In doing so the Russians won the support of a somewhat nervous West, which wanted the shelling stopped but feared Russian influence in the Balkans, and the support of the Serbs, who saw the Russians as friendly protectors.

Some in the West had always seen Russia as a valuable partner and a link to the Serbs. As early as July 1992, Lord Carrington noted that the United States and Russia might do better than the Western Europeans in driving the negotiations forward.[38] Russia took an active part in the London Conference on the former Yugoslavia in August 1992. When the new Clinton administration decided to work for better terms than those the Vance-Owen plan offered the Bosnian government,

Ambassador Bartholomew went to Moscow first to consult with the Russians.[39] Russia was also involved in the negotiations for a long-term settlement of the Croatian-Serbian dispute. The strategy was developed by Vitali Churkin and Charles E. Redman, the U.S. representative in the former Yugoslavia, and was premised on the normalization of daily relations between the Croats and the Serbs in Croatia, followed by a negotiation of a political settlement.[40] As a sign of their influence with the Krajina Serbs the Russians persuaded them to go to Zagreb to negotiate with the Croatian government using the Russian embassy there as a venue. Russia supported Croatian sovereignty over the Krajina areas.[41] Although the United States played the leading role in the negotiations between the Bosnian Croats and Bosnian Muslims concerning a federation between the two, as well as between Croatia and Bosnia concerning an economic confederation, Russia also was involved. Russia's primary mission was to mediate between the Bosnian Serbs and the other Bosnian communities. This remained the case until the events of 1995 shifted the balance of forces away from the Bosnian Serbs and gave a decisive opportunity to the U.S. diplomacy. The remaining question for Russia then became whether to participate in the Implementing Force (IFOR). Secretary of Defense Perry and Russian Defense Minister Grachev made it possible to answer that question affirmatively, with Russian troops reporting through their commander to an American general. This decision was fundamental for the future of peacekeeping in Europe.

1995—Year of Decision

Just before Christmas 1994, former U.S. president Jimmy Carter successfully brokered a four-month truce in the fighting. The Serbs were in a strong position territorially at this time, but the truce was the lull before the storm. By spring 1995, the Bosnian government army and the Croatian army were able to confront the Bosnian and Krajina Serbs from a position of military strength. As the Carter cease-fire broke down, fighting erupted all across the region. Event followed event: the Croatians recaptured territory in western Slavonia; the Krajina Serbs launched rocket attacks in May on downtown Zagreb; the Bosnian government forces fought to break the Serb stranglehold on Sarajevo; attacks and counterattacks followed one another in the Bihac pocket; Bosnian Serbs began to step up military pressure against the UN-protected Bosnian Muslim safe havens in eastern Bosnia; the Serbs violated the NATO-imposed heavy-weapon exclusion zone around Sarajevo. In response to this last challenge to NATO, on May 25 and 26, NATO aircraft attacked ammunition dumps near the Bosnian Serb capital of Pale. The Bosnian Serb response was to seize close to four hundred UN peacekeepers, many of them nationals of NATO countries. Extraction of all UN forces became a real possibility. On June 1, the British and the French announced their intention to deploy a well-armed rapid-reaction force to Bosnia to protect UN forces. On June 28, NATO approved a plan to help in the evacuation of these forces.

General Mladic of the Bosnian-Serb forces escalated the assault on the United Nations by attacking UN safe havens, capturing Srebrenica on July 11. The fall of Srebrenica was accompanied by a massacre by Mladic's forces of thousands of Muslim men and boys. Zepa fell on July 25. The next day the U.S. Senate voted to lift the arms embargo against Bosnia; the House followed suit on August 1. On August 4, Croatia launched a lightning strike against Krajina, which fell in two days. Nearly all the Krajina Serbs fled the territory for Serb-controlled areas in Bosnia and for Serbia itself. This, of course, relieved the Bihac pocket of the pressure Serbs had been placing on it.

With the military situation dramatically changed, the Clinton administration sent National Security Adviser Lake and Under Secretary of State Tarnoff to Europe on August 9 to discuss a U.S. peace plan. Thus began the Americanization of the diplomatic effort to reach a political settlement. Deputy Assistant Secretary of State Robert Frasure, however, had paved the way by patiently talking with Milosevic all during the summer of 1995 on quid pro quos for gradual lifting of sanctions. Assistant Secretary Richard Holbrooke took up the mission on August 14, traveling to the former Yugoslavia. Five days later, three senior American officials traveling with him, including Robert Frasure, were tragically killed on Mount Igman. On August 28, another Bosnian Serb mortar attack on civilians in Sarajevo killed thirty-seven people. The United Nations and NATO had been warning the Bosnian Serbs that there would be a retaliation if the Serbs attacked Gorazde, a large Muslim safe haven in eastern Bosnia, and if the Serbs continued to attack

Sarajevo from within the heavy-weapon exclusion zone. By this time, a redeployment of UN peacekeepers had made them less vulnerable to being taken hostage. The NATO retaliation was an air campaign that began on August 30 and ended on September 14. The air campaign was highly successful in changing the military balance to the Bosnian Serbs' disadvantage.

After these events a decision to involve U.S. ground forces in Bosnia became a serious possibility. Economic distress in Serbia resulting from international sanctions added a powerful argument in favor of a political settlement. On August 30, Holbrooke's effort to engage Milosevic in peace negotiations paid off: Milosevic agreed to speak for the Bosnian Serbs, whose leaders were divided and branded as war criminals, and assumed the mantle of peacemaker. This was a key procedural break in Holbrooke's negotiations. The economic pressure on Belgrade and Frasure's skillful handling of this pressure contributed to it.

Diplomacy had achieved several objectives during the 1994–95 period that paved the way for successful negotiations. These objectives included the following:

- a federation between the Bosnian Croatians and the Bosnian Muslims;

- an agreement that President Milosevic would negotiate on behalf of the Bosnian Serbs;

- an agreement on September 8, 1995, that Croatia and Serbia would recognize the territorial integrity of Bosnia;

- an agreement with the NATO allies that NATO air power would be used on a broad scale in response to Bosnian Serb challenges to UN Security Council decisions; and

- an agreement within the Contact Group on a peace plan that the United States could negotiate with the parties to the conflict.

On the military side of the equation, a new power balance was created that made the difference between success and failure in the effort to achieve a peace settlement:

- The army of Croatia demonstrated its prowess in its Krajina campaign and, in the process, decisively set back the Bosnian Serb cause in western Bosnia.

- The NATO air campaign significantly disrupted the military effectiveness of General Mladic's forces.
- The deployment of a heavily armed British-French rapid reaction force gave the United Nations an in-country fighting force that posed a new threat to Bosnian Serb forces around Sarajevo.
- UN peacekeepers were withdrawn from exposed positions so that NATO air power could be used without fear of peacekeepers being seized as hostages.
- Bosnian government forces had gradually strengthened their combat capabilities.

Late 1995, for all these reasons, was a time when the situation in the former Yugoslavia was highly fluid and the prospects for a settlement were promising.[42] The Bosnian Serbs were no longer dominating the field of battle. They were more evenly matched by their opponents, the Bosnian government forces and the Croatian army. It appeared that the time had come, finally, to intervene with U.S. troops if a settlement could be achieved.[43]

Success at Dayton

The U.S. government made decisions in 1995 that it had ducked in 1992–94, but not only because the situation on the ground had improved. If the balance of forces had been the only factor in the equation, the decision might have been postponed. The fact is that a crisis had arisen in the summer of 1995 that forced hard decisions. The mandate for UN peacekeepers deployed in Croatia was about to expire, and the Croatian government had said that it did not intend to renew the mandate. The Bosnian Serbs had brutally overrun Muslim-held towns in eastern Bosnia, humiliating the nations that provided UN peacekeepers. The U.S. Congress had given the administration a limited time to resolve the conflict before requiring that the arms embargo against Bosnia be lifted. NATO allies that had deployed troops in the former Yugoslavia had declared that they would pull their forces out under certain conditions, one of them being the lifting of the arms embargo; the U.S. administration in the circumstances was obliged to offer twenty thousand U.S. troops to cover an allied withdrawal. NATO began planning for a withdrawal from Bosnia.[44]

Thus, President Clinton was faced with a choice of using U.S. forces to cover a Dunkirk-like evacuation of NATO forces from the former Yugoslavia or using U.S. forces to support a political settlement. He opted for the latter; vigorous and skillful U.S. diplomacy by Secretary Christopher and Assistant Secretary Holbrooke used this decision to achieve a settlement.

The Dayton agreement adopted the same territorial formula, in percentage terms, as the 1994 Contact Group plan. As in earlier alternatives, Bosnia-Herzegovina would remain a single state within its current borders. There would be a central government with defined responsibilities and defined methods of sharing power among ethnic groups. Two "entities" would be created, each with its own presidency and legislature: the Federation of Bosnia and Herzegovina and the Serb Republic. Eastern Slavonia would be returned to Croatia. Sarajevo would be a united city within the Federation of Bosnia and Herzegovina; Gorazde would be linked to the federation by a land corridor. Other gains were recorded in the areas of human rights, cooperation with the War Crimes Tribunal, right of return of refugees, democratic elections, and arms reductions.

The U.S. government was uncomfortable with two earlier alternatives to Dayton, the Cutileiro plan and the Vance-Owen plan. In theory, however, these proposed solutions would have resulted in a situation not so different from what is likely to be the long-term result from the Dayton agreement. The Dayton agreement preserved American points of principle: a multiethnic state within the existing frontiers of Bosnia, a unified Sarajevo, a right of return for refugees, and war criminals to be brought to justice. But aggression seems to have reaped some reward, and the agreement has been badly mauled in the process of implementation. The question for historians to judge is whether an earlier military intervention by the United States would have yielded an outcome like that produced in 1995. Probably not.

Until 1995, the outside powers did just enough to create an argument about the principles that should govern the relations among three nations in Bosnia-Herzegovina. The dispute would have been settled on Serbian and Croatian terms, otherwise. The outside powers waited until the situation on the ground permitted a solution at minimum cost for them before they intervened with force. Intervention at earlier times might have exacted a much higher price. On the two occasions before Dayton when a political settlement seemed possible, the Bosnian Serbs were prepared for conflict and not likely to be deterred (1992), or they were at the zenith of their military campaign and not likely to hand back without a fight the territory they had won (1992–93). The judgment made by the major outside powers can be criticized but it is defensible.

The outcome may be encouraging to future aggressors or it may, in contrast, strengthen the idea that disputes should be resolved by peaceful means. Only time will tell. The result has set a precedent for international intervention in internal disputes of the sort that may occur again in post–Cold War Europe. Cooperation between Russia and the United States also is a significant precedent. This was not easily achieved, but the experience has been positive, despite sharp differences over policy toward the Bosnian Serbs. For this, Secretary of Defense Perry deserves great credit.

Will the agreement preserve what is left of the multiethnic character of Bosnia-Herzegovina? First answers are not encouraging. Most Serbs left the suburbs of Sarajevo that came under Bosnian government control in the Dayton accords, out of fear either of the Bosnian Muslims or of fellow Serbs. Muslims and Bosnian Croats, at least initially, failed to heal the wounds that opened up in Mostar. Elections were held in September 1997, with refugees returning temporarily to their home cities to vote. Ethnic cleansing and the shifts in populations it produced may mean that those officials who owed their election to the votes cast by refugees will essentially run governments in exile. If these trends continue and are not reversed, the result may be a Bosnia whose fate will not be much different from what it would have been under the Cutileiro plan or even the Owen-Stoltenberg plan.

Lessons Learned

Fragmenting societies can pose a threat to international peace and stability; the wars of the Yugoslav succession showed how this can happen. Learning from the experience should lead to

- a better mechanism for reconciling the interests and objectives of the major powers when subregional conflicts arise;

- earlier attention to internal disputes that might escalate to the level of armed conflict;
- clarity about which nation or which organization is responsible for galvanizing international action; and
- more emphasis on negotiating power-sharing arrangements, less on up-or-down votes.

These points are discussed in greater detail below.

Inadequate analysis. The case for vigorous diplomatic intervention prior to the breakup of the federation in Yugoslavia was not persuasive enough to carry the day. Why was that? For one thing the dispute was seen as an internal matter. Observers were divided on the question of whether the independence of several of the republics was desirable or unavoidable, but the inclination to hold the country together was strong. By 1991, Washington had become worried about the example that the fragmentation of Yugoslavia might set for the republics that still composed the Soviet Union. The impact on the Balkans or on Europe as a whole was hardly considered. There was no discussion of refugees streaming out of Yugoslavia into Germany or about the implications of the expansion of the war into Albania, not to mention the revival of the barbaric practice of ethnic cleansing, which was not foreseen. No effort was made to reach any collective judgment about what war in Yugoslavia might mean for international peace and security and consequently no basis was laid for collective diplomatic intervention.

If the international community makes no effort to reach a common assessment of a potential crisis, there can be no clarity about its desired objectives. This warning to future policymakers ought to fall in the category of truisms, but the absence of any clear objectives was one of the most serious failings of the international community's feeble diplomatic efforts up to the summer of 1995. It was not surprising that General Colin Powell, chairman of the U.S. Joint Chiefs of Staff, was moved to comment on the essential relationship between political objectives and military means.[45] The refusal of the Western allies to discuss Yugoslavia as a potential crisis area in 1990 in the face of a worsening situation there was part of a pattern of failure. If those powers that are able to take collective action to prevent crises have no idea what their aims are, they have little chance of dealing effectively with a crisis.

Ambivalence about internal conflicts. The case of Yugoslavia demonstrates that until an *internal* crisis reaches the stage where it presents a clear and present danger to states that are powerful enough to assume some responsibility for international peace and security, the international community is unlikely to intervene in a meaningful way. Even in 1992 it was possible to believe that the worst effects of the conflict could be contained. Identifying and coalescing around a direct threat to international peace and security is probably the most difficult issue nations face in enforcing norms and restraints, and it is particularly difficult in cases that can be thought of as civil war. If their own interests are not clearly and directly damaged by a crisis and its more obvious consequences, substantial grounds always will exist for governments to prefer the hands-off approach to an active, possibly military, intervention. An absence of conviction that there is a common interest works against even the most modest of diplomatic interventions.

Confusion regarding responsibilities. Who should have assumed responsibility for heading off the conflict in Yugoslavia? President Clinton and American pundits attacked the Europeans for not forcefully handling a problem on their doorstep. Europeans blamed Washington for its aloof attitude. Turf battles had started to develop among the international organizations and their leading members. NATO and the Western European Union and their supporters vied for the role of senior peacekeeper in Europe. Some European nations saw in the Yugoslav crisis a chance to strengthen the security side of the EC. This was encouraged by the United States, which had no desire to become involved. NATO, the most effective existing multilateral military organization in Europe, was not heavily involved in the early stages. Another organization that was cut out at first, both by Americans and by Europeans, was the United Nations. This was not an oversight. American spokespersons doubted publicly that there was a role for the United Nations.[46]

Ineffective meshing of U.S. and European intervention efforts. Two sets of negotiations concerning a settlement in Bosnia came close to a successful conclusion prior to the 1995 effort led by Assistant Secretary Richard Holbrooke. The first was led by Ambassador José Cutileiro in the spring of 1992. Former secretary of state Cyrus Vance and former British foreign secretary Lord Owen led the second negotiation in late

1992 and early 1993. There were differences in approach among them, but this can only partially explain why two of the efforts were frustrated while one succeeded. More relevant are the following factors:

- The United States fully supported the 1995 negotiation; it did not endorse the earlier solutions and, in fact, encouraged the Bosnian government to think that it could get a better deal.
- A second element not present in earlier periods was the use of force. The United States used air power on a large scale in Bosnia in 1995 and agreed to deploy thirty thousand ground troops to support implementation of the Dayton accords; both elements were either absent or highly conditional in the earlier efforts.

Some of the ambivalence about Yugoslavia within the ranks of the European Community came from a concern that the United States had opted out in the summer of 1991. Without the added strength of the United States, the nascent military cooperation of the EC was too untested to be relied upon as an effective vehicle to back up the negotiations. Nor could the United States have acted in Yugoslavia except in partnership with its European allies. Furthermore, a U.S.-Western European partnership without the active support of the Soviet Union, later Russia, would have run into serious difficulties, sooner or later. This conclusion, it should be underscored, means that leaving order-building diplomacy to the Western Europeans is not going to work for a long time to come. An incidental aspect of this warning sign is that rivalry among supporters of various international organizations also can prevent a broad united front. Competition among supporters of the Western European Union, NATO, and the CSCE contributed to policy paralysis.

Muddled answers to ethnic relationships. Two questions important for order-building diplomacy are these: (1) What can be done to resolve pressures for changing existing methods of dealing with ethnic groups well before the crisis stage is reached? (2) To what extent should the international community give encouragement to the norm of self-determination for ethnic groups? Yugoslavia was a learning experience in many respects—one of the lessons was how imperfectly we understand how to deal with minority rights.

Self-determination for ethnic groups has its limits. As Max Kampel-man notes, "The right of self-determination of peoples does not include the right of secession. These are two separate rights, which must be viewed separately."[47] The end of the Cold War has led to a revival of nationalist sentiment, partly because politicians have used it as a rallying cry and partly because it is a natural reaction to the foreign domination that many identified with the bipolar order. Underlying these factors are basic trends that will have a more lasting impact on attitudes toward self-determination by ethnic groups.

The most salient of these considerations is that sovereignty even for the most powerful nations operates differently than it did in the earlier decades of the twentieth century. There are more limitations on state sovereignty and, certainly in Europe, more recognition that most major internal actions have external effects. The communications and infor-mation revolutions also have tended to make state frontiers more porous than ever before. Local autonomy, in some circumstances, may be a more important value to people than the fortunes of the larger states of which they are a part. In a global economy in which central governments clearly have limitations in terms of protecting citizens and improving their well-being, local customs and ties offset the feelings of being alienated from a community too large to identify with in any tan-gible sense. Stronger local management of human affairs is a natural result of a stronger influence exercised by a global economy on the lives of individuals.

The destabilizing effect of armed conflict in Europe. Before the conflict erupted in Yugoslavia many observers regarded the situation as deplor-able but not a threat to international peace and security as long as war was confined to Yugoslavia. That view, at the least, was overly opti-mistic. The war added to the refugee crisis confronting Europe, Ger-many in particular. Good Russian-American relations were placed in some peril over the issue, which was exploited by Russian nationalists in a way that threatened the much larger stakes in the U.S.-Russian relationship. The first meeting of the NATO-Russian council in Sep-tember 1997 was a rather harsh ventilation of views over NATO's political objective in Bosnia, but the episode demonstrated the utility of a forum for debating the issues. The specter of a war that could include NATO allies and long-time foes Greece and Turkey has even been invoked. All this may be worst-case reasoning but it suggests that order-building diplomacy is a safer approach to international security than a policy that assumes war, once it breaks out, is of concern only to the initial participants. War has its own logic, not fully controllable even by combatants.

Intervention for humanitarian purposes. One of the saddest lessons of the Yugoslav crisis is that humanitarian assistance may operate against a settlement. It became quite apparent in 1993 that the troops sent in to ensure that food and medicine reached besieged civilians had become hostages of the Serbs. By threatening to attack British, French, Canadian, and other ground forces in Bosnia, the Serbs were able to force these governments to accommodate to Serbian strategic aims. No doubt thousands of lives were saved by the humanitarian assistance, but at the price of the denial of actions that might have pressured the Serbs to negotiate seriously.

The utility of public renunciation of the use of force. In the late summer of 1991, the European Community publicly debated the question of whether to intervene militarily in what was still a limited war between Serbia and Croatia. Because of British opposition, made known publicly, the EC put aside the idea that force would be used to buttress peacekeeping or peacemaking efforts.[48] Spokespersons for the United States also publicly ruled out the use of force. When a cease-fire was finally achieved between Serbia and Croatia through the good offices and skillful diplomacy of UN representatives Cyrus Vance and Herbert Okun, Serbia had occupied about one-third of Croatia. If Milosevic learned anything from the experience it must have been that he did not have to worry about external military intervention. When the Yugoslav People's Army in May 1992 provided the resources that enabled the Bosnian Serbs to fight the Bosnian government forces from a position of superiority, they had good reason to think it was safe to do so from a military standpoint. It is difficult to reach any other conclusion than that aggression was encouraged by the public renunciation of the use of force by both the EC and the United States.

Europe and U.S. Interests

Order-building diplomacy occasionally requires the threat or use of force. When such a situation arises, nations find it extremely difficult to accept the argument that norms and rules of behavior require them to sacrifice lives and resources. Norms have not generally been an adequate basis for justifying a military intervention. If the defense of international norms comes at too high a cost, the argument of direct national self-interest is the only rationale for intervention in disputes. Judgments by the Western nations, including the United States, on the question of intervening in a European dispute should proceed from an assessment of their strategic interests. Nowhere are U.S. strategic interests more important than they are in Europe. Rwanda, Cambodia, and Somalia are three of the most tragic examples of suffering known to human history. Humanitarian intervention by the United Nations in these cases was fully justified. Conflicts in Europe, however, *presumptively* pose a higher order of security risk for the Western nations. *Presumptively* is the operative word because a commonly held view in the United States was that the war in the former Yugoslavia was a problem for Europeans. The political leadership in the United States failed to mention in the case of Yugoslavia that two twentieth-century wars in Europe had established the United States as a major factor in European security affairs, and that the United States had a strong interest in a peaceful settlement in the Balkans. Even within Europe, rich in links with Yugoslavia, with a public much affected by the suffering in the former Yugoslavia, and absorbing a massive flow of refugees from Yugoslavia, governments were deterred from armed intervention in Yugoslavia because they thought the costs of doing so were too high to win public support. They also found the lack of American leadership disheartening.

But far worse than the disaster that did occur would have been a situation where Russia, the European Union, and the United States used armed force to support *opposing* factions in the former Yugoslavia. That this did not happen was one of the few positive aspects of the Yugoslav experience. Unfortunately, armed confrontation between Russia and the West was avoided not because of a firm belief in collective security but because of Russian weakness at the time. Improving international responses to conflicts arising from the fragmentation of societies is an important lesson of the Yugoslavian imbroglio. Also important is for the big powers to develop rules that help them respond to crises without coming into conflict with each other. Later chapters will deal with that challenge.

6

Transforming Nuclear Deterrence

Can Strategic Partners Be Nuclear Rivals?

When the Soviet Union collapsed and with it much of the bipolar order of the Cold War, a nuclear nightmare seemed close to coming true. Chapters 3 and 4 have addressed the two urgent problems that were immediately obvious: the rise of new nuclear powers—Ukraine, Kazakhstan, and Belarus—and the potential loss of control over warheads and fissile materials by the governments of the newly independent states, including Russia. Chapter 3 told the story of how the nuclear restraint regime of the Cold War helped to manage state-level nuclear proliferation. Chapter 4 argued that substate proliferation required new ways of thinking, new rules that would make internal practices a matter of international concern, a trend also evidenced in other areas. This chapter will discuss the great opportunity that the end of the Cold War presented to Russia and the United States: the possibility that the world's two greatest nuclear powers could lead the world into an era in which the salience of nuclear weapons in international relations could be much reduced.[1] Accomplishing this task and imprinting the norms and rules appropriate to a post–nuclear weapons era are essential to the achievement of a stable peace within the Euro-atlantic community.

History probably will record that the problem of state proliferation was handled brilliantly by the two U.S. presidents who confronted the problem—Bush and Clinton. History *may* record that the problem of controlling fissile materials was handled well, with a major assist from the U.S. Congress—Senators Lugar, Nunn, and Domenici in particular. The jury is still out on whether the United States, working with Russia, will seize—or perhaps even recognize—the unique opportunity the two former adversaries have to lead the world out of the age of nuclear weapons. History will not treat them or their leaders kindly if this opportunity is missed.

At a superficial level, the two nations speak a common language of cooperation, but at a deeper level there is a residue of suspicion and fear on both sides. Nowhere is this more apparent than in the issue of nuclear weapons, where Russia and the United States are still caught in the deterrence trap. Until mutual nuclear deterrence is no longer a determinant of many aspects of the U.S.-Russian relationship, there will be a threshold in the relationship that neither side will ever cross.

Much of this book concerns the centrality of past, present, and future U.S.-Russian relations in imprinting on the international system an order that points away from war and toward peace. Terminating U.S.-Russian nuclear rivalry, therefore, has a double imperative:

- A stable international order built on the logic of peace within the Euroatlantic community requires U.S.-Russian partnership; that will be difficult to achieve while the condition of mutual nuclear deterrence manifests itself as it does today.
- The global order can be influenced by a determined U.S.-Russian effort to enter a post–nuclear weapons era and a stable peace in their own relationship.

Arms Reductions and the Cold War's End

Just as the cause of human rights had a role in undermining the international system built up during the Cold War, so did arms control, as noted in chapter 3, play an important part in dismantling the military confrontation that had been an essential prop of the system. An arms reductions policy, it is safe to say, was consciously adopted as an instrument of change by Gorbachev. A long period of predictable and consistent Soviet policy and negotiating behavior on armaments came to an end with the accession to power of Mikhail Gorbachev. With the aid of his foreign minister, Eduard Shevardnadze, Gorbachev's fast-paced diplomacy overturned long-standing tenets of Soviet security policy. He accepted on-site inspections on Soviet territory, a global ban on the most advanced Soviet intermediate-range ballistic missile, and the first treaty to reduce and eliminate already-deployed nuclear weapons. He unilaterally cut back Soviet forces facing NATO and reciprocated a challenge by President Bush to withdraw short-range nuclear weapons from forward deployment and store or destroy them. A treaty that required asymmetric reductions in Soviet military equipment and established parity between NATO and Warsaw Pact conventional forces was negotiated under his leadership. He accepted the reunification of Germany, the unified country's right to be in NATO, and the withdrawal of Soviet forces from what had been the German Democratic Republic and, indeed, from all of East-Central Europe.

Toward the end of his time in power, events of historic proportions were coming at him so fast that he was overwhelmed by them. His critics believe that the agreements he entered into respecting Germany and East-Central Europe would not have been made had the Soviet Union been in a stronger position. Russian critics of the conventional and nuclear arms treaties believe that those treaties, especially START II, also were negotiated in a period of Soviet and Russian weakness and were therefore flawed from their inception.

The Soviet Union's economic health was poor when Gorbachev became general secretary. By shifting resources out of the military sector he hoped to modernize and revive the economy. Having this motivation, he was in a hurry to reach agreements, and the usual haggling over terms was cut short. Gorbachev and Shevardnadze also wanted to improve the Soviet Union's relations with the West and thought the East-West confrontation itself could be dismantled. This purpose became central to Gorbachev's "new thinking" paradigm and led him to view the U.S.-Soviet military equation from a new and very different perspective. From this perspective, ideas that had been anathema in the past, such as on-site inspection, became thinkable. The idea of eliminating all intermediate-range nuclear-armed missiles became negotiable.

Gorbachev was very much in control of security negotiations until the end of his tenure. On-site inspections were not palatable to the Soviet military or personally to Marshal Akhromeyev, Gorbachev's senior military adviser. The marshal was ordered to go to the Conference on Disarmament in Europe in Stockholm to accept the principle in 1986. Defense Minister Yazov vowed that the Soviet military would not carry out the provisions of the treaty on conventional forces in Europe. Gorbachev signed the treaty anyway.[2] From the Reykjavik meeting with President Reagan in 1986 through his signature of the START I treaty in 1991, Gorbachev showed that he was ready for unprecedented cuts in strategic nuclear forces. At Reykjavik, Gorbachev and Reagan seriously discussed the elimination of nuclear weapons.

The basic weakness of the Soviet state probably caused Gorbachev to believe that he had to do these things. It is clear, however, that Gorbachev had reached several conclusions that were not based exclusively on concerns about the Soviet Union's weakness. The reform of Soviet communism was seen by Gorbachev as necessary on its own terms, not only for economic reasons and not only because of the Soviet Union's performance in meeting Cold War pressures. The growth of a civil society in the Soviet Union meant that there were forces within the Soviet Union interested in reform. Gorbachev spoke for such people. He thought that the Soviet Union had no fundamental interest in continuing an ideological global confrontation with the West and that the Cold War, with all its burdens, was not a necessary condition of international life. He wanted to make wholesale changes in the rules of the international system. Over the years it had become clear what had to be done to do this. It was necessary, first of all, to expand the aims of the international system beyond that of war avoidance. To do that he had to start embracing Western values. This is precisely what he did with "glasnost" and "new thinking." Gorbachev, in short, sought to imprint a new design on the international system. One important element of his grand strategy was the demilitarization of East-West relations. Generally, rules of behavior are changed incrementally within a system that remains stable. This was the way the human rights norm gained ascendancy, as was described in chapter 2. Gorbachev sought change on a grander scale and, to a large extent, succeeded.

Although it added to the stress that the Soviet economy was already under, the Reagan defense program does not deserve all the credit for the series of events in the late 1980s that led to the final collapse of the Soviet Union. Nor is it wise to make the claim. It strengthens the hand of those Russians who believe that the major arms reductions agreements of the period were accepted by Moscow simply because of Soviet weakness. It ignores Gorbachev's intention to change fundamentally an international system that remained frozen in the Cold War mold.

Within his frame of reference, Gorbachev made several miscalculations. Two of the more serious ones were catering to hard-liners and believing that the nationalities problems could be kept under control during a time of radical transition. The arms reductions agreements he made with the West, however, were consistent with his worldview and contributed to the beginning of a new post–Cold War order among the major nations. It is essential to keep this in mind, especially since the impulse for change that Gorbachev injected into the international system has lost momentum and a reaction to that impulse may be gaining strength. Further nuclear arms reductions are essential in an order-building diplomacy aimed at consolidating and advancing the new rules of behavior that Gorbachev's initiatives, reciprocated by President Reagan, helped to establish. A peaceful, undivided, and democratic Europe probably will not be realized unless reductions in nuclear forces become a basic element in the process of change.

Unique American Leadership, Once Again

Gorbachev was matched in his radical break with the past by his first American negotiating partner, President Ronald Reagan. Since the beginning of serious U.S.-Soviet arms limitations talks in the late 1950s, American presidents had been influenced by "arms control" doctrines developed in the American academic community.[3] Thomas Schelling and Morton Halperin caught and even defined the essence of the doctrine when they wrote,

> The essential feature of arms control is the recognition of the common interest, of the possibility of reciprocation and cooperation even between potential enemies with respect to their military establishments. Whether the most promising areas of arms control involve reductions in certain kinds of military force, increases in certain kinds of military force, qualitative changes in weaponry, different modes of deployment, or arrangements superimposed on existing military systems, we prefer to treat as an open question.[4]

This agnostic attitude toward the idea of reducing nuclear weapons did not appeal to Reagan, who turned out to be the most viscerally antinuclear U.S. president of the nuclear age, a leader who, much like Gorbachev, had the unbounded confidence to think that he could change the existing international order. Arms control thinking of the 1950s and 1960s contributed to the major achievement of the Cold War: nuclear weapons were never fired in anger despite the bitter global confrontation between the Soviet Union and the United States. By 1980, however, U.S. nuclear strategy had become almost rococo in its attempt to compensate for the vulnerability of land-based missiles. The development by both sides of multiple, independently targeted reentry vehicles (MIRVs) provided incentives for a first strike. The requirements imposed by a counterforce second-strike option and readiness to fight a protracted nuclear war were driving U.S. strategic nuclear warheads toward the 10,000 range. Soviet strategic planners, with their forces concentrated on large land-based missiles, followed the U.S. lead in deploying MIRVs and began using their throw-weight advantage to multiply the numbers of warheads on each missile. This practice gave the Soviet Union numerical superiority in nuclear warheads and stimulated the arms race.

The time had come for a new approach, and Reagan insisted that his administration propose to the Soviets a negotiation on deep reductions in nuclear weapons. Ronald Reagan and George Kennan shared a common position on this issue. The disputes that arose between the State Department and the Defense Department in framing these proposals have been well documented.[5] The proposals that emerged from these struggles were not weighted toward negotiability and they ignored some fundamental tenets of arms stability, but they set U.S.-Soviet negotiations on a new course. Secretary of State George Shultz gained dominance in setting arms reductions policies during the critical last two years of Reagan's term of office, thus enabling Reagan's goals to be achieved. Gorbachev and Reagan broke with the pattern that had existed for nearly twenty years. The combination of the two personalities was unique. It led to trailblazing achievements that were unimaginable until these two men held power for a short time together.

President George Bush followed through by completing and signing the START I treaty with Gorbachev on July 31, 1991, concluding a framework agreement for START II with Russian President Yeltsin on June 17, 1992, and signing the START II treaty with Yeltsin on January 3, 1993. As noted earlier in this book, on May 23, 1992, Bush's secretary of state, James Baker, signed the Lisbon Protocol, which committed Belarus, Kazakstan, and Ukraine to eliminate the strategic nuclear weapons left within their territories after the breakup of the Soviet Union. And a major innovation in arms reductions procedure was accomplished by Bush and Gorbachev in the fall of 1991 when they agreed to take several parallel actions to remove tactical nuclear weapons from forward deployment. Secretary Baker's relations with Gorbachev's foreign minister, Eduard Shevardnadze, were particularly warm and productive. Shevardnadze himself saw good relations with the West as a key element in the Soviet Union's security and vigorously executed Gorbachev's policy of ending the U.S.-Soviet confrontation.

Yeltsin and Clinton

The golden age of cooperation in U.S.-Soviet/Russian nuclear arms control lasted from about 1986 through 1992. Shevardnadze resigned on December 20, 1990, warning of a coup by reactionary forces. The coup was attempted eight months later. Despite Yeltsin's triumph and the end of the Soviet era in December 1991, a nationalist-conservative backlash already was gaining strength in Russia by the time Bush and Yeltsin signed the START II treaty. Partly because of this trend and partly because of inevitable power struggles, Yeltsin and the Russian Congress of People's Deputies became locked in a bitter conflict that ended in a military assault, ordered by Yeltsin, on the parliament building in October 1993. The episode underscored how urgent and all-consuming the internal reordering of Russian society had become and how little time was left over for dealing with the longer-term threat of nuclear weapons or for changing the aims, structures, and procedures of the international system.

As described in chapter 3, the Clinton administration used its diplomatic energies to salvage the START I treaty and the Lisbon Protocol. It was successful in this, and instruments of ratification were exchanged in Budapest in December 1994. A year later (January 1996) the U.S. Senate gave its consent to the ratification of the START II treaty. No serious discussions or negotiations on further U.S.-Russian strategic nuclear arms reductions took place during the Clinton administration's 1993-97 term of office. The administration had decided that such talks should await the ratification of START II by the State Duma of the Russian Federation. Inaction on ratification in Moscow led to inaction on policy reviews in Washington. Neither the Yeltsin government nor the Clinton administration made discussion and negotiation of strategic nuclear arms control beyond START II a high priority, preferring instead to concentrate on consolidating progress toward democracy and a market economy, assuming that arms reductions demanded more than the political traffic would bear. With the Russian and American elections of 1996 behind them and deadlines for NATO enlargement hard upon them, however, the two governments began discussing guidelines for a START III agreement in the spring of 1997 and reached an understanding at a Clinton-Yeltsin meeting in Helsinki on March 21, 1997.

Current Russian Attitudes toward Nuclear Weapons

Trends in Russian thinking about the utility of nuclear weapons will complicate the process of transforming nuclear deterrence. Nuclear weapons are seen in Russia as one of the few remaining assets that make Russia a great power. Minister of Atomic Energy Viktor Mikhailov has said that "the only protection throughout this period will be nuclear weapons."[6] The experience in Chechnya, the reluctance of Russian young men and their families to respect conscription, the slow pace of military reform, the lack of resources for maintenance of equipment and for training, inadequate leadership at the top of the military hierarchy—all these factors, and others, have eroded Russian conventional capabilities and Russian confidence in those capabilities. Not surprisingly, President Yeltsin's June 1996 statement to the Federation Council and the State Duma on national security policy assigned a high priority to nuclear weapons:

> The Russian Federation [said Yeltsin] consistently pursues a policy of nuclear deterrence. A key role in its implementation is played by maintaining at a sufficient level the Russian Federation's nuclear potential

both at global level (the Strategic Nuclear Forces) and on a regional and local scale (operational-tactical and tactical nuclear weapons) as well as the potential for deterrence by non-nuclear means.

For the foreseeable future the Russian Federation preserves the status of a nuclear power in order to prevent nuclear attack or large-scale aggression with the use of conventional armed forces and armaments against it and/or its allies, and also to provide the new independent states of the Commonwealth with nuclear guarantees as one component in agreements on military questions.[7]

The prospect of enlarging NATO membership also has affected Russian attitudes toward nuclear weapons. An interview with Yuri Baturin, then President Yeltsin's national security adviser, was published in *Moscow Kommersant* on April 23, 1996, that is starkly clear on the subject:

[If NATO is enlarged,] our military will propose its countermeasures. Most likely, greater reliance on the nuclear deterrent, including lifting a score of obligations we unilaterally undertook in the past with respect to the elimination of tactical nuclear weapons and limitations of rail-based strategic platforms. Overall, the set of measures is quite extensive and, alas, capable of nullifying a lot of past achievements.

Another complicating factor was the revival of interest in the United States in a national ballistic missile defense system. The Russians saw this as a major impediment to proceeding with the strategic offensive arms reductions they are committed to make under START I and II. However, U.S. and Russian negotiators signed agreed statements on demarcation between theater and national ballistic missile defense systems on September 26, 1997. This removed one source of contention but left open the question of whether the United States will decide to deploy a national ballistic missile defense system in a few years.

There is no doubt that Russians also are sensitive to the existence of other, non-U.S. nuclear forces on or around the Eurasian continent. The inclusion of the other nuclear powers—the United Kingdom, China, and France—in nuclear arms control negotiations has been formally and repeatedly suggested by the Yeltsin government. However, no interest has been shown by the other nuclear weapons states, whose holdings of nuclear weapons are far below the level of nuclear weapons held by Russia and the United States. Russia has not pressed the matter.

From a Conditional Peace to a Stable Peace

October 1996 was the tenth anniversary of the meeting between Ronald Reagan and Mikhail Gorbachev at Reykjavik. At the time of that 1986 meeting, the pundits poked fun at it because the talks ranged so far beyond those ideas with which the experts were familiar and comfortable. President Reagan proposed to eliminate all ballistic missiles in the strategic forces over a ten-year period—that goal would have been achieved in 1996. President Gorbachev responded by proposing to eliminate *all* strategic nuclear forces. The talks deadlocked over Gorbachev's insistence that testing of ballistic missile defense systems be limited to the laboratory, and Reagan's refusal to accept that. The press could see the disappointment etched on the faces of the two presidents and their advisers—Secretary of State George Shultz among them—and drew what they thought was the correct conclusion—the conference had been a disaster. They were wrong.

On November 17, 1986, Secretary Shultz gave one of his finest speeches, explaining what he thought had happened. He said, "It may be that we have arrived at a true turning point . . . we can glimpse now, for the first time, a world freed from the incessant and pervasive fear of nuclear devastation." He spoke of "a safer strategic environment involving progressively less reliance on nuclear weapons." He was right—it was a true turning point. Over a five-year period three major U.S.-Soviet/Russian treaties came from that epiphany in Reykjavik: one eliminated a whole class of ballistic missiles and lifted the fear of nuclear devastation from millions of people in Europe and Asia; a second resulted in the first deep cuts in long-range nuclear weapons targeted on the United States and the Soviet Union; and a third was the START II treaty that required further deep cuts, including the elimination of the most destabilizing intercontinental ballistic missiles. A safer strategic environment involving progressively less reliance on nuclear weapons seemed within reach.

Since that time, a political revolution has occurred in the former Soviet Union and, because of that, a transformation has been wrought in U.S.-Russian relations. Without excessive exaggeration, we can speak of hopes for a vibrant U.S.-Russian partnership and even of a stable peace. The threats Americans see now do not come from Russian missile attacks but from terrorist gangs with suitcases. In fact, Russia and the United States are cooperating to tighten controls over fissile materials and fight nuclear smuggling. The two nations were joint supporters of the comprehensive nuclear test ban treaty, and they worked together to extend the nuclear nonproliferation treaty. They worked jointly with Ukraine and Kazakstan to eliminate strategic nuclear weapons in those new republics. They have traveled a long way since Reykjavik.

But the journey is not finished. In fact, the hardest part of the trip may lie ahead. "A world freed from the incessant and pervasive fear of nuclear devastation" is closer now, but until the United States and Russia escape from the nuclear deterrence trap no one can say that American-Russian relations have progressed beyond the stage of conditional peace. The Americans, the French, and the British do not conduct their affairs with cocked pistols at one another's heads. They have achieved a stable peace. Ballistic missiles armed with nuclear warheads remain on high alert in both Russia and the United States, locked into a posture that would allow national command authorities on either side to order a nuclear attack within minutes. Detargeting of ballistic missiles can be reversed in seconds.

Does this make any difference in the real world? After all, Americans and Russians are friends now. It does. It will be impossible for the United States and Russia to cross the threshold into a stable peace until they have broken the lock of the nuclear deterrence trap. Working with the Russian government under present circumstances is admittedly not easy, but George Kennan was quite right when he said in 1982 that "in the great question of nuclear weaponry there lies the deeper question of peace itself."

Several nations may be on a knife-edge between decisions that could take them toward the kind of world that President Reagan and Secretary of State Shultz glimpsed over ten years ago or, alternatively, toward a world of a global nuclear arms race, of nuclear smuggling and terrorism, and of proliferating nuclear weapons states. A full-scope approach to U.S.-Russian relations is what we should want. Arms reductions should no longer be the main item on the U.S.-Russian agenda, but they are an essential part of the process of achieving a stable peace between the two nations. And the issue will come back with a vengeance if negotiations between Russia and the United States on nuclear arms reductions break down. The outlook for resuming negotiations on nuclear arms reductions is promising, although as of this writing (fall 1997) the legislatures of the two countries have not yet spoken on the question of changes in the START II treaty and clarifications concerning the 1972 antiballistic missile (ABM) treaty.

Ratification of START II by the State Duma of the Russian Federation could usher in an era of further limitations and reductions in nuclear weapons. The concerns voiced by Russian critics of START II foreshadowed some difficulties ahead for START III, but also some opportunities for productive negotiations. The issues that arose in connection with the Duma's consideration of the START II treaty, in fact, suggested a possible rapprochement between U.S. and Russian views on what should be included in a START III treaty. The main element was a lower ceiling for warheads on deployed weapons systems so that Russia would be spared the expense of building many new single-warhead missiles to achieve START II ceilings. Active discussion of these matters between American and Russian officials began in the spring of 1997 and led to direct talks between Clinton and Yeltsin late in March that year.

The meeting in Helsinki on March 21, 1997, between Presidents Yeltsin and Clinton produced several important agreements designed to relaunch the stalled U.S.-Russian nuclear arms reduction negotiations. Reaffirming their common task to preserve the ABM treaty was one of them. A potential breakthrough in their relations in this area was their agreement to explore integrated cooperative defense efforts as regards theater missile defense. They also defined the key components of a START III agreement:

- Establishment, by December 31, 2007, of lower aggregate levels of 2000–2500 strategic nuclear warheads for each of the parties;
- Measures relating to the transparency of strategic nuclear warhead inventories and the destruction of strategic nuclear warheads and any other jointly agreed technical and organizational measures, to promote the irreversibility of deep reductions including prevention of a rapid increase in the number of warheads;
- Resolving issues related to the goal of making the current START treaties unlimited in duration;
- Placement in a deactivated status of all strategic nuclear delivery vehicles which will be eliminated under START II by December 31,

2003, by removing their nuclear warheads or taking other jointly agreed steps. The United States is providing assistance through the Nunn-Lugar program to facilitate early deactivation.[8]

Placing transparency and irreversibility of nuclear warhead dismantlement squarely in the context of START III gives it a more solid foundation than it had before. Deactivating strategic nuclear delivery vehicles to be eliminated under START II should be accomplished well before 2003, and the scope should be expanded. The two presidents also agreed that the deadline for the elimination of strategic nuclear delivery vehicles under the START II treaty will be extended to December 31, 2007. A protocol to the START II treaty codifying this arrangement was signed by Secretary Albright and Foreign Minister Primakov on September 26, 1997.

The presidents furthermore agreed that "their experts will explore, as separate issues, possible measures relating to nuclear long-range sea-launched cruise missiles and tactical nuclear systems, to include appropriate confidence-building and transparency measures."[9] This understanding provides an opening to work for the elimination of substrategic nuclear warheads, thus completing the process that President Bush and President Gorbachev launched in 1991.

START III and Beyond

Reducing nuclear weapons is no longer the only focus of the U.S.-Russian strategic dialogue. One of the most important developments of the 1993–96 period was the emergence of a variety of strategic nuclear issues as regular topics on the Russian-U.S. agenda: detargeting, safety of nuclear weapons, security of weapons and fissile materials, and problems connected with nonproliferation, to name a few. These discussions need to be broadened still further so that mutual nuclear deterrence will not block the evolution of a positive U.S.-Russian relationship. So long as thousands of nuclear weapons are held by the United States and Russia on a status of high alert and so long as the overall relationship falls considerably short of the trusting relationship that it can ultimately become, mutual nuclear deterrence and, hence, a conditional peace will continue to exist. But reductions alone will not suffice to transform deterrence, nor will very deep reductions be possible until other aspects of the deterrent relationship have been changed.

The decision to reduce the salience of nuclear weapons in U.S.-Russian relations as part of a broader strategy of limiting the role that these weapons play in international relations cannot be made on military grounds alone. This is a truly strategic decision, one that must treat military considerations as only part of a broader discussion of national interests in a rapidly changing world. Reducing reliance on the rapid launch of nuclear weapons would be a particularly effective way of turning away from nuclear war–fighting theories. This step, if taken jointly by the United States and Russia, would demonstrate that these two countries regard nuclear weapons as usable only to deter a nuclear attack. Of course, measures that would reduce reliance on rapid launch are reversible, which is why it is also necessary to create force structures at reduced levels that would be invulnerable to, and capable of retaliating to, an attack.

Reversibility is a virtue in a situation where hedging is still thought necessary. Most likely, implementing a policy of reduced reliance on rapid launch will have to proceed in stages while mutual confidence is being strengthened. The first steps in any process aimed at reducing reliance on early warning should be judged according to a wide variety of criteria, including the following:

- their impact on the need to launch on warning (this has implications for both counterforce targeting and for basing arrangements);
- the ease with which they can be reliably monitored;
- their effect on the skills of the military personnel responsible for strategic nuclear forces;
- their effect on the safety and security of nuclear weapons; and
- their impact on perceptions of the effectiveness of the nuclear deterrent.

A reduced reliance on rapid launch may create improved conditions for the hard decisions both governments will have to take if deep reductions in warheads are to be achieved.

A coincidence of factors suggests that by the first few years of the twenty-first century, Russia and the United States could be well advanced toward agreement on deep cuts in nuclear warheads and nuclear delivery systems. The service life of some Russian tactical and strategic nuclear weapons systems will have ended by then—unless prolonged to inflate the number of deployed warheads; negotiations for START III offer an excellent opportunity to avoid an accelerated Russian buildup of new weapons systems to replace the older models. START III negotiations should be completed long before 2003, when deactivation of missiles scheduled for elimination under the original START II treaty is to be completed. Deactivation of systems slated for elimination under START III could overlap with deactivations of START II. This situation will add urgency to the inclusion of other nuclear powers in arms control talks, and China should be the first of these powers to be brought into negotiations.

The September 1997 U.S.-Russian agreement on a demarcation between theater and national missile defense systems has important implications for other countries—most notably, China, which may have a new generation of strategic nuclear systems ready for serial production in a few years. A weakening of the technical barriers against the development of ballistic missile defense systems—a likely result of the demarcation agreement between the United States and Russia—need not be a cause for an arms race between two countries on friendly terms. China might reach conclusions about this U.S.-Russian understanding, however, that could influence the development of Chinese strategic nuclear forces.

As U.S. and Russian strategic nuclear forces are reduced, the need to engage all other nuclear powers in transparency and limitation measures will become more acute. The demarcation agreement adds more weight to the argument that the United States and Russia should now consider how to bring the United Kingdom, China, and France into discussions about the future of nuclear deterrence. For example, could some of the confidence-building measures agreed upon between Russia and the United States in the demarcation accord be applied on a broader basis? Could some of the transparency measures alluded to in the Helsinki understanding between Presidents Clinton and Yeltsin be negotiated with other nuclear weapons states? Delay in addressing these issues could result in a more competitive, less cooperative relationship with other nuclear powers.

Once START III has been negotiated—or once the number of warheads deployed by each country falls below fifteen hundred—future talks should focus on transforming nuclear deterrence on a global scale, and should probably take the form of several simultaneous negotiations dealing with separate but interrelated subjects. With a global nuclear arms race a possible scenario for the twenty-first century, participation in nuclear disarmament negotiations must no longer be confined to the United States and Russia. Of course, other nations have already been heavily involved in certain aspects of nuclear arms control—the comprehensive nuclear test ban, the nuclear nonproliferation treaty, and nuclear-weapon-free zones, to name just three. Now, though, they must become engaged in matters even closer to the heart of nuclear arms reduction, such as a global cutoff in the production of fissile material for use in weapons.

Limitations on warheads will have to be more rigorous. Nuclear warhead ceilings should cover *total* numbers of nuclear warheads—not just deployed warheads, but all warheads held by Russia and the United States. The ultimate objective of the U.S.-Russian negotiations, and of a multilateral nuclear reductions program, should be to reduce the total number of warheads to a few hundred. The U.S.-Russian Helsinki agreement on transparency in connection with warhead dismantlement is an important first step in this direction; however, when the number of warheads falls to between one thousand and fifteen hundred, warhead dismantlement will have to become obligatory and measures will have to be instituted to ensure irreversibility.

To date, treaties have not required reductions in the number of warheads *not* deployed with delivery systems. In a deep reductions program, however, it will be necessary to agree on a method of reducing nondeployed, as well as deployed, warheads under verifiable conditions. First, the problem of breakout—a rapid reconstitution of nuclear forces—can be managed by controlling all, not just some, warheads. Second, when the United States and Russia each deploy no more than fifteen hundred warheads, the nuclear forces of Britain, France, and China will become more relevant to U.S.-Russian programs. Focusing on warheads and bombs—including both strategic and substrategic weapons—will make a significant contribution to strategic stability and security and pave the way for deep reductions in nuclear forces.

The verification techniques for monitoring warhead dismantlement will require chain-of-custody techniques and inspection on demand when an agreement is reached to limit *total* warheads to a specific number. The problems of verifying the total number of warheads possessed by a country are so formidable that some experience with verifying the reductions process should be acquired before insisting that any country limit itself to a verified number of total warheads.

Expanding the scope of, and the number of participants in, talks on nuclear arms control will certainly complicate and probably slow the negotiating process. There is really no alternative, however, if we want to move beyond a conditional peace to a stable peace. The negotiating agenda after START III will become broader and more complex and will be decisively influenced by the actions and opinions of nations other than the United States and Russia. The negotiating net will be cast over a larger set of norms and rules of behavior and over a larger group of countries.

Success in these negotiations will be highly dependent on a transformation in political relationships in many regions of the world. Nuclear arms reductions are an essential but insufficient step in a grand strategy aimed at moving beyond a conditional peace to a stable peace. In the next two chapters, continuing our focus on Europe, we will review the mid- and long-term possibilities for basic changes in political and security relations among the nations of the Euroatlantic community.

7

Devising an Interim Security Order in Europe

Spheres of Interest and Collective Security

The war in the former Yugoslavia was allowed to continue for so long because the leadership within the Euroatlantic community judged the costs of military intervention to be too high. Finally in 1995, the cost-benefit ratio shifted in favor of intervention and events forced decisions. By then violations of the most basic precepts of civilization had occurred, bordering on genocide; "ethnic cleansing" had resulted in massive transfers of populations; the peacekeeping forces provided by the big powers had been humiliated. The war dramatized the absence of consensus even among like-minded nations on an intellectual and political framework that would help them analyze their stakes in the crises and conflicts that have erupted in or near Europe. The idea of collective security was evoked but discredited yet again by the failure of the major nations to act decisively early in the wars of the Yugoslav succession.

Collective security requires that governments perceive a flouting of broadly accepted international norms, particularly those related to the use of force to change borders, as a direct threat to their national interests. This is the beginning of the conceptual and practical difficulties inherent in collective security: governments find it difficult to discern long-term dangers; even when they do, they find it no less difficult to persuade wary publics that action is necessary. Of course, no government can possibly be excused from the responsibility of assessing the costs to the nation it represents of embarking on a collective security response to even the most flagrant violation of international rules. For this reason alone, collective security must be regarded as a model embracing a certain internal logic, as one approach available to the international community, but by no means a fully realized goal and least of all a condition of international life.

Spheres of interest are a normal and inevitable part of the international system. This chapter argues that the collective security model should gradually replace spheres of interest as the preferred approach to security in Europe, but also acknowledges that there is no way to banish the fact that great powers cast large shadows: power plus proximity equals influence. The question is whether features of both the collective security approach and the spheres-of-interest approach to security can be used over the next several years without one driving out the other. Although they should not be mutually exclusive, it is not easy to manage them simultaneously. Both collective security and spheres-of-interest models require serious commitments of leadership, resources, and public support. Both are difficult for democratic governments to create and implement effectively. Although it is quite likely that some combination of spheres of interest and collective security arrangements would be viable in Europe, this would require dominant powers to practice restraint and smaller states to manage their internal affairs very skillfully. In fact, that is perhaps the best we can hope for in the foreseeable future.

Spheres of Interest

In January 1994, at the beginning of his second year in office, President Clinton joined other NATO heads of governments in announcing that the alliance remained open to the membership of other European countries. It was a fateful decision and reflected a significant change in administration thinking. Moving the dividing line between East and West in Europe a few hundred miles to the east had not seemed, during the first year of the administration, to be a worthy outcome of Cold War sacrifices. The administration had opposed a German suggestion floated in 1993 that NATO membership should be offered in parallel with accession of new members to the European Union. It had stressed the idea, as had the Bush administration before it, of a Europe whole and free.

The NATO decisions of January 1994 actually gave more weight to a form of associate membership in NATO—the Partnership for Peace —which provided for joint training and transparency in defense budgeting. The Partnership was more successful than its critics expected in connecting Eastern European nations to NATO. But once the door had been opened to full membership in NATO—and to the security guarantees that went with it—the Partnership could not contain the pressures for NATO expansion. U.S. domestic politics also became a factor, as the Republican leadership in both houses of Congress staked out a position favoring NATO enlargement and criticized the Clinton administration for moving too slowly. By the end of 1994, the Clinton administration had launched a process within NATO that led inexorably to the Madrid Declaration of July 8, 1997, which announced that NATO members were inviting the Czech Republic, Hungary, and Poland to begin accession talks with NATO.

Nine other countries had applied for membership: Albania, Bulgaria, Estonia, Macedonia, Latvia, Lithuania, Romania, Slovakia, and Slovenia. The NATO countries had established criteria for membership that, in essence, required governments to be run along democratic lines, militaries to be under civilian control, and efforts to have been made to resolve disputes with neighboring countries. In practice, however, members of NATO were influenced in their decisions by other factors— geography, cultural affinities, and their own internal demography. The NATO governments, prodded by the United States, have declared that the first accessions to membership will not be the last. Romania and Slovenia are at the top of the list. The Baltic states have strong backing. In fact, NATO has declared that membership is not automatically ruled out for any emerging democracy in Europe. For the moment, Ukraine seems satisfied with a special relationship with NATO, rather than membership. Although President Yeltsin has said that membership in NATO for former republics of the Soviet Union is unacceptable to Moscow, President Clinton reportedly told him that membership for those countries cannot be excluded. President Clinton has said that Russia, too, might become a member of a common security alliance and, in a press conference held in Madrid on July 9, 1997, disputed the idea that territorial politics will be important in the twenty-first century:

You can only believe we're isolating Russia if you believe that the great power, territorial politics of the twentieth century will dominate the twenty-first century; and if you believe that NATO is inherently antagonistic to Russia's interest and that Russia inherently will have to try to exercise greater territorial domination in the next few years than it has in the last few. I dispute that.

I believe that enlightened self-interest, as well as shared values, will compel countries to define their greatness in more constructive ways. And the threats that we will share that will be genuine threats to our security will compel us to cooperate in more constructive ways.

To the east of Hungary, Poland, and the Czech Republic lie a number of nations whose security will be profoundly affected by the interaction of Russia and the West before and after formal NATO enlargement in April 1999. These nations include the Baltic states, Slovakia, Belarus, Ukraine, Moldova, Romania, and the Balkan states. At least three different models of NATO expansion can presently be foreseen:

- enlarge and then have a lengthy pause for a period of consolidation;
- enlarge in a series of relatively fast-paced accessions that would include most of the current applicants while Russia's relationship with NATO remains as defined in the NATO-Russia Founding Act; and
- enlarge gradually, ultimately including a firmly democratic Russia after a period of demonstrated stability.

The first model could occur because Russian opposition to accession to NATO of any newly independent state that emerged from the collapse of the Soviet Union will generate considerable hesitation, at least in Western Europe, about a second round of expansion that includes the Baltic states or Ukraine. This would not preclude invitations being issued in 1999 to Romania and Slovenia to join NATO, as was hinted at in the July 1997 Madrid Declaration.

The second model—expansion to include nearly all the applicants—could come about as Romania, Slovenia, the Baltic states, Slovakia, and possibly Bulgaria become viable candidates for NATO membership. Under these conditions, Ukraine might also reconsider its special relationship with NATO. This model is foreshadowed in the Madrid Declaration on Euro-Atlantic Security and Cooperation issued by NATO heads of state and governments on July 8, 1997.

The third model—expansion to include, ultimately, a democratic Russia—corresponds generally to what President Clinton has said publicly on several occasions, but it has few real supporters.

Under any scenario, there will be a group of countries in the neighborhood of Russia that will be left in an ambiguous status for a period of years. Russia always has seen and still sees this area as being within its sphere of interest. In particular, Russians see the newly independent republics that emerged from the collapse of the Soviet Union as an area of interest, at least for trade purposes and in some cases for security purposes, too. They consider that they have an obligation to those ethnic Russians who remained in the newly independent states after the collapse of the Soviet Union. These views and the activities that flow from them bring Russia and its neighbors into serious policy disagreements from time to time. This is inescapable. Most of Russia's neighbors, thinking of Moscow's past sins, will try to offset Russia's influence by establishing ties with the West, and the West probably will try to accommodate them. Russia's weakened condition may well put it on the losing side of this struggle for influence, but the result will increase Russia's alienation from the Western world unless compensating steps are taken.

Recentralizing the former Russian or Soviet empire is an unlikely outcome within the next several years despite nostalgic nationalist rhetoric in Russia; the repressive dominance of Cold War days almost certainly will not be replicated, if only because Russia lacks the power to exercise that kind of authority. However, George Kennan's view of Soviet thinking remains relevant to current Russian attitudes. Here is what he wrote on December 16, 1944:

> As far as border states are concerned the Soviet government has never ceased to think in terms of spheres of interest. . . . Our people . . . have been allowed to hope that the Soviet government would be prepared to enter into an international security organization with truly universal power to prevent aggression. We are now faced with the prospect of having our people disabused of this illusion.[1]

Few now conceive of the collective security model as a "truly universal power to prevent aggression." Its uses are much more limited. Otherwise, however, the attitudes that Kennan observed are much the same today; although Moscow is not in a position to exercise imperial domination over its western neighbors, resentments unfortunately may be felt on both sides over perceived affronts to national interests.

The new Eastern Europe—those countries left out of NATO—may ultimately be integrated into a Euroatlantic community through a "series of mutually supporting institutions and relationships," to quote from declarations made by Presidents Clinton and Yeltsin in Moscow on May 10, 1995, and in Helsinki on March 21, 1997. The building blocks of such relationships include the Partnership for Peace, the Euro-Atlantic Partnership Council, and membership in the European Union. The Organization for Security and Cooperation in Europe also will be useful, mainly for long-term conflict resolution and for the promotion of democracy; developing the tools necessary for peacekeeping or peace enforcement will be difficult for it, particularly since it lacks a military infrastructure. Subregional associations—comprising, for example, the nations around the Baltic Sea—might also serve the purpose of European integration.

Much more attention should be given to arrangements other than membership in NATO for the purposes of integrating the Euroatlantic community. NATO membership probably will not be available for most of the new Eastern Europe for many years.

And, if integration of essentially all European and North American nations into a Euroatlantic community cannot be achieved through these means, or can be achieved only over the course of several decades, other, less desirable outcomes are possible:

- Eastern Europe becomes a buffer zone between Russia, on the one hand, and an enlarged NATO and an expanded European Union, on the other hand.
- Eastern Europe comes to be dominated by Russian interests and loses some of its capacity for independent action.
- Eastern Europe becomes an area where Russia and the West engage in a protracted competition for influence.
- Eastern Europe becomes clearly identified as a Western sphere of interest, with the United States and the European Union committed to upholding their interests there, by force if necessary.

Historically, results such as these have been the norm within the European states system. But is this type of analysis now anachronistic? President Clinton's answer is that it may have outlived its validity with the end of territorial politics.

In fact, the Clinton administration's statements about NATO enlargement are rooted in ideas far removed from power politics. The policy problem is how to deal with what seem to be the unintended consequences of those statements. We need to understand well the premises of the U.S. policy, the weak points in those premises, and what it will take to deal with them. The administration's first premise is that extending security guarantees to certain East-Central European states will enhance stability and prosperity throughout Europe. The question of how far NATO enlargement will proceed, and for what purposes, is generating some uncertainty, however. A second premise is that blurring the distinction between those who do and those who do not receive U.S. security guarantees will reassure those left out, including Russia. This is a necessary part of a policy of reassurance, but those countries denied an Article V security guarantee, the Baltic states in particular, probably will not accept a blurring of the distinction between having a security guarantee and not having one. Many NATO members, new and old, will not accept that either. A third premise is that the distinction between members and nonmembers can be erased altogether, over the long term, as democratic Russia is integrated with the West. This is a policy that is compatible with a grand design aimed at achieving a stable peace in Europe. Its most serious weakness is that there is no consensus in the West that Russia should become an unqualified member of the Western system of states, and even raising the question causes a rush to the barricades.

It seems inevitable that an interim security order in Europe will include spheres of interest, as the big powers, encouraged in some cases by the smaller countries, stake out the frontiers of their security interests. During the current period of conditional peace, a collective security approach will not be seen by the great powers as a primary means of creating security for themselves. These powers can ignore external pressures and resist any attempt to impose sanctions. The usual solution where the vital interests of the great powers are concerned is to rely on alliance systems and clearly demarcated spheres of interest. The beginnings of this already can be seen in Central Europe and along the periphery of Russia.

Security for Russia, Germany, and other major nations can indeed be found in the spheres-of-interest model; historically, however, this model has often led Europe to division and confrontation. Russia will not always be as weak as it is today. Territorial politics (to use President Clinton's phrase) are not easily or fully restrained even by those who would like to concert the policies of the dominant powers, because in a time of conditional peace competition for influence is hard to put aside. Even in its most benign form a sphere of interest would exclude the weaker power, otherwise fully independent, from allying itself with potential enemies of the hegemonic power. In some cases, this is the model that may tacitly emerge even in the circumstances of Russia's weakened condition.[2]

Collective Security after the Cold War

The collective security model offers a hope, even though forlorn, of counteracting repressive spheres-of-interest policies, but its more likely attraction in the midterm will lie in its method of dealing jointly with intrastate threats to international peace and security. In Bosnia, something close to a collective security model was applied; intrastate or interstate disputes may arise elsewhere in the Balkans or in other parts of Europe where similar techniques could be applied. Even on the periphery of major powers, collective security is one tool available to small nations to offset the power wielded by larger nations. They can use collective security arrangements to build on the interest that great powers have in perpetuating a pattern of behavior that suits their general requirement for predictability, peace, and stability. The Organization for Security and Cooperation in Europe (OSCE) provides the organizational mechanism for doing this in a way that should certainly win the approval of Russia and the United States.

Classical definitions of collective security in Europe have been too narrowly constructed to be an operationally meaningful guide to policy analysis in the late twentieth century, especially where the use of military force is a consideration. Considerable weight should be assigned to the role of power in international relations, but this should not be the only consideration guiding national decisions. Security interests also can be served when governments develop and enforce broadly accepted international rules consistent with their national interests through collective action legitimized by representative international organizations.

The advantage of collective security as a conceptual model is that it is more appropriate than spheres-of-interest and balance-of-power politics for many post–Cold War security problems. Intrastate conflict is a new challenge for the international community, which has been moving fitfully toward the establishment of rules that in extremis justify intervention with military forces in internal affairs, as was discussed in chapter 5. Spheres-of-interest and balance-of-power politics are ill suited for dealing with conflicts that, although internal, threaten international peace and security. Even for state-on-state conflict close to the frontier of a great power, the collective security model may be appropriate. The OSCE may yet have a role in Nagorno-Karabakh, for example.

Applying the collective security model to disputes does not mean that the decision to intervene collectively, even for mediation purposes, is automatic, and still less does it mean that the decision to intervene with armed forces is an inevitable result. It is essential to distinguish clearly among the use of armed forces for

- crisis prevention;
- peacekeeping;
- protective security; and
- peace enforcement.

Peace enforcement lies at the higher end of the scale of violence in collective security operations and is rightly perceived through the lens of worst-case analysis. Governments *should* ask themselves whether a proposal for an observer mission or air strikes could lead inexorably to a requirement for peace enforcement at some stage; peace enforcement theoretically could require the suppression of conflict on a very large scale in the territory where fighting is taking place. There are many uses of military force in protective security and even in peace enforcement operations, however, that fall far short of that objective, yet which may still be valuable. If it is assumed that all peace enforcement operations inevitably will rise to the extreme end of the scale of violence, paralysis in decisionmaking will be the result.

The Premises of Collective Security

The collective security model, as conceived of in this chapter, is based on four premises: rules of behavior among nations, both tacit and explicit, should be encouraged; those rules should be respected and enforced; enforcement actions should enjoy the legitimacy conferred by broad international agreement; and those actions generally should be undertaken by multinational coalitions or multilateral organizations. Through the first years of the wars of the Yugoslav succession, the humanitarian assistance that was provided was not a case of applying the collective security model because it was not essentially aimed at developing or enforcing internationally accepted rules of behavior. It did buy time so that collective security operations could be activated when the situation was ripe for that. The economic sanctions against Serbia, on the other hand, could be regarded as a collective security measure since the sanctions were directed at rule development and enforcement. This was an example of order-building diplomacy. So, too, are efforts to bring accused war criminals to justice.

It would be easy to conclude that collective security as an enforcement mechanism offers little as compared with spheres-of-interest policies, which can rely on the big powers' willingness to defend their interests. Political theory is not very encouraging on this point. Hans Morgenthau, one of the great theorists of realism in American political science, was one of the first to analyze the concepts and shortcomings of collective security and its military implications. In his classic book, *Politics among Nations*, Morgenthau wrote that "the organizing principle of collective security is the respect for the moral and legal obligation to consider an attack by any nation upon any member of the alliance as an attack upon all members of the alliance." Morgenthau explained that the "alliance" to which he referred was a "universal alliance against potential aggression."[3] The principle of universality is generally cited to distinguish collective security, as manifested by the UN system, from a collective defense system like NATO whose membership is limited and where the presumptive aggressor during the Cold War was also clearly understood to be a particular state.

The conditions necessary to make collective security work, Morgenthau thought, were unlikely to exist in practice. The collective security model, as he saw it, required willingness to use military force, if necessary, in quarrels in which most of the "universal alliance" had no easily perceived direct stake. Furthermore, at least in Morgenthau's view, the collective security model was identified with defense of the status quo, and this view has been accepted by more recent writers.[4] In an era in which the status quo is being challenged at every turn, E. H. Carr's insight still resonates: "that few people do desire a 'world-state' or 'collective security,' and that those who think they desire it mean different and incompatible things by it."[5]

Carr was right, of course, in perceiving that the collective security model has many different shades of meaning, even considering only its military component. Applying the collective security model in the context of ethnic, nationalistic, communal, and internal power struggles, such as those in the former Yugoslavia, presents very different diplomatic problems from collective security in the context of great power relations or of aggression by one well-established state upon another. Ethnic conflicts are typically internal struggles conducted within the frontiers of an existing state. However, other nations have traditionally been viewed as having no authority to intervene in the internal affairs of a sovereign state. Yet intervention in internal affairs may have to be considered, as has already been demonstrated in the former Yugoslavia, to prevent a conflict from destabilizing the rest of Europe. The complex problems attendant upon the collapse of the Soviet Union and of the bipolar system require us to consider how internal intervention can be justified, gain public support, and be legitimized in cases of conflicts threatening international peace and security. The following observations point to a way of thinking about the collective security model that is relevant to today's security problems.

The collective security model should not neglect or ignore the distribution of military power in an international system. Relations among the largest states clearly will continue to be greatly influenced by power considerations, although perhaps not with the degree of intensity that prevailed between the United States and the Soviet Union during the

Cold War. Disputes in Europe and their outcomes will affect the evolution of the international order that is replacing the bipolar order of the Cold War. Balance-of-power considerations may figure in some of those situations. In others, they may not. Where they do not, joint intervention could be justified in terms of international peace and security. Even where a balance-of-power calculation is a factor, ground rules can be devised to constrain the roles of the big powers.

The collective security model can coexist with national policies aimed at maintaining a power equilibrium, but only if the latter policies do not drive the elements of trust and cooperation completely out of the international system. The collective security model should work well, in theory, in a system of democratic states, which much of Europe is becoming. There is evidence, disputed by some, that power balances among such states are less important in security calculations than their shared system of governance. But ethnic conflicts can arise even within such a system of states. For the time being, the power balance between Russia and the West suggests that war is unlikely. But in the end, Russia's continuing progress toward democracy is the best guarantee of security in Europe.

The collective security model need not be global or universal in scope. The OSCE, the largest European security organization, has over fifty members, more than the League of Nations and about the same as the United Nations in its early years. During the early 1990s, the OSCE was endowed by its participating states with structures and procedures so that it could be used for collective security purposes if the members so chose. Clinton and Yeltsin "underscored their commitment to enhance the operational capability of the OSCE" in their statement of March 21, 1997. Its status as a regional agency under Chapter VIII of the UN Charter gives it a claim to universalism; the UN Security Council could call on the OSCE to take necessary actions in the name of the global community of nations. The geographic coverage of the OSCE—from Vancouver to Vladivostok—affords ample scope for collective security. Other, ad hoc mechanisms on the same geographic scale as the OSCE have been devised to deal with peacekeeping. One of the most promising was the "contact group" established in the spring of 1994 to deal with negotiations concerning the war in Bosnia. Members of this group were the United States and Russia, and Britain, France, and Germany representing the European Union. This contact group proved to be effective despite differences among its members. A steering committee like this should be adequate to manage many types of collective security operations on a regional basis, informally, even within the OSCE, a consensus organization.

The collective security model need not be dedicated to defending the status quo. Any strategy of cooperation based on the collective security model would be doomed if the status quo were perceived to be its main focus. The Helsinki Final Act of 1975, the founding charter of the OSCE, proclaimed the principle of inviolability of frontiers, a major preoccupation of Europeans only too aware of the disasters that tinkering with frontiers could produce. But the Final Act also stated that frontiers could be changed peaceably and by agreement and it made human rights in each participating state a matter of concern to all signatories. In the end, the Final Act, as the Magna Carta of dissidents throughout Eastern Europe, contributed to ending the division of Europe and thus was one of the greatest conceptual assaults of modern times on the status quo. Military operations that have borne the hallmarks of the collective security model in both theory and practice have been used in the post–Cold War period to alter the status quo, not to defend it. The results have been at least a temporary aberration from the norms of self-determination and noninterference in internal affairs.

And so, finally, the collective security model need not be limited to relations between states: it may also address internal affairs within a state and, in fact, this will be its major function in the midterm. Over the long term, as democracy takes root throughout the continent, collective security should become the dominant mode of using force to keep the peace.

International Organizations and the Management of Collective Security

For better or worse, international organizations are generally the vehicles through which collective security decisions are made and peacekeeping operations managed. The procedures that the major nations use to make decisions about collective security can be as important as the merits of any given case in determining the success or failure of collective security. Although smaller nations find their voices in international organizations, for these multilateral creations to work effectively, great powers—Russia, the United States, and members of the European Union—also should try to concert their policies through bilateral as well as multilateral channels. Ideally, international organizations should be integrated into "a series of mutually supporting institutions and relationships," as recommended by Presidents Clinton and Yeltsin.

Ineffectual decisionmaking and weak management are charges laid at the doorstep of most international organizations, generally with much justification. Nonetheless, the key to improving performance in collective security operations lies in effective meshing of national and international security machinery. International organizations often are delegated managerial responsibility for implementing policies. Collective decisionmaking, therefore, amounts to an integration of national positions not only on basic policies but also on day-to-day operational issues. It is in the latter that much of the second-guessing and criticism about collective security operations arises, as we saw in the case of the United Nations' difficulties in the former Yugoslavia.

International organizations created by governments to act on their behalf in Europe all have their limitations. The OSCE is well positioned to conduct observer and mediation missions and to play a role in long-term conflict resolution efforts. Bosnia will be a test of how well the OSCE can perform in reconstructing civil institutions in that country. It will be a supremely difficult task and failure there should not become history's final verdict on the organization's possibilities. The OSCE's military role in peacekeeping is minimal at present. At their meeting of March 21, 1997, however, Clinton and Yeltsin declared that strengthening the OSCE met their interests, that its potential had yet to be fully realized, and that the OSCE's ability to develop new forms of peacekeeping and conflict prevention should be actively pursued. These sentiments were repeated in the NATO-Russia Founding Act of May 27, 1997. NATO enlargement may thus have the welcome result of focusing higher-level attention on the OSCE than has generally been the case.

NATO already has shown that it can be a powerful peace-enforcing instrument, but its uses in that mode are geographically limited: even with the Founding Act as legitimizer, it is doubtful that Russia will be comfortable with any effort involving NATO as a peace-enforcing mechanism in the territories of the former Soviet Union. A combined joint task force of NATO that included Russian troops for peace-keeping, however, might be a possibility, and the Partnership for Peace peacekeeping operations might prepare the ground for that. The Euro-Atlantic Partnership Council could become an important political management tool for that purpose.

The Commonwealth of Independent States has served as a device for Russian intervention, thus far with little pretense of being a truly impartial international force. The Western European Union is developing very slowly. Its long-run potential will depend on progress in consolidating the European Union and the perceived need for an alternative to NATO —if, for example, isolationism were to become a powerful force in the United States.

These, and the United Nations, are the organizations available for collective security purposes to the major nations. Their strengths and liabilities show that international organizations cannot act in the absence of leadership by the major powers.

Spheres of Interest and Collective Security under a Conditional Peace

Peace between Russia and the United States is still conditional—that is, neither side has traveled so far in its thinking about the other that war between them is totally excluded. The possibility is remote, but it is a possibility. Probably this situation will prevail for several years, during which time the spheres-of-interest–balance-of-power way of thinking about the relations between the two countries will be in conflict with the ideas of collective security. This will be the case above all in those areas in which Russia and the United States believe they have serious, even vital interests. In such areas the operations of collective security, with its emphasis on multilateral decisionmaking, may have difficulties making inroads against spheres-of-interest thinking backed by the threat of military force. Nonetheless, first steps in the transition process from collective defense to collective security already have been taken. Former secretary of state Henry Kissinger, noting this, has written that "the Founding Act seeks to graft a system of collective security on top of an alliance system."[6] Kissinger's opinion is that this will not work and that it dilutes NATO. If NATO is to enlarge to take in all European democracies, ultimately including Russia, it is undeniable that NATO's character will change fundamentally. In fact, Kissinger's observation that NATO already is becoming a hybrid collective security–collective defense system is quite accurate. The Founding Act is an important example of this and, more to the point, so is the experience in Bosnia.

In Paris, on May 27, 1997, President Yeltsin and NATO's heads of states and governments signed the Founding Act on Mutual Relations, Cooperation, and Security between NATO and the Russian Federation. This agreement created a NATO-Russia Permanent Joint Council that, in the words of the Founding Act, "will provide a mechanism for consultations, coordination and, to the maximum extent possible, where appropriate, for joint decisions and joint action with respect to security issues of common concern." The basic functions of this new mechanism will be defined more by practical experience than by the words of the Founding Act, but there is little doubt that a new collective security system is emerging.

Meanwhile, NATO's core functions are being redefined through the enlargement process and by the new realities caused by the collapse of the Warsaw Pact. In the past NATO provided five basic peacetime services to its members:

- deterrence—an attack on one is an attack on all (Article V);
- reassurance—people living under NATO's protective umbrella can feel safe and develop political self-confidence;
- integration—membership means being a part of the Western community of nations;
- reconciliation—former enemies have found it possible to become friends within the NATO family; and
- denationalizing defense activities.

The last four of these services rightly are being given the most emphasis today.

When the U.S. government explains the case for NATO expansion, its argument is cast in terms of reassurance, integration, and reconciliation. In its February 1997 report to Congress, the Clinton administration stated that "the purpose of enlargement is to integrate more countries into the existing community of values and institutions, thereby enhancing stability and security for all countries in the Euro-atlantic region." Secretary of State Albright, writing in the *Economist* in February 1997, commented that "we expect the new members to export stability eastward, rather than viewing enlargement as a race to escape westward at the expense of their neighbors." She argued that "NATO has taken a range of steps to ensure that the erasure of old lines of division does not leave new ones on the map."[7] The old core function of deterrence is being displaced by other requirements that are more political in character and more related to Article IV of the North Atlantic Treaty ("The Parties will consult together whenever, in the opinion of any of them, the territorial integrity, political independence or security of any of the Parties is threatened").

NATO is being transformed to deal with crisis management and with peace enforcement, as in Bosnia. Its future agenda will include global issues such as nonproliferation and terrorism. Russia now can cooperate in NATO through a variety of mechanisms. Because of the Founding Act and other mechanisms created since 1994, Russia can be, in effect, a "virtual member" of NATO. In addition, as promised in the Founding Act, the treaty on conventional forces in Europe will be adapted so that military buildups near Russia's frontiers will be precluded. Confidence-building agreements can address concerns about major military exercises. Other elements linking Russia and the West also are important. They include Russian association with the West through Russia's relations with the European Union and through Russia's membership in the OSCE.

One of the historic achievements of NATO is that it has "denationalized allied defense policies." It has done this by

- planning for collective force deployments and common operations;
- creating multinational formations;
- introducing common standards and procedures for equipment, training, and logistics;
- staging joint and combined exercises; and
- promoting infrastructure and logistics cooperation.

An enhanced Partnership for Peace can do most of these things and do them with Russian participation. Operations requiring military units, as in Bosnia, can be conducted under the aegis of combined joint task forces—"coalitions of the willing" as these forces have been called—because they can draw on NATO resources without every NATO country being involved. The traditional NATO benefits of reassurance, integration, and reconciliation can be open to members and nonmembers alike through a series of practical and workable devices.

Will Russia accept what it has been offered? Will having nearly everything NATO has to offer except Article V of the North Atlantic Treaty, the security guarantee, satisfy those other countries left out of NATO's enlargement? Can these beginnings of fundamental change in NATO be pursued over a period of years? The answers will depend on wobbly governments, personalities, a consensus within the West, American steadfastness in pursuit of a "grand design," and a host of other factors that are unpredictable.

Two critical areas in this regard are the Baltic states and Ukraine, areas where Russia and the West already are competing for influence. These cases can be used to illustrate several roles for collective security and spheres-of-interest policies. Three alternative developments are imaginable:

1. *A security arrangement dominated by a sphere of interest with little room or need for collective security operations.* In this scenario, despite Russian objections, NATO accepts applications for membership from the Baltic states. Russia might acquiesce but probably not without taking whatever defensive military countermeasures of which it is capable. In Yeltsin's terminology, a "Cold Peace" could be the result.

2. *A security arrangement dominated by spheres of interest where collective security could play an important but lesser role.* In this scenario, Russia succeeds in establishing the right to influence decisively the security arrangements made by the Baltic states and Ukraine, but the arrangements do not include military alliances between Russia and these countries, leaving some room for collective security operations (for example, observer missions).

3. *A security arrangement understood to be a transition to collective security where spheres of interest are expressed mainly by nonmilitary means.* In this scenario, the Baltic states and Ukraine are integrated into a Euro-atlantic community, including both Russia and the United States,

through a series of mutually supporting institutions and relationships. This would embrace the Partnership for Peace, the Euro-Atlantic Partnership Council, the European Union, the OSCE, and very likely some form of subregional security arrangements. Eventual membership in a transformed NATO for the Baltic states, for Ukraine, and for Russia itself would be a stated objective.

If Russia continues to make progress toward a stable democracy and a market economy, the vision that Clinton and Yeltsin have twice expressed should be applied to the Baltic states and Ukraine: "lasting peace in Europe should be based on the integration of all of the continent into a series of mutually supporting institutions and relationships that ensure that there will be no return to division or confrontation." Thus, of the scenarios outlined above, the third one is most compatible with a grand design based on achieving what the two presidents have called for, namely, "a stable, secure, integrated and undivided democratic Europe" (Helsinki, March 21, 1997). Because of internal politics in several of the concerned countries, it will be difficult to achieve. But the Madrid Declaration seems to point in this direction and, if creatively implemented, this model may win enough political backing to carry the day.

Policies aimed at creating a stable peace cannot be made in a vacuum, of course. In a world where conditional peace is the rule, it is possible that developments in what is still an unsettled Russia would warrant an enlargement of NATO to include at least the Baltic states. Certainly the Baltic states think that. A stable peace could hardly be imaginable, however, even as a long-term policy goal, if an unconditional U.S. military commitment to the Baltics and possibly to Ukraine through the mechanism of Article V of the North Atlantic Treaty were required because of circumstances in Russia.

Spheres of Interest and Collective Security under a Stable Peace

There is a difference between spheres of interest in a state of *conditional* peace as opposed to spheres of interest in a state of *stable* peace. In the former, spheres of interest may be backed up by a threat to use military force because resort to force is still a factor in big-power relations.

Under a stable peace, military intervention may be required from time to time to deal with threats to international peace and security arising from struggles over power sharing in an ethnically divided society—a future Bosnia, for example. Since progress toward a stable peace will hardly proceed in lock-step, for a long time to come there will be pockets in Europe where a state of conditional peace will persist. Therefore, the possibility of armed conflict between neighboring countries —an Albanian-Serbian conflict over Kosovo, for example—cannot be excluded. Such conflicts could occur even after most of Europe had achieved a state of stable peace. In such cases, military intervention under a collective security arrangement might be required. But military action as a recourse by the major powers against one another would be excluded, as a rational policy option, just as it is now among members of the European Union, for example.

However, in a state of stable peace between Russia and its neighbors, or between Germany and its neighbors, spheres of interest would continue to exist. They would be maintained by the effects of cultural, trade, and other ties. A Euroatlantic community in which most of the European OSCE nations, including Russia, are run along Western democratic lines, and democracy is firmly entrenched, is the only way in which the small nations of Eastern Europe can escape from the threat posed by contending spheres of interest backed by military force. These nations, of course, must make the transition from a conditional to a stable peace among themselves. If the logic of peace does not prevail among them, they can still fall victim to communal conflict and border wars.

Europe has changed and will change more in the future. But successful implementation of a grand strategy will take a great deal of time:

- time to consolidate an enlarged NATO and adapt to the requirements of a new strategic concept;
- time to test the efficacy of the NATO-Russia Founding Act and for democracy in Russia to become more deeply entrenched;
- time for attitudes in the West to change.

For a long time to come, a hybrid system of security will prevail, part collective security and part collective defense, and there will be a considerable overlap between the two. In an ideal world, this mixed system of security strategy concepts would be an interim arrangement, a system that would be necessary during a time of conditional peace but that would gradually yield to a pure collective security strategy as a stable peace spreads across Europe. In the next, and final, chapter we will discuss what policies are required if Europe is to become truly undivided and democratic.

8

Achieving a Stable Peace in Europe

A Grand Design for the Twenty-First Century

A Long-Term Goal

Steady, purposeful U.S. policy over a long period of time yielded an outcome in the Cold War that fulfilled the fondest hopes of the founders of the strategy of containment. A tenacious commitment to this grand strategy was possible because it corresponded to U.S. foreign policy ideals and aspirations, to the need to avoid nuclear war, and, above all, to the moral element in U.S. traditions. The American public will not support any strategy for very long if it does not fit well with Americans' perceptions of themselves. The United States has the power to be a global policeman or a global balancer, aligning first with one state then another in accordance with the ebb and flow of power calculations. But strategic concepts like these would be rejected and would guarantee a return to isolationism. If these ideas will not serve to engage the American people in heroic efforts for peace, which will?

In October 1996 President Clinton offered the vision of "a peaceful, undivided, and democratic continent" of Europe, and in March 1997 President Yeltsin joined him in this grand design. In this chapter, I will argue that this is both a *desirable* and a *feasible* goal for U.S. policy and the only way to build conditions for a stable peace in Europe. An undivided and democratic Europe will be exceedingly difficult to achieve, and the steps necessary to achieve it will be controversial. The measures needed to move toward it will require public support in North America and Europe every step of the way. The concept implies that the norms, rules, and structures that would impress the logic of peace on relations among nations of the Euroatlantic community will come to be accepted throughout that region. In this chapter, we are considering processes that Russia and the West might set in motion to encourage the idea that war is "subrationally unthinkable."[1] The question for all of us is whether war between Russia and the West could ever become as unthinkable as it already has become among the Western democracies, and whether we should try to make it so. President Clinton acknowledged the daunting nature of the challenge: the opportunity to build such a new Europe exists now, he said, "for the very first time since nation-states first appeared in Europe . . . it has never happened before." This is a grand design worthy of the highest aspirations of the American people.

A Long-Term Strategy

To pursue the Clinton grand design, a long-term strategy will have to be devised, the American people will have to be persuaded that it makes sense, and the U.S. administration will have to begin the long process of converting it into rules of behavior that will survive several future administrations. In all likelihood, international organizations will have to be adapted or created to carry the policy forward.[2] I argued in the last chapter that we are seeing the tenuous beginnings of this in the transformation of NATO. I believe that the strategy should be aimed at two objectives:

- strengthening the constitution—the rules and institutions—of the group of Western states that has steadily consolidated its cultural, economic, political, and defense activities over the past four decades; and

- constructing the constitution—the common set of rules and expectations about the behavior of states within the system—of the entire Euroatlantic community (that is, all European and North American nations).

The distinction I make between these two overlapping and interrelated communities is based on a factual situation, not on ideological or power considerations. In the West, conditions have developed that can fairly be called a stable peace. Those nations have begun to approach the Kantian idea of an international community—a "Federation of Peace." In Europe as a whole, however, nothing like that has been achieved. There is still a conditional peace. Cooperation has emerged, but for quite limited purposes. The relationships are more like a Grotian society of nations where cooperative relations are based on formal or legal understandings concerning state-to-state relations.[3]

The operational conclusions that flow from this observation differ from analyst to analyst. One opinion is that the distinction is immutable and that U.S. policy should be based on that assumption.[4] Of course, there are good arguments to support the view that Russian governmental traditions and Russia's Eurasian geography mean that the West ends at Poland's eastern frontier. But I would argue that the Russian people themselves should decide whether or not they wish to become a part of the West. Perhaps the Russians would prefer to keep their distance from the West—there is such a tradition in Russia, and it is still strong. The key point, however, is that the West should not force this outcome on the Russians; to the contrary, it should urge the opposite.

A strategy posited on the unchanging character of the differences that have separated Russia and the West is a self-fulfilling prophecy. The basic premise of such a strategy is that Europe never can become undivided and democratic. The trouble with such a status quo strategy is that it offers no vision of the opportunities available to construct a security system in which power is constrained not just by countervailing power but also by the exercise of democratic control over national decisions. Security in Europe is not just a question of military limitations and reductions. The essence of European security lies in the process of creating an inclusive community of democratic nations. In this sense, free elections are as much a security measure as are ceilings on the numbers of tanks.[5]

Until all of the European nations have become democracies where conflicts, internal and otherwise, are addressed through rules rather than resort to force, there will continue to be pockets where peace is only conditional. Obviously the state of stable peace is not going to become universal in Europe for a long time to come. U.S. policy should be to expand that zone of stable peace steadily and persistently, recognizing

that a goal of an undivided and democratic Europe will be more difficult to achieve if great and proud nations such as Russia are told that
they will forever be excluded from the society of democratic nations.

New Factors in the International Equation

The weight of European experience with the states system since the
Peace of Westphalia in 1648 is on the side of the pessimists. Strong
national ambitions have overcome all restraints imposed on them. Democratic governments have not always remained democratic. Europe has
not ceased being a place where nations struggle for power and influence.
Given the nature of nation-states and of the states system, as exempli-
fied by centuries of European history, a conclusion that conflict among
the European states is inevitable sooner or later is clearly warranted. If
war was prevented by the bipolar stalemate of the Cold War in Europe,
then the collapse of bipolarity should be accompanied by a renewal of
rivalries and, eventually, of conflicts.

History suggests two possible models for Russian relations with the
West in the midterm. One might resemble the relations between Russia
and the West while the nineteenth-century Concert of Europe was
functioning well—cooperation in the interest of stability. Or, the model
might resemble the one that preceded and followed World War II—
distrust steadily degenerating into hostility. Neither offers the prospect
of a stable peace: the reasons for this judgment are obvious in the case
of the twentieth-century model; the nineteenth-century model was
based on a balance-of-power equilibrium, and no thought was given to
moving beyond it.

Although history must be our guide as we consider the prospects for
a stable peace in Europe, it is not an infallible guide. Two structural
changes affecting the very definition of Europe have occurred in recent
decades and have altered the circumstances that led to wars in Europe
in the past. One is the arrival of the United States as a European power,
and the other is the rise of the European Union. These developments
may represent a historical discontinuity. Through the Monroe Doctrine,
the United States and Great Britain collaborated after the Napoleonic
Wars in deterring the spread of European imperialism in the Western
Hemisphere, but the United States at that time played no direct role in

Europe. After World War I, the United States withdrew from Europe. World War II changed all that. The United States has taken on a new role in Europe in power terms only in this century and really only since the 1950s. The United States has become a force that determines the equilibrium of Europe.

Those who have suggested that the European states system has been changed forever by the events of the 1940s and 1950s may have been right, even though the division of Germany, on which their assumptions and predictions were largely based, is no longer a factor.[6] The division of Germany probably was a less important element in creating a stable order in Europe than the advent of the United States as a continuing player in nearly every aspect of European life. That can be seen more clearly now with the collapse of Soviet power in Europe and the end of the confrontation that obscured the real character of the changes in Europe. The United States, no longer so critical in the defense of Western Europe, is still seen by Europeans as a stabilizing force in Europe, a powerful economic motor for all developed nations, and the only multipurpose global superpower. The presence of the United States as a European power changes the basis for measuring and judging the nature of an equilibrium in Europe and for estimating the chances that order will win out over anarchy.

Will that remain so? Through an economic, political, and cultural network, the nations of Western Europe and North America have become linked at many levels, in addition to the governmental level. This fact is what gives meaning to the notion that a Western order already exists. It is not overt military threats or balance-of-power calculations that still bring forth "the New World to redress the balance of the Old," but the more benign pressures of a strong tradition of cooperation, shared values, the idea of "the West."

The larger Euroatlantic community has entered a phase of institution building not unlike the disappointing efforts that followed other major European convulsions. A significant difference, however, is that now, for the first time in history, Moscow and Washington are both involved in creating organizations that will link North America and all the states of Europe. The United States exercised a major influence over the creation of security organizations—the League of Nations and NATO, to cite two of them—at the end of both world wars. American withdrawal from European affairs doomed post–World War I organizations, whereas the intense involvement of the United States in Europe for the last half century has produced some of the most successful organizations in European history.

The last time that Russia played an active and relatively cooperative role in all-European organization building was at the end of the Napoleonic Wars. Even in the brief heyday of the Concert of Europe, dealings among the European partners were as difficult as those faced by today's governments. The Concert offered certain rules and a *process* for resolving problems, not ready-made answers.[7] Other members of the Concert —France, Prussia, Austria, and Britain—found life with czarist Russia disquieting at times. But, as Henry Kissinger has pointed out, "it did not have the ideological fervor of its Communist successors, and it proved possible for long periods to deal with it as an important member of the European concert powers."[8]

The rise of the European Union (EU) is another important reason why history cannot be an infallible guide to the prospects for replacing anarchy with order. There has been nothing like the EU as it exists today, to say nothing of the Union of the future that is now being planned and constructed. If the EU were merely interdependence writ large, its impact on war and peace could be assessed in terms of historical experience with economic interdependence. The EU is more than that. States in Western Europe have pooled their sovereignties and this change has introduced a new factor into European relations. EU members have devised a strategy of cooperation out of which they have created order. Institutionalized economic cooperation already has subordinated national laws and prerogatives to those of the EU. The fiscal and monetary policies of the EU—matters still jealously guarded by national governments—increasingly are bound together by economic realities, as well as by formal agreements. Political cooperation has reached the point where common policies are commonplace, although defense cooperation has been much more difficult to achieve.

Policy Requirements of a Long-Term Strategy

The European Union is a necessary but not a sufficient answer to the problem of creating order in Europe. The possibility cannot now be excluded, unlikely though it seems, that the EU will disintegrate under the pressure of popular nationalist sentiments in member states. *The Great Illusion*, Norman Angell's famous book first published in 1909, used economic arguments to attack the idea that war was a profitable venture. The "delicate interdependence of the financial world," Angell argued, deprived the victor in a war of any real advantage, because "the financial and industrial security of the victor [is] dependent upon financial and industrial security in all considerable civilized centers."[9] Logical though he might have been, World War I broke out a short time later. The EU's political, economic, and defense institutions are still being built. Its internal structure lacks a democratic system of governance, and progress toward deeper integration may slow down as difficulties in implementing the Maastricht Treaty multiply. Furthermore, the EU's weak foreign policy and security machinery will limit what it can do externally for many years to come.

The European societies of states must include the United States if the conditions for order in Europe are to be met. The EU and the United States, with other nations, have been and still are "the West," the main contributor to order in Europe and with a constitution that is strong and well tested. But more can and should be done to lock in the gains achieved over the past four decades. Why? Because stable peace in the West makes an important contribution to peace everywhere in Europe. And because a Western commonwealth that is a success in every endeavor will be a magnet for Russia and for all of Eastern Europe.

Strengthening the Constitution of the West

The goal of building a Europe that operates along Western lines is essentially what is called for by the appeal for an undivided and democratic Europe. An essential step would be to strengthen the constitution of the West:

* first, by building a Western economy that is so strong that it is both attractive to the rest of Europe and able to absorb economies that are less competitive;

* second, by ensuring that the United States will remain a strong and active member of the Western democracies; and

- third, by continuing the process of building a single market and pooling sovereignties within the European Union.

Bolstering the political economy of the West. The United States has led the way in establishing the North American Free Trade Agreement, and U.S. trade with the Asia-Pacific region is booming. These factors, combined with the globalization of the marketplace, could relegate U.S.-EU economic relations to the status of a second-order problem—a sharp contrast to the central place that U.S.-European economic relations occupied for much of the Cold War. The New Transatlantic Agenda agreed upon between the EU and the United States in December 1995 committed the United States and the EU to closer ties but to nothing that would change the business-as-usual approach that both sides are taking to their economic relations. Such a history-defying goal as a peaceful, undivided, and democratic Europe cannot be accomplished without a more ambitious economic platform than now seems contemplated by Washington.

A more far-reaching economic agenda will also be necessary because, as Fred Bergsten has pointed out, when the euro replaces national currencies "a bipolar currency regime dominated by Europe and the United States, with Japan as a junior partner, will replace the dollar-centered system that has prevailed for most of this century. A quantum leap in transatlantic cooperation will be required to handle both the transition to the new regime and its long-term effects."[10] An example of a quantum leap was proposed by Canadian prime minister Jean Chrétien, who advocated a Transatlantic Free Trade Area. Nothing has come of his proposal to date. To be sure, both the U.S. and the Western European economies will probably thrive, especially in comparison with those of Russia and Eastern Europe, even without more dramatic integration of the economies of the North Atlantic. A key to a truly unified Europe, however, is likely to be found in the international political economy. And this almost certainly means some preferential system of trade between North America and an expanding EU.[11] This will require, among other things, a major shift in current U.S. foreign policy, which is focused on a Latin American free trade area, and probably a shift in public opinion, as well.

Keeping America in Europe. The durability of the U.S. presence in Europe is fundamental to the success of a policy aimed at strengthening the West and building links with the larger Euroatlantic community. U.S. staying power in Europe, fortunately, is not just a function of whether U.S. foreign policy in the future will motivate the kind of steadiness of purpose we have witnessed during the past forty years. U.S.-European economic relations are so embedded in the international political economy that the basis for interaction should be there for many years.

The political aspects of the relationship are a little more shaky, on both sides of the Atlantic. Some Europeans see the European Monetary Union as a means of combating American hegemony. Differences of varying degrees of seriousness exist between the United States and Europeans over extraterritoriality (witness the tussle over the Helms-Burton legislation), Bosnia, Iran, the Middle East, Africa, and some aspects of Russian policy. Policies adopted and actions taken unilaterally by the United States without adequate consultation with its European allies have been a source of constant complaint by Europeans for decades.

A deepening political relationship between the United States and Western Europe will not divide Europe; to the contrary, it will help to unite Europe by acting as a powerful magnet to attract Russia. The very process of agreeing on the goal of an undivided and democratic Europe requires a high degree of integration of the foreign policies of the Western nations. The sustained effort over years necessary to achieve that goal will be even more demanding. Ideas have been advanced for an Atlantic Union, and although this is consistent with my own aspirations, the present feasibility of this goal is dubious.[12] It would entail too many institutional changes to be politically realizable. As a long-term goal, a union or, perhaps better, a commonwealth could be an expression of an undivided and democratic Europe; the first step, however, should be to build on what now exists. Even that process will be extremely difficult to carry out in a time of weak governments and public indifference.

A first achievable step would be an intensification of the U.S.-EU consultation on global security issues, such as proliferation of weapons of mass destruction, terrorism, and regional conflicts that threaten international security. This type of consultation also will take place in the NATO-Russia Permanent Joint Council created by the Founding Act, but this will not eliminate the need for consultations in a U.S.-EU framework. Several of the global issues of interest are law enforcement and intelligence problems rather than military matters and are more easily discussed in a U.S.-EU forum. A deepening of interparliamentary ties through NATO and through the OSCE also would be a productive way of improving communications within the Western commonwealth. Revamping NATO to provide a more distinct role for Europeans also should be pursued.

Strengthening the European Union. The progress made so far in building the EU has helped to realize Thomas Mann's aphorism: a European Germany, not a German Europe. The Germans like it that way and so does the rest of Europe. The achievements of decades do not need to be undercut by efforts to tie North America more closely to Europe. An enhanced mechanism for political consultation among all the democracies of the West should not weaken the political consultations among EU members. To the contrary, the infusion of a global view would make those consultations more valuable so long as it does not imply a formal global defense strategy for NATO, a strategy that would be singularly inopportune at a time when the coherence of NATO is being severely tested by the addition of new members.

Serious policy questions have arisen in connection with the effort to create a common currency in the EU, primarily in regard to the limited latitude the Maastricht criteria afford governments to deal with unemployment problems in Europe. The outlook in the fall of 1997 is for the euro to go forward nonetheless. Little has been done to correct the lack of democratic governance within the EU's common institutions. Forging a truly common foreign policy or a rudimentary security policy has yet to be achieved, and the effort was an embarrassing failure where it mattered most in the former Yugoslavia. But it is important to keep the principle and the practice of pooling sovereignties alive. It is beneficial for relations within Western Europe and it will provide useful lessons for the Euroatlantic community. Any American attempt to undercut the "European idea" would be resented and would surely backfire.

Strengthening the Euroatlantic Community

A society of Euroatlantic states that includes Russia and the other Eastern European OSCE states will be linked for some time by rules and institutions that differ in quality from those that link the United States and the European democracies, old and new, even at this stage of their relationships. States of the broader Euroatlantic community have achieved some notable successes in concerting their policies—as, for example, in regard to Bosnia. But that community is functioning at best as an informal concert of sovereign nations; the roots for a deeper relationship are not yet in place. Between Russia and the West there is, as yet, no *stable* peace. Russia and the West are still in a state of *conditional* peace, relying on deterrence in their mutual relationships, not yet abandoning thoughts of the use of force against each other as a conceivable contingency in extremis. Changing that situation will take time. Political turbulence in Russia is likely to persist for some years, making the transition more difficult to achieve and links between Moscow and the West more flimsy and provisional than they should be.

A Euroatlantic community that operates according to the logic of peace requires the achievement of an undivided and democratic Europe. The two main ways by which this can be accomplished are

- first, by transforming security relationships; and
- second, by building stronger economic relationships.

Security relationships. A priority task is to pursue the nuclear agenda set forth in chapter 6. Unless there is a transformation in nuclear deterrence in the U.S.-Russian relationship, a stable peace will not be possible and the legacy of the Cold War will continue to limit the political process of normalizing their relations.

Ultimate full membership for Russia in a transformed NATO should be understood to be the long-term goal, but other steps that would point toward a stable peace are more pressing matters. These other steps should stress the idea that the Euroatlantic area is a single security space, as described in the previous chapter. The NATO-Russia Founding Act will accomplish some of this. Russian participation in a much-enhanced Partnership for Peace and in future combined joint task forces should be encouraged. The Euro-Atlantic Partnership Council, linking members of the Partnership for Peace more closely than before, is a very important step, especially if the council develops into a major policy management tool that could operate closely with the OSCE.

In the meantime, the OSCE should continue to be the main instrument for conflict resolution in Europe and for the promotion of democracy in the area beyond the reach of NATO. It should have a legitimizing role in authorizing military interventions for peacekeeping purposes, while recognizing that no one would permit the OSCE to have peace-enforcing responsibilities like those laid out in the UN Charter (Chapter VII). A greatly strengthened OSCE secretariat and inter-parliamentary union would be useful improvements.

Economic relationships. For the Eastern European states the most valuable security measure would be rapid economic development. This should be the priority area for the United States and, indeed, for all the Western democracies. But this, of course, requires internal reform, and this is where the obstacles to economic development are most pronounced. Membership in the EU has become a possibility for some of the Eastern European states, but not for all. The EU has invited several Central and Eastern European countries to begin negotiations on accession, a positive step but one that will take several years to complete.

The decline in Russia's economy may have bottomed out and Russian membership in the World Trade Organization and in the Organization for Economic Cooperation and Development has become a possibility in the near future. Reform in Russia still has a long way to go, however, and there, as in Eastern Europe, investment has been slow in coming. The reasons, again, are largely internal, and progress will be limited while these problems—lack of a legal framework for conducting business, inability to collect taxes, support for large, inefficient industries—are sorted out.

The economic health of the Western democracies is an essential part of the process of stimulating economic reform in the East. It is not just a question of the West being a valued trading partner for Russia and Eastern Europe, but also of being a model that works. Internal reforms in Russia and Eastern Europe can come only if the people and leaders of those countries want reforms to come and are prepared to pay the price. At least a part of their motivation has to come from seeing the merits of Western political and economic systems. A commonwealth of Western democratic states interconnected through political, economic, and security links should be a powerful attraction for Russia and other European OSCE nations in the process of transforming themselves to democracies and free market economies.

Is an Undivided and Democratic Europe a Feasible Goal for the United States?

A long-term strategy aimed at the goal of an undivided and democratic Europe can succeed only if it enjoys legitimacy in the eyes of the American people and the Congress. Many Americans take very seriously the words of John Quincy Adams about America's role in the world: "She is the well-wisher to the freedom and independence of all. She is the champion and vindicator only of her own." Building a commonwealth of Western democracies in Europe and North America that is so attractive that Russia will wish to accept its norms and code of behavior and to take the difficult internal steps necessary to do so is not a minimalist foreign policy. It goes well beyond the task of managing power and conflict in international relations. It will have to be presented to the American people as a proper response to changes now sweeping the world, and the people may not be convinced. The basic arguments are, first, that the strategic goal (or "grand design") of an undivided, democratic Europe matches American values and, second, that it is realistic and feasible.[13] A Europe whole and free is a goal compatible with American democratic values as these are expressed in our Declaration of Independence, the UN Charter, and the ten principles of the Helsinki Final Act. But is a Europe undivided achievable? If a strategy aimed at achieving a highly desirable goal is perceived as impractical, that strategy will be relegated to the realm of do-goodism.

The question of whether the American public and the Congress would regard the achievement of an undivided and democratic Europe as a realistic goal—one worth pursuing for generations, if necessary—can be divided into four elements:

- Why bother?
- Will Americans support this or any other grand design?
- How should a peaceful, undivided, and democratic Europe be defined?
- How burdensome will it be?

First, why bother?[14] Because the division of Europe into the indefinite future will inevitably accentuate latent big-power rivalries. Because American indifference concerning democracy in Europe is not compatible with America's status as a leading member of the Western world. And because peace in Europe ultimately will depend on Russia's becoming a democratic state within the Euroatlantic system. The process of making the transition from authoritarianism to democracy can be risky, provoking—as we have already seen in the Balkans and in Russia itself—virulent nationalism.[15] But the risk has to be taken.

Second, will the American people place their trust in *any* grand design the U.S. government may present to them? This is not an era for heroics. The end of the era of big government may be the end, also, of the era of large conceptions in American foreign policy. The level of confidence that Americans have in their federal government is at an all-time low. Former Speaker Tom Foley has referred to a dangerous denial of legitimacy to those who would lead the country. He supported this with public opinion polls that showed only 19 percent of the public believed the government could be trusted to do the right thing all or most of the time, in contrast to 75 percent who thought so in the 1950s and 1960s.[16] This attitude is not cheering news, but it does not necessarily translate into an opinion that the U.S. government should be less active in the international arena. A study conducted by the University of Maryland on this question concluded that "the minority that calls for the U.S. government both to reduce its role and to disengage from the world is too small to represent the dominant political sentiment."[17] In fact, polls taken in mid-1997 suggest that isolationist sentiment may already have peaked and be on a declining trajectory. Attitudes among elite groups, in particular, have shifted dramatically. Sixty-one percent of the experts on security affairs who were polled said they were "satisfied with the way things are going in the world," as compared to only 15 percent in 1993.[18] The public response will depend very much on the skill with which the strategic concept is presented from the "bully pulpit" and the demands it makes on the American people.

Third, how does one define "a peaceful, undivided, and democratic continent"? It would be natural for the United States to encourage the enlargement of the Western world to include all the European OSCE countries. The politics of exclusion would not fit the reforming instinct of America's engagement in world politics and would not show the honor due to the new buds of democracy in Russia and in East-Central Europe. George Kennan addressed a similar question in 1951:

> These, then, are the things for which an American well-wisher may hope from the Russia of the future: that she lift forever the Iron Curtain, that she recognize certain limitations to the internal authority of government, and that she abandon, as ruinous and unworthy, the ancient game of imperialist expansion and oppression.[19]

These seem to be achievable goals toward which Russia is already moving. But, of course, the Kremlin still wields too much arbitrary authority to be called democratic, and Russia's interest in its neighbors could, with cause, be labeled expansionist. Probably, a consensus among Americans could be found for the judgment that Russia's political and economic reforms are too new and too shaky to rule out the emergence of an authoritarian, nationalist, and expansionist Russia in the next decade. The two Europes will exist for quite a while roughly in their present form. During this time Russia's future will come into focus.

The fourth question is how burdensome a strategy calling for an undivided and democratic Europe is likely to be in resources and risks. If that question were asked when the strategy of containment was adopted by the U.S. government, that strategy might have been discarded as impractical. In fact, critics such as the dean of American columnists at that time, Walter Lippmann, thought it was impractical. He believed that

> the strategical conception and plan which Mr. X recommends is fundamentally unsound, and that it cannot be made to work, and that the attempt to make it work will cause us to squander our substance and our prestige.[20]

Probably a similar criticism could be made of the "strategical conception" advanced in this book. But the strategy I have outlined relies heavily on diplomacy and on economic relations. It should not be necessary to contemplate the use of American military forces on a scale beyond that which already has been used in bringing peace to Bosnia.

Does the Strategic Concept Fit Perceived American Interests?

A strategic concept should be feasible, even though long term, and it should resonate with the American people. A strategy of working for an undivided and democratic Europe fits those two basic requirements. But at another level of analysis, it must be asked whether the concept is congruent not only with fundamental U.S. values but also with the way policy-oriented members of American society see basic U.S. interests. The severest critics of such a strategy are likely to be those who would favor a less forward U.S. foreign policy. According to one opponent of a "globalist strategy":

> Our interests are to defend our society from attack, to temper violence and alleviate distress where we can, to join with others to combat the social and biological degradation of the planet, and to make real for all Americans the promise of the values we profess.[21]

And two American specialists on Asian economic affairs have argued that "Americans must begin to recognize that Cold War–style military power today is relevant to only a small and narrowing spectrum of policy problems."[22]

These views are typical of many Americans who would prefer that the nation's government concentrate on economic policy and pursue a less interventionist or a less unilateralist policy abroad. And these are the people who are interested enough in foreign policy to write about it. There are many Americans for whom a U.S. government foreign policy is an irrelevance, an anachronism, or an undesirable encumbrance. For such people, no strategic concept is likely to be acceptable. A policy based on the achievement of an undivided and democratic Europe will have to deal with the following reservations:

- The domestic affairs of other countries are beyond the proper scope of U.S. foreign policy. *Implication:* Democracy as a foreign policy objective is misguided.
- The use of U.S. military force should be confined to direct threats to U.S. vital interests. *Implication:* Deploying U.S. forces in response to concerns about long-term big-power relations or international norms is unnecessary.

- Russia's transition to democracy will be difficult and lengthy, but Russia does not present any direct threat to the United States. *Implication:* Russia can become the object of benign neglect.

- U.S. relations with our European allies are dominated by economics, not political or security concerns. *Implication:* It is a distraction from the nation's real business to set objectives such as peace, unity, and democracy.

- Our real security problems are no longer in Europe. *Implication:* Europe should help the United States in other parts of the world while Europe itself is assigned a lower priority.

Presidential leadership and a bipartisan coalition in the Congress supported the grand strategy that rebuilt and defined Western Europe after World War II. Can those conditions be met in today's America? I believe that the essential elements for success are present.

Polls show that a strong majority of Americans favor including Russia in NATO. With the qualification that Russia should first demonstrate that it is a stable democracy, 65 percent of those polled favor Russian membership. A report of a conference held at Stanford on September 19 and 20, 1997, signed by former Secretary of State Christopher and former Secretary of Defense Perry and others, said in part that "NATO should remain open in principle to membership by all states of the Euro-Atlantic Partnership Council without exception, contingent upon their meeting NATO's stringent standards for admission." A statement on NATO enlargement issued on September 9, 1997, signed by every living former secretary of state, emphasized the importance of Russia's role in the Euroatlantic region: "NATO has made clear its desire to develop cooperative security relations among all of the states of the Euro-Atlantic region, including Russia." In a similar vein, the Center for Strategic and International Studies, in a major report on U.S. foreign policy published in September 1996, stated that "if Russia isolates itself from a cooperative approach toward European security, that result should stem from its own decision, not from a failure to reach out." Skeptics of NATO enlargement within the American academic community have written persuasively about the possibilities of Russia's membership in NATO. Here are two illustrative arguments. First:

> Russia should be brought into NATO for the same reasons West Germany was in 1955: to encourage the right behavior and prevent it from pursuing an independent hostile foreign policy.

And another:

> Integrating Russia into NATO will help avoid the emergence of a new gray zone in the heart of Europe.

This summary of how ordinary American citizens and centrist specialists in international affairs see U.S. national interests shows that a strategic concept aimed at securing an undivided and democratic Europe should at least pass the plausibility test.[23] U.S. administrations will not lack a public opinion base well disposed to a Europe that is undivided and democratic.

With the end of the Cold War and because of historically unprecedented circumstances, Europe, Russia, and North America have been given an opportunity to create a system that might, over time, help the nations participating in it to achieve a stable peace. Transforming latent public support into the kind of enduring commitment that was the hallmark of U.S. conduct in Europe during the Cold War will require unswerving leadership by successive U.S. administrations. But the goal of a peaceful, undivided, and democratic Europe is feasible and it deserves the support of the American people.

The argument of this book has been that the primary task of American statecraft is to create a system of norms, rules, and structures that encourages the settlement of disputes without resort to force, or at least in accord with an understood set of rules—tacit or otherwise. During the Cold War there were rules that steered the United States and the Soviet Union toward peaceful outcomes to their disputes. These rules were derived from a first principle: a nuclear war could not be won and must never be fought. The rules of behavior that sprang from this principle helped to consolidate a U.S.-Soviet bipolar order. But the political power of ideas and rules is fleeting in historic terms. By the late 1960s, a thirst for change began to appear across the continent of Europe. Ultimately, the new thinking of that time led to dramatic changes in the international agenda. The way a government treated its own citizens became a legitimate issue for international oversight. Many factors undermined the bipolar order in Europe, but human rights were one of the most important.

Events during the last years of the Bush administration and the first years of the Clinton administration showed that some principles and rules carried over from the Cold War, especially the nuclear restraint regime, could help to avoid conflict in the new era. An example: the successful U.S.-Russian-Ukrainian negotiations in 1992–94 concerning Ukraine's nuclear status. There were *two* major ingredients in the recipe for that success: active and persistent U.S. mediation, and a nuclear restraint regime that was well understood and well entrenched.

New threats to international peace and security have appeared that were not evident or did not exist during the Cold War. Unprecedented types of cooperation across national boundaries are helping to put in place a system of principles and rules that addresses the very real threat that weapons of mass destruction could fall into the hands of criminals and terrorists.

An enormous human tragedy took place in the former Yugoslavia and almost irreparable damage was done to the standing of basic principles: peaceful settlement of disputes, respect for frontiers, self-determination, and national sovereignty. The lessons of Bosnia come down to the simple fact that norms and rules are not enough, that codes of behavior are not self-enforcing. But even in Bosnia, despite policy differences between Russia and the United States, the two nations found ways for their soldiers to serve side by side to sustain the shaky peace.

Strategic partners, as the United States and Russia could become, are likely to have difficulties living up to that role if they are also rivals in nuclear weaponry. Russia and the United States cannot cross the threshold from a conditional to a stable peace while they maintain thousands of nuclear weapons on a day-to-day launch-on-warning alert and while they hold many others in reserve "just in case." Reductions in the numbers of nuclear warheads loaded on missiles and bombers will not be enough. Nuclear deterrence itself must be transformed.

The European security regime of the next decade probably will be based on the principles of collective security—broadly defined as a multilaterally sanctioned use of force—and on spheres of interest—a recognition that big powers cast large shadows in their own neighborhoods even if hegemonic domination is not their intent. Under the current conditional peace, neither of these two concepts in its pure form is likely to meet all of Europe's requirements for security. Some harmonious fusing of the two ideas will have to be worked out, a process that already has started with the transformation of NATO.

If this is the midterm prospect, what ideas should guide long-term U.S.-Russian security relations in Europe? Consensus on a framework for American relations with the nations of Europe has not yet appeared in the United States. But President Clinton has provided a strategic concept that could deservedly be called a grand design by speaking of "an opportunity to build a peaceful, undivided, and democratic continent." The logic of this grand design should mean that a democratic Russia will become eventually a full and equal member of a Euroatlantic community of democracies, not excluded from any organization that would help to create a single security space in North America and Europe. It could mean, as the president has said, a "common security alliance," in which Russia and the United States are both involved. Secretary Albright was certainly right when she wrote that "Europe cannot finally be whole and free until a democratic Russia is fully part of Europe."[24] If this was seriously intended, the interim security arrangements that the West adopts should be guided by the rule of doing no harm to the prospects for achieving the goal of an undivided and democratic Europe.

Can NATO help to create a Europe that is undivided, peaceful, and democratic? In principle, yes. NATO could accept Russia as a member if it met the standards that other new members have met. NATO could make a transition from a military alliance defending a Western—principally American—sphere of interest to an effective security organization serving other purposes.

The difficulty in NATO's making this transition, and thus becoming an instrument for unifying Europe, is that NATO carries too much historical baggage. No matter how convincing the claims may be that new, more cooperative relationships with Russia can be fostered through NATO and its enlargement, the hard fact remains that NATO's residual function, its legacy from the Cold War, is to act as a hedge against a recurrence of Russian imperial ambitions. Many U.S. senators see it this way and have supported NATO enlargement for that reason, and that reason alone. Many Russians believe that Russia, a continental power, is simply too large to be just another NATO member.

Integrating Europe is not conceptually coterminous with NATO enlargement. Many other mechanisms can support the process of integration. But if NATO enlargement becomes in practice a series of new demarcation lines being drawn across the map of Europe, each new line leaving Russia more isolated from the rest of Europe, then NATO enlargement will become the antithesis of uniting Europe. Even a resounding success for the NATO-Russia Permanent Joint Council will not overcome that obstacle.

A policy of progressive enlargement of NATO makes sense if its purpose is to convert NATO into a twenty-first-century version of a collective security mechanism. But achieving that goal requires a steady, long-term effort based on a consensus in the United States and in the West as a whole that NATO should mature into a servant of an undivided and unified Europe.

Can a Euroatlantic alliance founded on the principle that an attack on one is an attack on all (Article V of the North Atlantic Treaty) really include Russia? If Russia continues to evolve toward true and deeply rooted democracy, Article V will have no relevance so far as conflict within the Euroatlantic community is concerned. In any event, Article V, it is important to note, is operative only in Europe and North America, not in Asia. A U.S. alliance with Russia would be as normal as a U.S. alliance with Germany. Its purpose would be to provide a basis for common defense planning and for peace enforcement in pockets of instability remaining in Europe, and to facilitate training and logistics for operations in out-of-area contingencies by coalitions of the willing. The latter would be North Atlantic Treaty Article IV operations (consultations in the event of a security threat) and, for out-of-area operations, would almost certainly require a UN resolution to be politically feasible. They would thus, by definition, be collective security operations in which Russia might participate.

A more serious problem is whether there is or could be a consensus within the West that if Russia met every democratic criterion one could pose, it could be invited to join an essentially Western alliance. Deputy Secretary Strobe Talbott once wrote that "the extraordinary transformations that have taken place should make us reluctant to exclude possibilities for the future—and ambitious in pursuing them."[25] There are those who would prefer to keep NATO as it is, or change it as little as possible, for reasons ranging from concerns about Russian reactions to concerns that NATO's core collective defense function will be transmogrified into a collective security function. For these people, the first wave of NATO enlargement should be the last. Most Russians probably see it that way too.

Those who view the world through the prism of realpolitik will continue to view Russia as a sometime friend or a sometime enemy, but in any case a nation so potentially powerful and so strategically situated (astride Eurasia) that an alliance-in-being should be maintained to offset Russia's great strength. And there are those for whom Russia is an alien power in Europe, a nation that was bypassed by the Renaissance and the Reformation, a nation whose history, traditions, and values are so un-Western that a dividing line always will exist somewhere east of Poland. These attitudes are truly the main barriers to Russia's inclusion in a common security alliance.

The challenges of achieving an undivided and democratic Europe can best be understood by facing up to the dilemmas that U.S. policymakers must resolve if they are to establish a long-term policy in support of that goal.

1. *If the United States makes the necessary substantial investments of its prestige, diplomatic energy, and resources in leading Europe toward a stable peace, will it sacrifice U.S. interests elsewhere?*

   An unprecedented opportunity now exists to unite a democratic Europe, but imminent threats to U.S. security lie elsewhere—in the Middle East, for example, or in Asia. The absence of a military threat in Europe should enable us to work mainly with political and economic tools in that region. NATO enlargement should be seen in that light, not as a process requiring a heavy investment of military resources, which should be directed to more troubled regions, with help from those nations that see themselves as actors on the global stage.

2. *Should the United States use NATO as an instrument for integrating a democratic Russia with the democratic West, or do NATO's core functions preclude that?*

If NATO's core functions today and in the future are denationalizing defense planning, reconciling former enemies, and integrating nations of the Euroatlantic community into a single security space, then membership in a transformed NATO should be open to a democratic Russia. If we consider peacekeeping and out-of-area operations to be the main functions of NATO in the future, this also argues for Russia's membership. But we must recognize that NATO is only one instrument for building a stable peace in Europe and that time must pass before political change makes broader membership in NATO a practical choice.

3. *How should the United States establish coherence between a phased enlargement of NATO and its goal of an undivided and democratic Europe?*

A network of interlocking organizations already exists that provides multiple channels for harmonizing potentially conflicting interests within the Euroatlantic community. Much more attention should be paid to the non-NATO arrangements. The question of what to do about NATO enlargement after 1999 should not be answered by accepting that membership should be frozen at nineteen. The door should be left open for additional members, but no timetable should be set, now or later.

4. *What policy toward Western Europe would best promote the U.S. goal of integrating Russia with the West while securing Western Europe's cooperation in addressing other global problems, economic as well as military in nature?*

The members of the European Union and other democratic nations of Western Europe do not all agree on the goal of a cohesive Euroatlantic community. Considerable effort will be required to gain their full support for an undivided and democratic Europe as a fact, not just a slogan. At the same time, Western European support for U.S. objectives elsewhere in the world cannot be taken for granted. Realistically, we will have to make choices about what we ask them to do since their complete alignment with every U.S. policy objective is unachievable.

The most important thing the U.S. administration can do is to set the policy framework and persuade the American people and the Europeans, both East and West, of its soundness. If it fails to do this, policies will surely be hijacked by people whose vision of the future is quite different. Many features of the policy have been outlined already by the administration, but its key tenet—a peaceful, undivided, and democratic Europe—is not yet accepted by the public because that goal has not been cemented into the vital center of American foreign policy, no consensus at home or abroad supports it, and the means so far arrayed to achieve it fall pitifully short of the effort that it will require. Compared with that effort, the enlargement of NATO now under consideration is at best a down payment and at worst another obstacle to the achievement of a stable peace. A stable peace in Europe should be given priority in recognition of the common values that always have linked Europe and North America and the need to secure what amounts to our home base.

The long-term goal that President Clinton proclaimed accords with the aspirations of the American people. Achieving a stable peace in Europe, as President Clinton has suggested, "for the very first time since nation-states first appeared in Europe," is a prize worth the high stakes that are on the table in this game. It would be a feat greater than Franco-German reconciliation and more lasting even than the success of the Cold War's containment policy. The investment of American effort may have to be on a scale comparable to what the nation put into containment, perhaps not in terms of financial costs but certainly in terms of long-term commitment and prestige. NATO enlargement in 1999 will be just the end of the beginning.

Notes

Foreword

1. Patrick Morgan, *Deterrence: A Conceptual Analysis* (Beverly Hills, Calif.: Sage, 1977).

2. See, for example, Herbert Simon, *The Sciences of the Artificial* (Cambridge, Mass.: MIT Press, 1969); also Davis B. Bobrow, *International Relations: New Approaches* (New York: Free Press, 1972); George Kent, "Political Design," University of Hawaii, Dimensionality of Nations Project, Research Report no. 63, 1972; and Ernest Haas, *Collective Security and the Future International System*, University of Denver Monograph Series in World Affairs, vol. 5, no. 1, 1967–68.

3. "Clinton's Opening Statement and Response at His News Conference," *New York Times*, March 8, 1997.

Introduction

1. From President Clinton's State of the Union address of February 4, 1997. For the full text, see *Washington Post*, February 5, 1997, A18–19.

2. I am using "order" to imply a relationship among a set of nations that is based on principles recognized by all of them. My thinking has been influenced by Hedley Bull, particularly his classic work, *The Anarchical Society: A Study of Order in World Politics* (New York: Columbia University Press, 1977). For an excellent study of tacit "rules of prudence and of explicit codes of conduct," see Graham T. Allison and William L. Ury, with Bruce J. Allyn, eds., *Windows of Opportunity: From Cold War to Peaceful Competition in U.S.-Soviet Relations* (Cambridge, Mass.: Ballinger, 1989). My views are generally in line with those expressed in that book.

3. I am indebted to Alexander George for encouraging me to develop this conceptual approach to a relationship between Russia and the West. He defines "stable peace," a term he borrowed from Kenneth Boulding, as a relationship between two states in which neither considers the use of military force, or even the threat of it, in a dispute. Deterrence and compellance by military force are simply excluded, and both sides know it. Professor George defines "conditional peace" as a conflict relationship in which war is possible from time to time and in which deterrence plays the predominant role generally. He also introduces the concept of "precarious peace" to refer to peace between antagonists that is really only the absence of war for the time being.

4. In *Stalin and the Bomb: The Soviet Union and Atomic Energy, 1939–1956* (New Haven, Conn., and London: Yale University Press, 1994), David Holloway concludes that "it was only after the death of Stalin, when repression eased, and after the first hydrogen bomb tests, which heightened scientists' understanding of what they had created, that signs can be observed of a new attitude to nuclear weapons" (p. 319). Quoting Malenkov's March 12, 1954, statement that "modern weapons mean the end of world civilization," Holloway concludes that Malenkov "changed his assessment of nuclear war between 1952 and 1954 as a result of the development of thermonuclear weapons" (pp. 336–337).

5. President Clinton's speech in Detroit, Michigan, October 22, 1996. See chapter 7, page 162, for an interesting insight into the president's thinking on the subject of cooperating with, rather than isolating, Russia.

1. Inventing Rules of Behavior for the Nuclear Era

1. On December 2, 1942, Enrico Fermi's experimental nuclear reactor produced a self-sustaining nuclear chain reaction, the first ever caused by human intervention in nature's processes. Many events could qualify as the beginning of the nuclear era; this was one of the most dramatic. Harvard University president James B. Conant was informed in a message, "Jim, you'll be interested to know that the Italian navigator has just landed in the new world." A decade later—indeed several decades later—American leaders were still trying to come to grips with the implications of this new world. See Richard G. Hewlett and Oscar E. Anderson, Jr., *The New World, 1939/46* (University Park: Pennsylvania State University Press, 1962), 112.

2. Bertrand Russell, "The Prevention of War," in Morton Grodzins and Eugene Rabinowitch, eds., *The Atomic Age* (New York: Basic Books, 1963), 100–106; Herman Kahn, *On Thermonuclear War* (Princeton, N.J.: Princeton University Press, 1960); and Herman Kahn, *Thinking about the Unthinkable* (New York: Horizon Press, 1962).

3. Marc Trachtenberg, "A Wasting Asset: American Strategy and the Shifting Nuclear Balance, 1949–1954," *International Security* 13, no. 3 (winter 1988–89): 5–49; and Russell D. Buhite and William Christopher Hamel, "War for Peace: The Question of an American Preventive War against the Soviet Union," *Diplomatic History* 14, no. 3 (summer 1990): 367–384.

4. "United States Objectives and Programs for National Security," NSC 68, April 14, 1950, 6. The document has been declassified. NSC 68 is partially reproduced in P. Edward Haley, David M. Keithly, and Jack Merritt, *Nuclear*

Strategy, Arms Control, and the Future (Boulder, Colo., and London: Westview Press, 1985), 43–49.

5. For a classic study of containment, see John Lewis Gaddis, *Strategies of Containment* (New York and Oxford: Oxford University Press, 1982).

6. NSC 68, 19–20.

7. Based on an account in Department of State, *Foreign Relations of the United States* (hereafter *FRUS*), *1952–54* (Washington, D.C.: Government Printing Office), vol. 2, pt. 1.

8. General Andrew J. Goodpaster, recorded interview by Malcolm S. McDonald, April 10, 1982, Eisenhower Library, Oral History # 477, 14.

9. General Lauris Norstad, recorded interview by Dr. Thomas Soapes, November 11, 1976, Eisenhower Library, Oral History #385, 40.

10. For an excellent summary of the episode, see McGeorge Bundy, *Danger and Survival: Choices about the Bomb in the First Fifty Years* (New York: Random House, 1988), 255–260. For a contemporaneous criticism of the implications of the speech, see Henry Kissinger, *Nuclear Weapons and Foreign Policy* (New York: Harper, 1957), especially chaps. 8 and 9.

11. Sir John Slessor, *Strategy for the West* (New York: William Morrow, 1954).

12. *FRUS, 1952–54*, vol. 2, pt. 1, 805.

13. Slessor, *Strategy for the West*, 16.

14. *FRUS, 1952–54*, vol. 2, pt. 1, 532–533.

15. See, for example, Admiral Carney's statement to this effect at the NSC meeting of October 29, 1953, in *FRUS, 1952–54*, vol. 2, pt. 1, 572.

16. *FRUS, 1952–54*, vol. 2, pt. 1, 597.

17. Maxwell Taylor, *The Uncertain Trumpet* (New York: Harper, 1960), 38–42. But note General Goodpaster's comment that Eisenhower retained the full power of decision for himself (see note 34 below, Goodpaster letter).

18. For a comprehensive discussion of U.S. and Soviet nuclear command and control systems, see Bruce G. Blair, *The Logic of Accidental War* (Washington, D.C.: Brookings Institution, 1993). Blair believes that "little doubt exists that past presidents, beginning with Dwight D. Eisenhower, delegated to key military commanders the authority to carry out nuclear war plans under some circumstances" (p. 46). For another very useful discussion related to this issue, see Scott D. Sagan, *The Limits of Safety: Organizations, Accidents, and Nuclear Weapons* (Princeton, N.J.: Princeton University Press, 1993). Sagan states that "President Eisenhower delegated authority to U.S. military commanders in the mid-1950s to use such *defensive* nuclear weapons immediately in the event of an attack" (p. 92). Sagan is referring to the U.S. Army Air Defense Command.

19. Memorandum of Conference with the President, August 11, 1960, prepared by A. J. Goodpaster, memorandum dated August 13, 1960. Declassified June 10, 1980, NLE: MR Case no. 79-103, document no. 5.

20. *FRUS, 1952–54,* vol. 2, pt. 1, 546.

21. Memorandum dated January 4, 1954, for the Secretary of State, the Secretary of Defense, and the Chairman, Atomic Energy Commission. Subject: Policy Regarding the Use of Nuclear Weapons. Declassified in 1988 at my request.

22. NSC 162/2, October 30, 1953, the Senator Gravel edition of the Pentagon Papers.

23. *FRUS, 1952–54,* vol. 2, pt. 1, 695–696.

24. Ibid., 815, 833–844.

25. Ibid., 795–799.

26. Eisenhower recounts in his *Mandate for Change* (Garden City, N.Y.: Doubleday, 1963 [pp. 312–313]) that he told Secretary of War Stimson that Japan was already defeated and that the United States should avoid shocking world opinion.

27. See, for example, *FRUS 1952–54,* vol. 2, pt. 1, 397.

28. Ibid., 461.

29. Robert H. Ferrell, ed., *The Eisenhower Diaries* (New York: W. W. Norton, 1981), 311–312.

30. Memorandum for the Record, February 10, 1956, prepared by Col. A. J. Goodpaster, Eisenhower Library. Declassified April 15, 1980.

31. Quoted in Fred I. Greenstein, *The Hidden-Hand Presidency: Eisenhower as Leader* (New York: Basic Books, 1982), 257. Letter to Richard L. Simon, Simon and Schuster, Inc. Compare this with Reagan's later statement that a nuclear war cannot be won and must never be fought.

32. Memorandum of Conference with the President, January 16, 1959, prepared by Brigadier General A. J. Goodpaster, Eisenhower Library. Declassified August 22, 1979.

33. *Public Papers of the Presidents of the United States: Eisenhower, 1959,* (Washington, D.C.: Government Printing Office), 252.

34. General Andrew J. Goodpaster read this account and made the following comment:

> I would draw a distinction, I believe, between what Eisenhower approved for defense budgets, preparations, and operational plans and concepts on the one hand, and how he envisaged his actions in directing and conducting military activity (including nuclear) should conflict actually occur, on the other. Dealing with the first set of issues was a continuing largely bureaucratic struggle. On the second, he had no doubt and left no doubt that he would be actively in charge,

and retained the full power of decision for himself. The efforts we often saw to force his hand on the first by tying him down on the second just as often got nowhere with him. Nor did he allow ongoing foreign policy judgments and decisions to be forced by such considerations. He was willing to allow the premises for budgets and the like to be argued over, but without by any means losing his freedom of decision on current international issues or—prospectively—conduct of military affairs. (Letter to the author, February 7, 1997)

35. See Thomas C. Schelling, *The Strategy of Conflict* (Cambridge, Mass.: Harvard University Press, 1960), 260:

We are dealing with the theory of unwritten law—with conventions whose sanction in the aggregate is the need for mutual forbearance to avoid mutual destruction, and whose sanction in each individual case is the risk that to breach a rule may collapse it and that to collapse it may lead to a jointly less favorable limit or to none at all, and may further weaken the yet unbroken rules by providing evidence that their "authority" can not be taken for granted. . . . What makes atomic weapons different is a powerful tradition that they *are* different . . . there is a tradition for their non-use—a jointly recognized expectation that they may not be used in spite of declarations of readiness to use them, even in spite of tactical advantages in their use.

36. Bundy, *Danger and Survival,* 587.

37. *Public Papers of the Presidents of the United States: Kennedy, 1961* (Washington, D.C.: Government Printing Office), 232.

38. Theodore C. Sorensen, *Kennedy* (New York: Harper and Row, 1965), 609–610.

39. Raymond Garthoff, *Intelligence Assessment and Policymaking* (Washington, D.C.: Brookings Institution, 1984), 44.

40. Sorensen, *Kennedy,* 513.

41. For an excellent discussion of Acheson's report and its aftermath, see David N. Schwartz, *NATO's Nuclear Dilemmas* (Washington, D.C.: Brookings Institution, 1983), 150–179.

42. *Public Papers of the Presidents of the United States: Kennedy, 1961,* 254–255.

43. Papers of President Kennedy, National Security Files, box 313, folder NSC Meetings, 475–507, Kennedy Library.

44. For a summary and an analysis of McNamara's Athens and Ann Arbor speeches, see Schwartz, *NATO's Nuclear Dilemmas,* 156–165. A long excerpt from the Ann Arbor speech can be found in Robert Art and Kenneth Waltz, *The Use of Force* (Lanham, Md.: University Press of America, 1983), 148–150.

45. Bundy, *Danger and Survival.*

46. An excellent analysis of this dilemma can be found in A. L. George and Robert O. Keohane, "The Concept of National Interest: Uses and Limitations," in Alexander George, ed., *Presidential Decisionmaking in Foreign Policy* (Boulder, Colo.: Westview Press, 1980).

47. John Lewis Gaddis, *The Long Peace: Inquiries into the History of the Cold War* (New York: Oxford University Press, 1987), 240–241; and Schelling, *Strategy of Conflict*, 257–266.

2. Challenging the Bipolar Order

1. Gordon Craig and Alexander George suggest that this order was a primitive international system, incorporating certain restraints and norms, maintained through the Cuban missile crisis by crisis management and deterrence procedures. See Craig and George, *Force and Statecraft: Diplomatic Problems of Our Time*, 3d ed. (Oxford: Oxford University Press, 1995), 105.

2. See Gaddis, *The Long Peace*, 237–243.

3. For a somewhat similar analysis, see Allison and Ury, eds., *Windows of Opportunity*. See also Stanley Hoffman, *Primacy or World Order* (New York: McGraw-Hill, 1981).

4. See, for example, Fred Hiatt, "U.S. Faults Russia on POW Data," *Washington Post*, September 3, 1993, A27; and Paul Lashmar, "Stranger than 'Strangelove': A General's Forays into the Nuclear Zone," *Washington Post*, July 3, 1994, C9.

5. For an excellent discussion of arms control and its relation to the firebreak, see Jennifer E. Sims, *Icarus Restrained: An Intellectual History of Nuclear Arms Control, 1945–1960* (Boulder, Colo.: Westview Press, 1990).

6. For a discussion arguing that the speech was intended to have this effect, see Raymond L. Garthoff, *Détente and Confrontation*, rev. ed. (Washington, D.C.: Brookings Institution, 1994), 133–134. A former speechwriter for Brezhnev has confirmed to me that the timing was deliberate. I drafted an instruction for the U.S. ambassador in Moscow immediately upon hearing of the Brezhnev speech, asking him to raise the matter with Gromyko. Thereafter, the State Department informed the Senate that discussions were under way with the Soviets on the issue of reciprocal troop reductions.

7. Winston Churchill, *Triumph and Tragedy* (Boston: Houghton Mifflin, 1953), 226–227.

8. As Craig and George point out, the bipolar structure of the Cold War went well beyond the "two-alliance variant of the European balance-of-power system at the turn of the century" (Craig and George, *Force and Statecraft*, 106).

9. Gaddis, *Strategies of Containment*, 14–15.

10. For general background, see Frederick H. Hartmann, *Germany between East and West: The Reunification Problem* (Englewood Cliffs, N.J.: Prentice-

Hall, 1965), 70–71; Ferenc A. Vali, *The Quest for a United Germany* (Baltimore: Johns Hopkins University Press, 1967), 160–161; and W. W. Rostow, *Europe after Stalin: Eisenhower's Three Decisions of March 11, 1953* (Austin: University of Texas Press, 1982), 70–73. For a valuable recent discussion of whether the 1952 note was a lost opportunity, see Ruud van Dijk, "The 1952 Stalin Note Debate: Myth or Missed Opportunity for German Reunification," working paper no. 14, Cold War International History Project, Woodrow Wilson International Center for Scholars, Washington, D.C., May 1996.

   11. Henry A. Kissinger, *White House Years* (Boston: Little, Brown, 1979), 409–424.

   12. Ibid.

   13. Gaddis, *The Long Peace*, 240–241.

   14. See Henry Kissinger, "Reflections on Containment," *Foreign Affairs* 73, no. 3 (May/June 1994): 113–130; and Michael Howard, "The World According to Henry," *Foreign Affairs* 73, no. 3 (May/June 1994): 132–140.

   15. Margaret Thatcher, *The Downing Street Years* (New York: HarperCollins, 1993), 792–799; and "Mitterand, in Kiev, Warns Bonn Not to Press Reunification Issue," *New York Times*, December 7, 1989, A21.

   16. A. W. De Porte, *Europe between the Superpowers: The Enduring Balance*, 2d ed. (New Haven, Conn.: Yale University Press, 1986); and John J. Mearsheimer, "Back to the Future: Instability in Europe after the Cold War," *International Security* 15, no. 1 (summer 1990): 5–56.

   17. Gaddis, *Strategies of Containment*, 274–308.

   18. James M. Naughton, "Ford Sees 35-Nation Charter as a Gauge on Rights in East Europe," *New York Times*, July 26, 1975.

   19. On June 30, 1973, members of the North Atlantic Council met with President Richard Nixon in San Clemente, California. Present also were Secretary of State Kissinger, State Department Counselor Helmut Sonnenfeldt, and Assistant Secretary of State for European Affairs Walter Stoessel. Participants in the conference have reported to me that Secretary Kissinger said the CSCE should not become a cosmic event that could lead the public to believe spectacular results had been achieved. His view was that the Soviet Union was not going to be eased out of Eastern Europe by some sort of declaration and that the sooner the conference was over, the better.

   20. This and the several references to State Department and embassy telegrams and memoranda that follow are based on documentation that I requested and received under the Freedom of Information Act. Telegram from Department of State to Paris, July 18, 1969; telegram from the American embassy, Paris, to Department of State, July 22, 1969 (Paris 11066).

   21. Telegram from Department of State to U.S. Mission NATO, April 21, 1969.

22. *Public Papers of the Presidents of the United States: Nixon, 1970* (Washington, D.C.: Government Printing Office), 131.

23. Ibid.

24. Department of State memorandum of conversation of November 12, 1969, Secretary Rogers and FRG defense minister Helmut Schmidt.

25. Key participants in the State Department during these years were Assistant Secretaries for European and Canadian Affairs Martin Hillenbrand and Walter Stoessel; Deputy Assistant Secretary George Springsteen; Ralph McGuire and Edward Streator, director and deputy director, respectively, of the Office of Regional Politico-Military Affairs (RPM); Arva Floyd, officer-in-charge of political affairs, RPM; and Leo Reddy, of that office. Reddy was the line action officer in RPM and later served in the same capacity in the U.S. Mission to NATO. He originated many of the ideas for NATO consultations. At the U.S. Mission, Ambassadors Robert Ellsworth and Donald Rumsfeld were closely involved with CSCE matters. George Vest, deputy chief of mission and chargé d'affaires, later took on the responsibility for getting the multilateral CSCE talks under way. John Maresca, then in the office of the NATO secretary general, was much involved with the NATO work on CSCE and later served in a leading role throughout the CSCE multilateral negotiations. Laurence Eagleburger, political adviser in the U.S. Mission, and myself as his successor, represented the United States in the Senior Political Committee at NATO headquarters; we were directly responsible for negotiations with allies and interaction with the State Department. Gerald Helman represented the United States in the Political Committee and handled many of the human rights issues. Tom Niles, Steve Ledogar, and Ted Wilkinson all worked on various aspects of the CSCE during 1974, my last year at the mission. The interaction between RPM and the U.S. Mission was intense and productive. At the Washington end, during this time, Arva Floyd was the prime initiator of instructions to the U.S. Mission.

26. John J. Maresca, *To Helsinki: The Conference on Security and Cooperation in Europe, 1973–1975* (Durham, N.C.: Duke University Press, 1985), 158.

27. Speaking notes left at the Department of State by Soviet Ambassador Dobrynin on November 19, 1969.

28. Department of State memorandum of conversation of November 28, 1969, Assistant Secretary of State Martin Hillenbrand and Finnish ambassador Olavi Munkki.

29. Telegram from Department of State to Ambassador Robert Ellsworth, April 18, 1970. The February 18 statement is the president's 1970 report to Congress on foreign policy.

30. Telegram from Department of State to U.S. Mission NATO, October 29, 1970.

31. Telegram from U.S. Mission NATO to Department of State, March 12, 1972 (USNATO 1058).

32. Telegram from U.S. Mission NATO to Department of State, March 26, 1971 (USNATO 1283).

33. Telegram from U.S. Mission NATO to Department of State, March 26, 1971 (USNATO 1279).

34. Telegram from U.S. Mission NATO to Department of State, March 26, 1971 (USNATO 1283).

35. Telegram from Department of State to U.S. Mission NATO, July 30, 1971.

36. Letter dated July 2, 1971, from Frank Shakespeare to Department of State, and letter of August 4, 1971, from John Irwin II to Shakespeare.

37. Telegram from U.S. Mission NATO to Department of State, July 1, 1971 (USNATO 2787).

38. Telegram from U.S. Mission NATO to Department of State, September 24, 1971 (USNATO 3954).

39. Telegram from Department of State to the embassy in Bonn, September 16, 1971 (State 170072).

40. Telegram from Department of State to U.S. Mission NATO, October 2, 1971 (State 181563).

41. The description of this report is from a text sent by the Department of State (E. J. Streator) to various agencies for final clearance on October 30, 1971. Some further revisions might have been made but, if so, are unavailable to the author. This text already had been discussed and revised in the interagency process.

42. Telegram from U.S. Mission NATO to Department of State, November 27, 1971 (USNATO 4962).

43. Telegram from U.S. Mission NATO to Department of State, November 24, 1971 (USNATO 4916).

44. Memorandum from Bureau of European Affairs (EUR/RPM: Ralph J. McGuire) to CSCE Task Force Working Group on Freer Movement. Subject: Public Affairs Guidance for CSCE—Freer Movement of People, Ideas and Information. November 19, 1972.

45. Maresca, *To Helsinki*, 44. In his foreword to Maresca's book (p. ix), William E. Griffith suggests why Moscow accepted the demanding human rights provisions:

the initial lack of enthusiasm for the whole conference shown by Dr. Kissinger helped working-level diplomats to compromise and unconsciously helped the Soviets to believe that the results would cause them no problems. . . . Had the Soviets realized how much détente would decline, and how much their final, reluctant agreement to the human rights provisions in Basket III of CSCE would come home to haunt them, they would hardly ever have agreed to the Final Act at all.

46. Telegram from George Vest, U.S. delegation, Multilateral Preparatory Talks, dispatched from U.S. Mission NATO, December 20, 1972 (USNATO 5465).

47. Memorandum to the President from Secretary of State William Rogers. Subject: CSCE Multilateral Preparatory Talks. December 20, 1972.

48. The CSCE story, of course, continues to this day and its possibilities are far from being exhausted. Several other studies have been published about later stages of the process.

49. Thomas Risse-Kappen, "Ideas Do Not Flow Freely: Transnational Coalitions, Domestic Structures, and the End of the Cold War," *International Organization* 84, no. 2 (spring 1994): 185–214.

50. Maresca said it most eloquently: "This group of middle-grade career diplomats understood instinctively and unanimously the concepts they could not, under any circumstances, compromise. . . . We probably owe a great deal to this anonymous group of diplomats, who acted for the most part on the basis of their own collective best judgment" (*To Helsinki*, p. 158).

3. Testing the Utility of Nuclear Restraints after the Cold War

1. I was U.S. chief negotiator for the Safe and Secure Dismantlement of Nuclear Weapons (SSD) from March 1993 through March 1994. Other key people, to whom I extend my thanks once more, were Gloria Duffy and Jim Turner, my DOD and DOE deputies; Mike Stafford, executive secretary and chief of staff; and Jack Beard, our chief counsel.

2. For an excellent account of the Bush administration's diplomacy concerning German reunification, see Philip Zelikow and Condoleezza Rice, *Germany Unified and Europe Transformed* (Cambridge, Mass.: Harvard University Press, 1995). The authors remark that "the Bush administration was riveted on the institutions—principally NATO—that had sustained the Western alliance and American power in Europe for forty-five years" (p. 368). As that book shows, the existence of an organization, NATO, was central to the ability of the United States to imprint an order on the international system.

3. Herbert Simon's ideas of "bounded rationality" and "satisficing" help one appreciate how the imperfect understanding of all the facts in a case induces decisionmakers to rely on simplified models that incorporate principles and rules. Simon developed and explained these concepts in several works. See, for example, Herbert A. Simon, *Administrative Behavior: A Study of Decision-Making Processes in Administrative Organization,* 3d ed. (New York: Free Press, 1976). In this book he writes of "the theory of intended and bounded rationality—of the behavior of human beings who *satisfice* because they have not the wits to *maximize*" (p. xxviii). Robert Keohane has provided an analysis of how these concepts encourage decisionmakers to rely on "rules of thumb" to guide their decisions in his book *After Hegemony* (Princeton, N.J.: Princeton University Press, 1984). See especially chapter 7, "Bounded Rationality and Redefinitions of Self-Interest."

4. For a useful discussion of the nuclear restraints as an international regime, see Roger K. Smith, "Explaining the Non-Proliferation Regime: Anomalies for Contemporary International Relations Theory," *International Organizations* 41, no. 2 (spring 1987): 253–279. The question posed by the events of 1991–94 in the former Soviet Union was whether a nuclear restraint regime could outlive the specific conditions that gave rise to it.

5. For an excellent and pioneering exploration of this problem, see Kurt M. Campbell, et al., *Soviet Nuclear Fission: Control of the Nuclear Arsenal in a Disintegrating Soviet Union,* Harvard CSIA Studies in International Security, no. 1 (Cambridge, Mass.: Center for Science and International Affairs, Harvard University, November 1991).

6. Francis X. Cline, "Rift Over Military Widens at Meeting of Ex-Soviet Lands," *New York Times,* February 15, 1992, 6; Virginia I. Foran, "Ukrainian Holdout: The Real Problem with the Treaty," *Washington Post,* January 3, 1993, C3. Foran wrote that "Kiev must be made to understand that its intransigence threatens the collective security of the post–Cold War world." See also Sam Nunn, "Will Ukraine Save Itself?" *Washington Post,* January 3, 1994, A19.

7. This description is drawn from a White House fact sheet dated September 27, 1991, published in the *NATO Review,* no. 5 (October 1991): 11.

8. This summary is drawn from a *Novosti* report of President Gorbachev's televised address of October 5, 1991, published in *Survival* 33, no. 6 (November/December 1991): 569–570.

9. *Soviet Nuclear Threat Reduction Act of 1991,* Public Law 102–228, *Congressional Record,* November 27, 1991, S 18798.

10. From the text prepared for delivery as released by the Office of the Assistant Secretary/Spokesman, U.S. Department of State. Baker's reference to "Ukraine's determination to become nuclear-free" presumably refers to the July 16, 1990, declaration of the Ukrainian parliament not to accept, produce, or acquire nuclear weapons, and the October 24, 1991, statement of the parliament on the nonnuclear status of Ukraine. See *RFE/RL Research Report 2,* no. 8, February 19, 1993, 71–73, for a chronology on the control of former Soviet nuclear weapons.

11. However, it was not always smooth sailing for the HEU deal. Commercial considerations were an inevitable part of the picture and led to a certain amount of rancor between the U.S. and Russian entities concerned with the issue. The State Department frequently was called upon to intercede. Dr. James Timbie was the key State Department official in these matters and a key player in nuclear arms control in general.

12. This was generally understood to be an affirmation of Ukraine's intention to denuclearize, but some Ukrainians later suggested that it referred only to those weapons that had to be eliminated under the terms of START I.

13. The Nunn-Lugar umbrella agreement, negotiated with each of the four recipient states, established the basic legal framework for Nunn-Lugar assistance to that state. Subsequent implementing agreements authorized and defined the various programs of assistance.

14. Foreign Broadcast Information Service [hereafter FBIS]-SOV-93-064, April 6, 1993, 21–22. The Russian government must have thought that its Moscow announcement and the U.S.-Russian statement in the Vancouver Declaration were consistent with each other; no doubt the Ukrainians thought so too.

15. At the beginning of these negotiations, 46 SS-24 ICBMs, 130 SS-19s, 21 Bear H bombers, and 13 Blackjack bombers were deployed on Ukraine's territory.

16. Probably the Kravchuk government's perception that the United States had to be an active partner in the nuclear negotiations made it easier for the Russian-Ukrainian nuclear dialogue to proceed with little or no linkage to other issues in the Ukrainian-Russian relationship, including the division of the Black Sea fleet. Some ideas, such as techniques of compensation, did percolate from one negotiation to another, but there was no effort to link the various sets of talks.

4. Bringing Order Out of Chaos

1. John Deutch, Statement for the Record to the Permanent Subcommittee on Investigations of the Senate Committee on Government Affairs, March 20, 1996, 9. Text provided by the subcommittee.

2. Joseph Nye, dean of the Kennedy School at Harvard University, is one of those observers who have made this point. See, for example, his concluding remarks at a conference sponsored by Harvard and Los Alamos on nuclear, biological, and chemical weapons proliferation, held in Washington, D.C., on May 23, 1996.

3. For a particularly cogent discussion of this point, see Peter J. Katzenstein, "Coping with Terrorism: Norms and Internal Security in Germany and Japan," in Judith Goldstein and Robert O. Keohane, eds., *Ideas and Foreign Policy: Beliefs, Institutions, and Political Change* (Ithaca, N.Y., and London: Cornell University Press, 1993). Katzenstein points out that nations respond to terrorist threats in ways that are influenced by the normative context within their societies. Institutionalized norms, he argues, affect national behavior both directly—by setting standards for appropriate behavior—and indirectly—by offering a way of organizing action. Using Germany and Japan as examples of different cultural contexts, Katzenstein observes that "the abstract universalism that typifies Germany's domestic norms has made it easy for German officials to view the German state as part of an international community of states seeking to protect itself against subversive attacks." In contrast, "the social embeddedness of Japanese law and its situational logic have made it more difficult for Japan than for Germany to involve itself actively in furthering the evolution of international legal norms prohibiting terrorism."

4. V. V. Bogdan, executive officer of MINATOM, said in late 1995 that the atomic energy sector had been stabilized better than others and that the backbone of its scientific potential had been retained. He reported that the state order for the weapons directorate had received only 70 percent financing and that other directorates had received even less. Exports from the MINATOM sector, he said, amounted to $1.2 billion in 1994, and the goal for the year 2000 was $3 billion (FBIS-UMA-96-119-S, June 19, 1996). Interview by *Vooruzheniye, Politika, Konversiya*, December 18, 1995.

5. Aleksandr Golts, "Alarm Bell Should Send Signal of Hope from Moscow," *Krasnaya Zvezda* (Moscow), April 19, 1996, 1 (FBIS-SOV-96-077, April 19, 1996).

6. Bogdan, *Vooruzheniye, Politika, Konversiya*. Also see an article by Anatoliy Stepanovich Diakov, of the Moscow Physico-Technical Institute, on the problems of dealing with fifty to one hundred tonnes of weapons-grade uranium that will be released by reductions in nuclear weapons in Russia. *Nezavisimaya Gazeta* (Moscow), April 11, 1996, 1-2 (FBIS-SOV-96-093-S, May 13, 1996).

7. "Federal Counterintelligence Service Worried by Activity of U.S. Researchers in Russia," *Nezavisimaya Gazeta* (Moscow), January 10, 1995, 3 (FBIS-SOV-95-008, January 12, 1995).

8. Presidential Edict No. 71, *Rossiyskaya Gazeta* (Moscow), February 1, 1996, 3 (FBIS-SOV-96-026, February 7, 1996).

9. Telegram from U.S. embassy in Moscow, December 20, 1995, no. 39891.

10. The full text of the White House fact sheet, entitled "Nuclear Materials Security" and issued by the Office of the Press Secretary on October 23, 1995, is as follows:

Following their meeting in Hyde Park, Presidents Clinton and Yeltsin issued a joint statement noting the importance they attach to ensuring the security of nuclear weapons and materials and welcoming the joint report they received from the Gore-Chernomyrdin Commission discussing how the U.S. and Russia can work together to strengthen security for nuclear material. This report follows up on the Presidents' May 10 summit statement on nonproliferation.

Joint cooperative efforts to bolster security and accounting for nuclear material made significant advances in Russia in 1995, including:

- expanding cooperation from a handful of facilities to more than a dozen, enhancing the safety and security of tons of nuclear material;
- creating a new material protection, control and accounting training center at Obninsk;
- improving national-level oversight of nuclear material security, including regulations, licensing and inspections;
- creating nuclear material protection, control, and accounting systems at four facilities—Elektrostal (a nuclear fuel plant), Arzamas-16 (a nuclear weapons laboratory), Kurchatov and Obninsk (nuclear research centers)—to serve as models for such systems at other facilities; and
- accelerating direct cooperation between U.S. and Russian nuclear labs to improve nuclear materials security.

For 1996, the U.S. and Russia have agreed to expand their cooperation as follows:

- expansion of intergovernmental cooperation to five of the largest civilian sites handling weapons-usable material in Russia, located in Dmitrovgrad, Obninsk, Podolsk, Mayak and Elecktrostal;
- expansion of direct lab-to-lab cooperation to additional key facilities including labs at Chelyabinsk-70, Krasnoyarsk-26 and Sverdlovsk-44;
- further development of the Obninsk training facility; and
- additional training, technical assistance and equipment to improve Russia's national material control and accounting system.

These projects will draw on the $30 million in Nunn-Lugar funds and $17 million in lab-to-lab funds currently available. The Administration has requested an additional $70 million in nuclear material security funds from Congress for these projects in FY 1996.

The U.S., using $140 million in Nunn-Lugar funds, has been cooperating with Russia on the design and construction of a safe, secure and ecologically-sound storage facility for fissile material from dismantled nuclear weapons. Another $32 million in Nunn-Lugar funds is being spent to enhance security in the transportation and storage of the increasing numbers of nuclear weapons destined for dismantlement.

11. See, for example, the issue of land mines, as described by Jessica Tuchman Mathews, "The New, Private Order," *Washington Post,* January 21, 1997, A11.

12. Richard G. Lugar, "Weapons of Mass Destruction and Cooperative Threat Reduction" (remarks before the Harvard and Los Alamos–sponsored conference on nuclear, biological, and chemical weapons proliferation, May 23, 1996).

13. Richard G. Lugar, speech to United We Stand, Dallas, Texas, August 12, 1995. A task force of the Council on Foreign Relations took the same view in 1996.

14. *Izvestiya,* April 11, 1996, 1, 3.

15. Hedley Bull observed that resort to violence on an international scale by groups other than the state could be a sign of the transformation of the states system into a secular reincarnation of the medieval order. He thought that these new forms of war could not be allowed to lie permanently beyond the compass of the rules of the states system. (Bull, *The Anarchical Society,* 258, 193.)

5. Principles, Leaders, and the Use of Force

1. See Josef Joffe, "America's in the Balcony as Europe Takes Center Stage," *New York Times,* December 22, 1991, IV:5.

2. For a provocative discussion on this subject, see Edward N. Luttwak, "Where Are the Great Powers?" *Foreign Affairs* 73, no. 4 (July/August 1994): 23–28.

3. Warren Zimmermann, "The Last Ambassador," *Foreign Affairs* 74, no. 2 (March/April 1995): 16.

4. The Maastricht Treaty on European Union was completed on December 11, 1991, signed on February 7, 1992, and entered into force on November 1, 1993. The European Community thereafter became the European Union.

5. James E. Goodby, "Peacekeeping in the New Europe," *Washington Quarterly* 15, no. 2 (spring 1992): 156. Research for this article shaped my thinking about Yugoslavia. I am grateful for the opportunity given to me by the *Washington Quarterly.*

6. John Zametica, *The Yugoslav Conflict,* Adelphi Paper no. 270 (London: International Institute for Strategic Studies, 1992), 62.

7. William Drozdiak, "Europeans' Balkan Stance Attests to Rising German Influence," *Washington Post,* December 18, 1991, A15.

8. William Drozdiak, "EC Envoys Agree on Recognition of Croatia, Slovenia Next Month," *Washington Post,* December 17, 1991, A15.

9. Chuck Sudetic, "Bosnia Fears It's Next in Yugoslavia's Civil Strife," *New York Times,* December 28, 1991, A6.

10. David Gompert, "How to Defeat Serbia," *Foreign Affairs* 73, no. 4 (July/August 1994).

11. Chuck Sudetic, "Vance Appeals to Serbs to Halt Bosnia Fighting," *New York Times,* April 16, 1992, A1.

12. Blaine Harden, "Serbs, Croats Agree to Carve up Bosnia," *Washington Post*, May 8, 1992, A17.

13. Susan L. Woodward, *Balkan Tragedy* (Washington, D.C.: Brookings Institution, 1995), 311.

14. José Cutileiro, letter to author, May 20, 1996.

15. Chuck Sudetic, "Yugoslav Groups Reach an Accord," *New York Times*, March 19, 1992, A9.

16. Warren Zimmermann, conversation with author, February 21, 1996; and Cutileiro, letter to author. Ambassador Cutileiro recalls that a U.S. view in March 1992 was that four constituent units would be preferable to the three he had worked out.

17. International Conference on the Former Yugoslavia (ICFY), "Report of the Co-Chairmen on Progress in Developing a Constitution for Bosnia and Herzegovina," October 25, 1992, 1, paragraphs 2–3, submitted to the UN secretary-general by them on October 26, 1992. Sudetic, "Yugoslav Groups Reach an Accord," A9. José Cutileiro, "Horrors Built on Delusion," *International Herald Tribune*, August 15–16, 1992, 4.

18. Department of State, "U.S. Meeting with Bosnian Foreign Minister," *Dispatch* 3, no. 34 (August 24, 1992): 671.

19. Some Americans directly involved in the diplomacy of this time believe that a U.S. military response to the shelling of Dubrovnik would have had a serious effect on Serbian plans.

20. ICFY, "Report of the Co-Chairmen on Progress in Developing a Constitution for Bosnia and Herzegovina," 1, paragraphs 2–3.

21. Ibid.

22. Ibid., 6.

23. ICFY, "Report of the Secretary-General on the Activities of the ICFY," S/25221, February 2, 1993, 3.

24. ICFY, "Report of the Secretary-General on the Activities of the ICFY," S/25479, March 26, 1993.

25. David Binder, "Talks in Geneva on Bosnia Hit an Impasse," *New York Times*, January 31, 1993, A1.

26. Paul Lewis, "Bosnian Peace Talks Yield No Progress," *New York Times*, February 8, 1993, A10.

27. John M. Goshko, "U.S. Takes More Active Balkans Role," *Washington Post*, February 11, 1993, A1.

28. ICFY, "Report of the Secretary-General on the Activities of the ICFY," S/25479, March 26, 1993.

29. Ibid., annex V, "Statement of Izetbegovic of March 25, 1993."

30. ICFY, "Report of the Secretary-General on the Activities of the ICFY," S/25709, May 3, 1993, annex V. William Drozdiak, "Big Powers Give Final Endorsement to Partition Plan for Bosnia," *Washington Post,* July 6, 1994, A21.

31. David B. Ottaway, "Mediator Backs Partition for Bosnia," *Washington Post,* June 18, 1993, A1.

32. A. M. Rosenthal, "Needed: U.S. Goal in Bosnia," *New York Times,* February 2, 1993, A19.

33. Drozdiak, "Big Powers Give Final Endorsement," A21. David B. Ottaway, "Winds of War Blow in Balkans Despite Latest, American-Backed Plan," *Washington Post,* June 24, 1994, A29. Alan Riding, "Bosnian Serbs Said to Reject Mediator's Partition Plan," *New York Times,* July 21, 1994, A3.

34. See NATO Press Release 15.94, February 9, 1994.

35. Blaine Harden, "Yugoslav Republics Fear Crackdown," *Washington Post,* August 20, 1991, A8.

36. Paul Lewis, "Russia a Barrier to NATO Air Strike," *New York Times,* February 9, 1994, A12. See also Roger Cohen, "Bosnia Talks Show No Gain as Serbs Assail Deadline," *New York Times,* February 11, 1994, A6.

37. John Kifner, "Serbs Withdraw in a Russian Plan to Avert Bombing," *New York Times,* February 18, 1994, A1.

38. Seth Faison, "European Envoy to Ask Balkan Leaders to Talks," *New York Times,* July 10, 1992, A6.

39. Elaine Sciolino, "U.S. Faces Delicate Task in Intervening in Negotiations on Bosnia," *New York Times,* February 12, 1993, A10.

40. David B. Ottaway, "U.S. Bosnia Plan Relies on Russia's Help in Croatia," *Washington Post,* March 20, 1994, A32.

41. *RFE/RL Daily Report,* no. 63, March 31, 1994.

42. To put it in other terms, the situation had become metastable: the time had come when a *relatively* small input could create *relatively* large results. See Irving Lachow, "The Metastable Peace: A Catastrophe Theory Model of U.S.-Russian Relations," in J. E. Goodby and B. Morel, eds., *The Limited Partnership: Building a Russian-U.S. Security Community* (Oxford: Oxford University Press, 1993).

43. Michael Dobbs, "Holbrooke's Parting Shot—For Now," *Washington Post,* March 3, 1996, C1.

44. In terms of William Zartman's theory of ripeness in negotiations, a mutually hurting stalement had been achieved in 1995 and a series of events had occurred that presented a crisis bounded by a deadline. See I. William

Zartman, *Ripe for Resolution* (Oxford and New York: Oxford University Press, 1985).

45. See Colin L. Powell, "U.S. Forces: Challenges Ahead," *Foreign Affairs* 71, no. 5 (winter 1992–93): 36–41; and Richard Cohen, "Better Listen to Colin Powell," *Washington Post*, January 5, 1993, A15.

46. See the statement by an administration official quoted in John M. Goshko, "Yugoslavia Is Puzzling Problem for U.S., Allies," *Washington Post*, September 22, 1991, A31.

47. Max Kampelman, "Secession and Self-Determination," *Washington Quarterly* 16, no. 3 (summer 1993): 5.

48. See also William Drozdiak, "Lack of an Armed Option Limits EC's Yugoslav Peace Initiative," *Washington Post*, September 5, 1991, A23.

6. Transforming Nuclear Deterrence

1. This chapter is an elaboration of the arguments I made in my first panel discussion as Payne lecturer at Stanford in October 1996 and in a second panel discussion at Stanford in November 1996, chaired by former Secretary of State George Shultz. While at Stanford I coauthored (with Hal Feiveson of Princeton University) a paper entitled *Ending the Threat of Nuclear Attack*, published by Stanford's Center for International Security and Arms Control. Many of the points made in that paper also are included in this chapter.

2. Ambassador Oleg Grinevsky, former Soviet CDE and CFE negotiator and later Russian ambassador to Sweden, is the source of both these statements.

3. For an excellent exposition of this doctrine, see Sims, *Icarus Restrained*.

4. Thomas C. Schelling and Morton H. Halperin, with the assistance of Donald G. Brennan, *Strategy and Arms Control* (New York: Twentieth Century Fund, 1961), 2.

5. One of the best accounts is Strobe Talbott, *Deadly Gambits* (New York: Alfred A. Knopf, 1984).

6. Michael R. Gordon, "Russia Atom Aides Buy I.B.M. Supercomputer Despite U.S. Curbs," *New York Times*, February 25, 1997, A11.

7. *Nezavisimaya Gazeta*, June 14, 1996, 7–8.

8. "Joint Statement on Parameters on Future Relations in Nuclear Forces," White House press release, Helsinki, March 21, 1997. This document is reproduced in H. Binnendijk and J. E. Goodby, eds., *Transforming Nuclear Deterrence* (Washington, D.C.: National Defense University Press, July 1997).

9. Ibid.

7. Devising an Interim Security Order in Europe

1. George F. Kennan, *Memoirs, 1925–1950* (Boston: Little, Brown, 1967), 222.

2. The author is indebted to Alexander George for his observations concerning the various forms spheres of interest can take (letter to the author, September 25, 1996).

3. Hans J. Morgenthau, *Politics among Nations* (New York: Alfred A. Knopf, 1953), 142.

4. Morgenthau, *Politics among Nations*, 332; Josef Joffe, "Collective Security and the Future of Europe," *Survival* (spring 1992): 37.

5. E. H. Carr, *The Twenty Years' Crisis, 1919–1939* (New York: Harper and Row, 1964), 10.

6. Henry A. Kissinger, "NATO: Russia's De Facto Veto," *Washington Post*, July 12, 1997, A20.

7. Madeleine K. Albright, "Enlarging NATO," *Economist*, February 15–21, 1997, 21–23. Testifying before the Senate Appropriations Committee on October 21, 1997, Secretary Albright said: "First, a larger NATO will make us safer by expanding the area in Europe where wars simply do not happen . . . second . . . it will make NATO stronger and more cohesive . . . third . . . the very promise [of a larger NATO] gives the nations of central and eastern Europe an incentive to solve their own problems." Albright's statement was issued by the Office of the Spokesman, Department of State.

8. Achieving a Stable Peace in Europe

1. This idea has been explored at length by John Mueller in his book *Retreat from Doomsday: The Obsolescence of Major War* (New York: Basic Books, 1989). His thesis is that war is an idea grafted onto human existence, and like other discredited ideas, such as dueling or slavery, it can be—and is—disappearing as a thinkable option. Professor Mueller's thesis is not the basis for the discussion in this book, which is focused more on the question of how Russia and the West might consciously design a transition to a stable peace. After all, Mueller himself says that "if the thesis propounded here about the obsolescence of war is correct, the Soviets have little to worry about. That they might have some difficulty swallowing this idea is, however, understandable" (p. 262).

2. In the summer of 1991, *The Washington Quarterly* published an article that I had written on the organizing principles of U.S. foreign policy to replace containment in Europe and provide a long-term purpose for American diplomacy. The article was entitled "Commonwealth and Concert"—metaphors for strategic concepts that should inform American policies toward the old

democracies of Europe and toward Europe as a whole. This section adapts the arguments I made in that article to current conditions.

3. U.S. foreign policy analysts and scholars are as divided as any other sector of the U.S. public on the questions of where post–Cold War Europe is headed, where it should go, and what the United States can do about it. Much of the confusion is traceable to fundamentally different views of the international system. In *The Anarchical Society* (2d ed., p. 23), Hedley Bull summed up the main schools of thought as follows:

> Throughout the history of the modern states system there have been three competing traditions of thought: the Hobbesian or realist tradition, which views international politics as a state of war; the Kantian or universalist tradition, which sees at work in international politics a potential community of mankind; and the Grotian or internationalist tradition, which views international politics as taking place within an international society.

4. In the opinion of a *Washington Post* commentator (Stephen S. Rosenfeld, "To Protect What Is Ours," *Washington Post*, December 27, 1996, A23), "first we should be talking about Primo Levi's civilization of Europe, the ideas and institutions that, however imperfectly applied define what needs most to be defined and favored in the West. A line already is drawn in Europe—a line of culture and tradition, the abiding realities. On one side is Europe, and on the other side is Russia." See also Henry Kissinger, "NATO: Make It Stronger, Make It Larger," *Washington Post*, January 14, 1997, A15. Kissinger wrote that "Russia is in, but not of Europe; it borders Asia, Central Asia, and the Middle East, and it pursues policies along these borders that are difficult to reconcile with NATO objectives."

5. This argument is one I made in a lecture at the National War College, Washington, D.C., on April 15, 1990. The lecture, expanded and revised, was published under the title "The Diplomacy of Europe Whole and Free," in Samuel F. Wells Jr., ed., *The Helsinki Process and the Future of Europe* (Washington, D.C.: Woodrow Wilson International Center for Scholars Press, 1990).

6. Anton de Porte, *Europe between the Superpowers: The Enduring Balance*, 2d ed. (New Haven: Yale University Press, 1963).

7. In *Force and Statecraft* (p. 30), Craig and George identify the rules of the Concert as follows: "no single state should be allowed to increase its possessions except with the consent of others; . . . a high degree of restraint on the part of single powers; . . . a willingness to accept the validity of existing treaties; . . . a willingness when single powers seemed on the point of seeking unilateral aggrandizement . . . to participate in concerted action to restrain them."

8. Henry Kissinger, "No Illusions about the USSR," *Washington Post*, January 22, 1991, A13.

9. Norman Angell, *The Great Illusion: A Study of the Relation of Military Power in Nations to Their Economic and Social Advantage*, 3d ed. (London: William Heinemann, 1912), 31.

10. C. Fred Bergsten, "The Dollar and the Euro," *Foreign Affairs* 76, no. 4 (July/August 1997): 83–95.

11. This idea is seen as "a subtle threat to the global trading system" by a leading expert in the field of trade, C. Fred Bergsten. He believes that the implication of a Transatlantic Free Trade Area is that free trade is acceptable so long as it is limited to countries of roughly equal income levels. See C. Fred Bergsten, "Globalizing Free Trade," *Foreign Affairs* 75, no. 3 (May/June 1996): 107–108. I do not accept that characterization. On those grounds, NAFTA could be criticized because it does not include the low-income Caribbean nations. Free trade areas and an effort to globalize free trade are not incompatible but instead are mutually reinforcing.

12. A creative proposal for an Atlantic Union is that of Charles A. Kupchan. He describes it in "Reviving the West," *Foreign Affairs* 75, no. 3 (May/June 1996): 92–104. Although I believe that the Maastricht accord will be reinterpreted so that it will not be achieved exactly as envisaged, I do not believe that the European Union should be sidetracked, or that it could be. Nor do I believe that NATO's Article V guarantee should be dropped. These two suggestions, in my view, would kill the chances that an Atlantic Union could be negotiated any time soon.

13. On the need for both desirability and feasibility of a long-range goal in order to gain domestic support, see Alexander L. George, "Domestic Constraints on Regime Change in U.S. Foreign Policy: The Need for Policy Legitimacy," in Ole Holsti, Randolph Siverson, and A. George, eds., *Change in the International System* (Boulder, Colo.: Westview Press, 1980), 233–262.

14. A brief and trenchant analysis of why the United States should invest in international order in general has been made by Joseph Nye. He cited transnational interdependence, geopolitical interests, and order as a collective good. Joseph Nye, "What New World Order?" *Foreign Affairs* 71, no. 2 (spring 1992): 83–96.

15. For an excellent analysis of this problem, see Edward D. Mansfield and Jack Snyder, "Democratization and War," *Foreign Affairs* 74, no. 3 (May/June 1995): 79–97.

16. Thomas S. Foley, "A Second American Century?" (keynote address to the Woodrow Wilson International Center for Scholars' conference "End of the American Century?" June 3–4, 1996; published as a working paper by the Wilson Center, Washington, D.C., in September 1996).

17. Steven Kull and I. M. Destler (principal investigators), "Misreading the American Public on International Engagement" (Center for International and

Security Studies and Its Program on International Policy Attitudes, University of Maryland, College Park, Md., October 18, 1996), 11–12.

18. Tyler Marshall, "Isolationist Sentiment in U.S. Tapering Off, Poll Says," *Los Angeles Times*, October 10, 1997, A5. The poll was conducted by the Pew Research Center for the People and the Press and sampled five hundred opinion leaders, as well as the general public.

19. George F. Kennan, "America and the Russian Future," *Foreign Affairs* 69, no. 2 (spring 1990): 157–166. First published in *Foreign Affairs* in April 1951.

20. Walter Lippmann, "The Cold War," *Foreign Affairs* 65, no. 4 (spring 1987): 869. This article is an excerpt from a series of articles that Lippmann wrote for the *New York Herald Tribune* in 1947. Lippmann proposed as an alternative to containment a negotiation directed at securing the withdrawal of Soviet troops from Eastern Europe.

21. Ronald Steel, "The Internationalist Temptation" (an essay presented at the Woodrow Wilson International Center for Scholars' conference "End of the American Century?" June 3–4, 1996; published as a working paper by the Wilson Center, Division of International Studies, Washington, D.C.).

22. Chalmers Johnson and E. B. Keehn, "The Pentagon's Ossified Strategy," *Foreign Affairs* 74, no. 4 (July/August 1995): 114.

23. Polling data are quoted in Center for International and Security Studies, *The Foreign Policy Gap* (College Park, Md.: Center for International and Security Studies, University of Maryland, October 30–31, 1997); the polls were taken at various times between January 1994 and September 1996. The Stanford report was circulated by the office of William Perry, Stanford University. The "New Atlantic Initiative" statement, which was signed by former secretaries of state, was printed in the AEI newsletter for October 1997. The Center for Strategic and International Studies report was *Foreign Policy into the Twenty-First Century: The U.S. Leadership Challenge* (Washington, D.C.: CSIS, September 1996). The two quotations from American scholars are, first, Bruce Russet of Yale University, "The Basis for Peace in the Twenty-First Century" (paper prepared for dedication of the George Bush School of Government and Public Service, Texas A & M University, September 10, 1997); and second, Charles A. Kupchan of Georgetown University, "Doing the NATO Shuffle," *Washington Post*, August 31, 1997, C1.

24. Albright, "Enlarging NATO."

25. Strobe Talbott, "Why NATO Should Grow," *New York Review of Books*, August 10, 1995, 6.

Index

ABM systems. *See* Antiballistic missile systems

Acheson, Dean, report to Kennedy by, 31

Adams, John Quincy, 193

Administrative Behavior (Simon), 214–215n3

After Hegemony (Keohane), 215n3

Aggression, problem of rewarding, 132

encouraging by renouncing use of force, 138

Ahtisaari, Martti, in ICFY, 122

Akhromeyev, Marshal, 143–144

Albania
conflict with Serbia, 178
NATO membership and, 161

Albright, Madeleine
on inclusion of Russia, 200
on NATO, 174–175, 223n7

Alliance, in collective security vs. collective defense model, 168, 169

The Anarchical Society (Bull), 224n3

Angell, Norman, 187

Antiballistic missile (ABM) systems
demarcation agreement on (August 1997), 155
preserving ABM treaty, 152

Arab-Israeli relationship, as "precarious peace," ix

Arms control, as explicit rules, 43

Arms reduction. *See* Disarmament; Nuclear disarmament

Arms supplying, Eisenhower's views on, 18–19

Arzamas-16, nuclear security at, 218n10

Asia, U.S. participation in Europe vs., 203, 204

Aspin, Les, proposal to Ukraine by, 80

Atlantic Union, proposals for, 189, 225n12

"Atomic archipelago," 93

Atomic Energy Commission (AEC), transfer of weapons to Defense Dept. from, 24

Aum Shinrikyo sect, nerve gas attack by, 8, 94

Austrian State Treaty of 1955, German unification and, 42

Authorization for use of nuclear weapons
Eisenhower and, 19–24
Kennedy and, 29, 31
U.S.-Soviet rules and, 39–40
USSR disintegration and, 70–74

Autonomy, Yugoslav conflict lessons, 137

Avoidance of war, as U.S.-Soviet rule, 39, 44, 45

Baker, James
on nuclear restraint challenge, 69, 72, 215n10
preventive diplomacy by, 70, 147
strategic warhead negotiations by, 74

Balance-of-power policies
collective security model vs., 167, 169–170, 179

Balance-of-power policies *(cont.)*
  in nineteenth century, 184
  spheres-of-interest model vs., 10,
    210*n*8
  U.S.-Russian relationship and, 173
Balkan states, NATO enlargement
    and, 161, 162. *See also specific
    states*
Ballistic missiles, disarmament and,
    149, 150, 151
Baltic states
  See also specific states
  Euroatlantic community and, 164
  NATO enlargement and, 161,
    165, 176–177
Bartholomew, Reginald
  Bosnia conflict role, 127–128
  preventive diplomacy by, 70
Baturin, Yuri, on nuclear weapons, 149
Bay of Pigs, Vienna summit and,
    31–32
Behavioral rules. *See* Rules of behavior
Belarus
  Lisbon Protocol and, 74–75, 78,
    147
  NATO enlargement and, 162
  nuclear disarmament aid to, 71–72
  nuclear weapons control issues,
    66, 72
  START I treaty and, 73, 89
  U.S. uranium purchase and, 73, 75
Belgium, Ukrainian disarmament aid
    by, 89
"Belligerent reprisal," 108
Bergsten, C. Fred
  on currency change, 188
  on free trade, 225*n*11
Beria, German unification proposed
    by, 42
Berlin
  1948 blockade of, 15, 39
  Khrushchev's threat to, 28, 32, 39
  Quadripartite Agreement on, 60

U.S.-Soviet rules and, 38–39, 45
Berlin Wall, 39
Bihac region, 1995 fighting in, 128,
    129
Biological weapons
  international norms and, 108
  substate entity problems, 95
  terrorism and, 94, 96–97
  U.S.-Russian cooperation and, 96
  U.S.-U.K.-Russian agreement on,
    96
Bipolar order
  challenges to, 37, 46–64
  Helsinki Final Act and, 46–47
  redefinition of after Cold War, 66,
    169–170
  renewal of conflict after, 184
  rules of behavior in, 35, 37–43, 44
Black Sea fleet, Russian-Ukrainian
    conflict over, 77, 78, 80, 216*n*16
Blair, Bruce G., 207*n*18
Boban, Mate, 118–119
Bohlen, Charles, on spheres-of-
    interest policy, 41
Bombers, in Ukraine, 81, 83, 216*n*15
Border inviolability, in Helsinki Final
    Act, 171
Bosnia-Herzegovina
  See also Yugoslavia, former
  British-French force in, 129, 131
  cantonization plans for, 120–122,
    126
  confederation plan and, 115
  "Contact Group" plan for, 126,
    130, 132
  Dayton agreement on, 131–133
  decentralization plan for, 123–126
  diplomatic approaches to
    (1991–95), 119–126
  "ethnic cleansing" in, 119, 122
  ethnic pluralism in, 117, 118, 133
  historical context and, 113–114,
    116–119

Bosnia-Herzegovina *(cont.)*
    international leadership failure in,
        112–114
    NATO role in, 175
    1990 election results in, 117
    OSCE intervention in, 172
    partition plan for, 119–120
    referendum call for, 118
    Russia and, 126–128, 199
    UN peacekeepers in, 116–117,
        118, 128, 129, 130, 131
"Bounded rationality," 91, 92, 214–
        215n3
Brandt, Willy
    Ostpolitik policy, 37, 42, 47, 60
    and seeds of change, 47
Brezhnev, Leonid
    CSCE and, 46, 53
    1972 summit with Nixon, 61
    Nixon's "era of negotiations" and,
        47, 49
    Ostpolitik and, 47
    SALT I agreement and, 68
    on U.S. troops in Europe, 40–41,
        210n6
Brezhnev doctrine, 46, 49, 53, 54
Brioni Declaration (July 7, 1991), 115
Britain. *See* United Kingdom
Budapest, START I ratification in,
        67, 89, 147
Budapest Appeal (March 1969), 47
Budapest Warsaw Pact meeting
        (June 1969), 53–54
Budget concerns. *See* Military budget
Bulgaria, NATO enlargement and,
        161, 162
Bull, Hedley, on Grotian society,
        224n3
Bundy, McGeorge
    on authorization to use nuclear
        weapons, 31
    on Eisenhower legacy, 29
    on "existential deterrence," 34

Bureau of European Affairs, on
        CSCE, 59, 61–62
Bush, George
    newly independent states and,
        69–70, 73, 75, 78, 141
    nuclear disarmament and, 68, 71,
        74, 76, 146–147
    Nunn-Lugar program and, 71–72,
        76, 78, 100
    on peace in Europe, 111
    post–Cold War order and, 66, 67
    preventive diplomacy by, 70–71
    START I treaty and, 68, 75, 146
    START II treaty and, 68, 146–147

Canada, Ukrainian disarmament aid
        by, 89
"Cantonization," as alternative for
        Bosnia, 120–122
Carr, E. H., on collective security,
        169, 223n5
Carrington, Lord Peter
    on Russian role, 127
    Yugoslav peace attempts, 116–117
Carter, Jimmy, Bosnian truce role,
        128
Central Intelligence Agency (CIA)
    on fissile materials, 93
    nuclear security role, 107
Chain-of-custody techniques, 157
Chechnya, Russian disarmament
        and, 148
Chelyabinsk-70, nuclear security at,
        220n10
Chemical weapons
    international norms and, 96, 108
    substate entity problems, 95
    terrorism and, 94, 96–97
    U.S.-Russian cooperation and, 96
    U.S.-U.K.-Russian agreement
        on, 96
Cheney, Richard, strategic warhead
        negotiations by, 74

Chernomyrdin, Viktor
  Gore-Chernomyrdin Commission, 102, 103
  trilateral accord and, 86
China
  disarmament negotiations and, 149, 155–157
  U.S.-Russian relationship and, 155
  U.S.-Soviet rules and, 39
Chrétien, Jean, Transatlantic Free Trade Area proposed by, 188
Christopher, Warren
  Bosnia conflict role, 124, 132
  visit to Kiev by, 83–84
Churchill, Winston, on spheres of interest, 41
Churkin, Vitali, Bosnian conflict role, 127, 128
CIA. See Central Intelligence Agency
CIS. See Commonwealth of Independent States
Civil war, aggressive acts vs., 113–114
Classified information, new international norms and, 99
Clinton, Bill
  Bosnia conflict and, 124, 125–126, 129, 131, 132, 135
  on cooperation for nuclear deterrence, 8
  on Euroatlantic community, 164
  "grand design" of, xi–xii, 3–4, 10–11, 181, 182, 198, 200, 204
  Helsinki meeting with Yeltsin (March 1997), 3–4, 9, 148, 152–153, 155, 164, 175
  Hyde Park summit with Yeltsin (October 1995), 103, 105, 217–218n10
  on international organizations, 171–172
  meeting with Kravchuk, 85, 87
  Moscow summit with Yeltsin (January 1994), 87–88
  Moscow summit with Yeltsin (May 1995), 102, 164
  NATO enlargement and, 160, 161, 162, 163, 174
  newly independent states and, 69–70, 141
  nuclear disarmament and, 148, 175
  on nuclear security, 101
  Nunn-Lugar program and, 71–72
  OSCE and, 170
  on peace in Europe, 111
  post–Cold War order and, 67
  START I treaty and, 79, 147
  START II treaty and, 147–148
  START III treaty and, 148
  on territorial politics, 164, 166
  Ukranian crisis and, 67, 76, 78–79, 80, 85, 89
  U.S.-Russian-Ukrainian trilateral accord, 76, 87–88
  Vance-Owen Bosnia plan and, 124, 125–126
  Vancouver summit with Yeltsin (April 1993), 79, 101, 218n14
"Coalitions of the willing," 176, 202
"Cold Peace," 176
Cold War
  conditional peace in, x
  détente and, xi, 45
  Gorbachev and ending of, 144, 147
  "grand design" in, 3
  Helsinki Final Act and, 63
  nationalism revived after, 137
  nuclear deterrence policies, 33–34
  nuclear restraint after, 7, 65–91
  "stable peace" goals and, 4–5
  U.S.-Soviet cooperation in, 43–45
  U.S.-Soviet rules in, 35, 38–43, 45
Collective security
  balance-of-power policies vs., 167, 169–170
  Baltic states issues, 176–177
  conditional peace and, 173–177

Collective security *(cont.)*
  in conditional vs. stable peace, 178
  "contact group" and, 170
  defined, 10, 199
  democracy as aid to, 170, 171
  economic sanctions and, 168
  European Union and, 170,
    189–190
  international organizations and,
    171–173
  long-term strategy for, 189–190
  need for, 10
  norms enforcement required for,
    159–160
  OSCE and, 170
  as policy guide, 166–167
  premises of, 168–171
  spheres of interest and, x–xi, 160,
    165–166, 179, 199-200
  Ukraine issues, 176–177
  U.S.-Russian relationship and, 173
Combined Joint Task Force, Russian
    participation in, 191
"Commonwealth and Concert"
    (Goodby), 223*n*2
Commonwealth of Independent
    States (CIS)
  creation of, 72
  nuclear weapons control and, 70,
    72–73
  Russian intervention and, 173
  START I treaty and, 72, 73
Communications revolution, Soviet
    breakdown and, 63
Compellance, in stable peace, x
Conant, James B., 206*n*1
Concepts, importance of, 38
Concert of Europe, current situation
    vs., 184, 186, 224*n*7
Conditional peace
  collective security and, 173–177,
    178
  as current status, 183

defined, x, 4, 205–206*n*3
for European Union, x–xi
moving to stable peace from,
    150–157, 173, 177, 179, 204
rules enforcement and, 111
spheres of interest and, 165–166,
    173–177, 178
Conference on Disarmament in
    Europe (1986), 143–144
Conference on Security and Cooper-
    ation in Europe (CSCE), 46,
    48–63
  See also Helsinki Final Act
  criteria for acceptability of, 50–51
  final preparations, 60–63
  human rights issues, 46–47, 49, 53,
    54–55. *See also* "Freer movement"
  Moscow summit and, 61
  NSSM 138 on, 58–59
  security-related issues, 60, 63
  Yugoslav failure and, 112, 136
Conflict resolution, OSCE role in,
    172
Congress of People's Deputies
  START I treaty and, 70
  Ukrainian crisis and, 77, 84
  Yeltsin's dissolution of, 84
Constitution, for Euroatlantic com-
    munity, xiii, 182
"Contact Group" Bosnia plan, 126,
    130, 132
  collective security and, 170
Containment, 15
  in Eisenhower strategy, 17
  seen as impractical, 195
  success of strategy of, 181, 204
Conventional forces
  CSCE preparations and, 60–61
  firebreak doctrine, 40, 44
  Kennedy's buildup of, 32
  NATO enlargement and, 175
  nuclear weapons use debate and,
    20, 21, 30–31, 32

Cost issues. *See* Military budget
Craig, Gordon
  on bipolar order, 210n1, 210n8
  on Concert of Europe, 224n7
Crimea
  Massandra accords, 82–83, 86
  Russian-Ukrainian conflict and, 80
Criminal activities, nuclear threat
  and, 69, 94
"Critical date"
  Eisenhower and, 24–26
  in Truman policy, 15–16
Croatia
  See also Yugoslavia, former
  confederation plan rejected by,
    115
  declaration of independence by,
    116
  diplomatic approaches to Bosnia
    and (1991-95), 119–126
  "ethnic cleansing" strategy of, 119,
    122
  historical context, 114–119
  normalization attempts in, 128
CSCE. *See* Conference on Security
  and Cooperation in Europe
Cuba, U.S.-Soviet rules and, 39, 45
Cuban missile crisis
  policy impact of, 29
  U.S.-Soviet rules and, 41, 44
Cultural exchanges, CSCE and, 49,
  53–54, 57
Currency change, effects of, 188, 190
Cutileiro, José, Bosnian cantonization
  plan by, 120–122, 132, 133,
  135, 220n16
Czechoslovakia
  1948 coup in, 15
  1968 invasion impact, 47, 52
  bipolar order challenged in, 37
  UN Charter and, 38
Czech Republic, NATO enlargement
  and, 161, 165

Davis, Lynn
  in Kiev negotiations, 84
  trilateral accord role, 86
Dayton agreement, 131–133
Decisionmaking, rules as aid to, 90–91
Defense Department. *See* Department of Defense
Defense policies, denationalization
  of, 175–176
Defensive use of nuclear weapons,
  authorization for, 23–24,
  207n18
De Gaulle, Charles, CSCE and, 48
Demarcation accord, going beyond,
  155
Democracy
  collective security enhanced by,
    170, 171
  as Euroatlantic community goal,
    11, 181, 183–184, 194
  as policy goal, 196, 197
  stable peace and, 178, 183–184
Denationalization of defense policies,
  175–176
Denmark, Ukrainian disarmament
  aid by, 89
Department of Defense
  Eisenhower's concerns about,
    27–28
  nuclear disarmament role, 71–72
  transfer of weapons from AEC to,
    24
"Design exercise," peace model as, xi
Détente
  bipolar order and, 45
  CSCE preparations and, 48, 58,
    59
  long-range policy planning and, xi
Deterrence
  See also Nuclear deterrence
  in conditional peace, x
  "general," ix, x
  "immediate," ix, x

Deterrence *(cont.)*
    in precarious peace, ix
    stable peace and, x, 151, 199
Deutch, John, 216*n*1
Developing world, intervention in,
        Eisenhower's views on, 18–19
Diplomacy
    See also Order-building diplomacy
    Gorbachev/Shevardnadze suc-
        cesses, 142–143
    importance of objectives in, 134
    importance of shared values in,
        38, 63–64, 214*n*50
    international aid for disarmament,
        88–89
    involving other nuclear powers in,
        155–157
    in long-range strategy, 195
    for nuclear security, 101–103
    in nuclear succession crisis, 67,
        70–71
    preventive, 70–71
    rewarding aggression through, 132
    rule-building, 97
    rules as aid to, 90–91
    rules enforcement and, 111–112
    top-down approach, 104, 109
    Yugoslav conflict approaches,
        119–126, 127–128, 129, 130,
        132–133
    Yugoslav conflict failure, 111–114,
        117–119
    Yugoslav conflict lessons, 133–138,
        168
    Zartman's ripeness theory, 221*n*44
Diplomatic mission access, in
        Helsinki Final Act, 55
Disarmament
    See also Nuclear disarmament
    CSCE preparations and, 60
    current status of, 148–149
Dmitrovgrad, nuclear security at,
        103, 218*n*10

Dobrynin, Anatoli, CSCE and, 52
Domenici, Senator. *See* Nunn-Lugar-
        Domenici legislation
Dubrovnik, response to attack on,
        122, 220*n*19
Dulles, John Foster
    "critical date" views, 25
    on "massive retaliation," 18
    nuclear weapons authorization
        debate and, 20, 21, 22, 23
    Radford and, 26

Eagleburger, Lawrence, 121, 212*n*25
"Early deactivation," in Ukrainian
        proposal, 81
Early warning systems, reducing
        reliance on, 154
Eastern Europe
    challenges to bipolar order in, 37,
        63–64
    Cold War human rights issues, 7
    CSCE preparations and, 50, 52,
        53, 54
    economic development recom-
        mendations, 192
    Euroatlantic community and, 164
    European Union membership
        for, 192
    Gorbachev and, 143
    Helsinki Final Act and, 46–47, 171
    NATO enlargement and,
        160–166
    Ostpolitik and, 47
    in Partnership for Peace, 161
    U.S.-Soviet rules and, 39,
        41–42, 45
Eastern Treaties, CSCE preparations
        and, 60
East Germany. *See* German Demo-
        cratic Republic
EC. *See* European Community
Economic aid, Eisenhower's views
        on, 18–19

Economic interdependence
  currency change and, 188, 190
  proposals for strengthening,
    192–193, 204
  prospects for stable peace and, 186
Economic sanctions, in collective
    security model, 168
Economic strength, proposals for
    bolstering, 188
Eisenhower, Dwight
  "critical date" and, 24–26
  firebreak doctrine and, 40
  historical context and, 16
  Khrushchev and, 32
  leadership of, 43
  legacy of, 28–29
  nuclear age policies, 13–14, 16–29
  on nuclear deterrence, 16, 17, 33
  nuclear weapons authorization
    and, 19–24, 28–29, 208–
    209n34
  Project Solarium and, 16–17
  in Suez crisis, x
  U.S.-Soviet relations and, 6, 43
Elections, Dayton agreement and,
    132, 133
Elektrostal
  nuclear security at, 103, 218n10
  test project at, 101
Ellsworth, Robert, CSCE and, 52,
    56, 57, 212n25, 212n29
Enforcement
  See also Intervention
  ambivalence and, 135
  collective security model and, 167,
    168
  need for, 8–9, 111–112, 159–160
  objectives required for, 134
  opposition to U.S. participation
    in, 196
  spheres of interest and, 10
  Yugoslav conflict lessons, 138,
    139–140, 159–160, 199

"Era of negotiations"
  bipolar order and, 37, 47, 48
  Brezhnev and, 47, 49
  U.S. Mission to NATO and,
    50–51
Estonia, NATO enlargement and,
    161
"Ethnic cleansing," 118–119
  cantonization plan and, 122
  collective security model and, 169
  lessons of Yugoslavia, 134, 159
Ethnic pluralism
  Bosnia intervention approaches
    and, 119–126, 133
  possibility of conflict with, 178
  Yugoslav conflict lessons, 117,
    118, 136–137
EU. See European Union
Euro, transition of currency to, 188,
    190
Euroatlantic community
  constitution for, xiii, 182
  defined, 3
  democracy as goal for, 181
  Eastern Europe and, 164
  free trade proposals for, 188
  long-term strategy for, 182–184,
    200
  norms enforcement required in,
    8–9, 10
  peace model for, xi, xii, 10–11
  proposals for strengthening,
    190–193
  security system development for,
    xii–xiii, 10, 200–204
  stable peace as goal for, 10–11,
    141, 181
  U.S. as part of, 185–186
Euro-Atlantic Partnership Council
  Baltic states and Ukraine in, 177
  long-range goals and, 164, 175,
    191
  peacekeeping role for, 173

Europe
  proposals for strengthening,
    187–190
  Russian differences with, 183,
    224n4
  structural changes affecting,
    184–185
  U.S. interests in, 197
  U.S. presence in, 188–190. *See also*
    Overseas forces
  U.S. role in security of, 139, 185
  U.S.-Soviet conflict rules, 38–39
European allies
  See also North Atlantic Treaty
    Organization
  Eisenhower and, 19
  Kennedy policies and, 33–34
European Community (EC)
  See also European Union
  Bosnian cantonization plan and,
    120, 121
  Bosnian partition plan and, 120
  Bosnian referendum call by, 118
  CSCE preparations, 55–56
  1991 Yugoslav peace conference
    (The Hague), 115–116
  transition to European Union,
    219n4
  Yugoslav conflict lessons, 135,
    136, 138
  Yugoslav republics recognized by,
    116
European Monetary Union, U.S.
  influence and, 189
European security conference. *See*
    Conference on Security and
    Cooperation in Europe
    (CSCE); Helsinki Final Act
European Union (EU)
  See also European Community
  Atlantic Union proposal and,
    225n12
  Baltic states and Ukraine in, 177

  in collective security model, 170,
    189–190
  "contact group" and, 170
  creation of, 219n4
  Eastern European states and, 192
  economic agenda for, 187, 188
  nationalism as threat to, 186–187
  proposals for enlarging, xiii, 164,
    192
  proposals for strengthening, 190
  prospects for stable peace and,
    186
  types of peace in, x
  Yugoslav conflict and, 112, 135,
    136. *See also* Yugoslavia, for-
    mer; *specific countries*
"Existential deterrence," 34

Family reunification, in Helsinki
    Final Act, 55
Federal Bureau of Investigation (FBI),
    nuclear security role, 107
"Federation of Peace," 183
Fermi, Enrico, 206n1
Finland
  Helsinki site offered by, 47–48
  Ukrainian disarmament aid by, 89
Firebreak doctrine, 40, 44
First-use policies, 23, 30, 33–34
Fissile material
  See also Fissile materials trafficking
  P-8 summit (1996), 106
  recommendations for controlling,
    106–109
  Russian success at controlling,
    105–106
  storage issues, 88, 93–94
  top-down approach to control of,
    104, 109
  U.S. Congress and control of,
    141–142
  U.S.-Russian cooperation and,
    101–103, 150–151

Fissile material *(cont.)*
USSR disintegration and control
of, 65, 69, 93, 98, 217*n*6
Fissile materials trafficking
See also Fissile material
dangers of, 69
international norms and, 106, 109
U.S.-Soviet cooperation and, 7–8,
108–109
"Flexible response" strategy, 29–32
Floyd, Arva, 212*n*25
Foley, Tom, on confidence in government, 194
Force, use of
aggression encouraged by renunciation of, 138
for collective security, 10
in conditional vs. stable peace,
x, 4–5
enforcement of rules by, 8–9,
139–140
in "logic of peace," 4
Force and Statecraft (Craig and
George), 224*n*7
Foreign policy, importance of concepts in, 38
Founding Act. *See* NATO-Russia
Founding Act
"Four Policemen," xi
France
Bosnia conflict role, 129, 130
in "contact group," 170
CSCE and, 47, 48, 50, 53, 60, 61
disarmament negotiations and,
149, 155–157
nuclear weapons development
by, 32
Ukrainian disarmament aid by, 89
Frasure, Robert, Bosnia conflict role,
129, 130
Freedom of the press issues, CSCE
preparations and, 55, 57. *See
also* "Freer movement"

"Freer movement"
CSCE preparations and, 50, 52,
53, 54, 56, 59, 63
German position on, 58
security issues vs., 60
seeds of change and, 61–62
specifics, 55, 56–57
Free trade, prospects for stable peace
and, 188, 225*n*11
Frontier inviolability, in Helsinki
Final Act, 171

GDR. *See* German Democratic
Republic
General deterrence, ix, x
"General war," Eisenhower policy on,
19, 20, 22
Geneva International Conference on
the Former Yugoslavia (ICFY),
122–124
George, Alexander, 205–206*n*3
on bipolar order, 210*n*1, 210*n*8
on Concert of Europe, 224*n*7
German Democratic Republic (GDR)
CSCE and, 52
Gorbachev and, 143
UN Charter and, 38
U.S.-Soviet rules and, 39
Germany
See also German Democratic
Republic; West Germany
in "contact group," 170
European Union and, 190
Gorbachev and, 143
international vs. internal security
and, 216–217*n*3
refugee problem in, 134, 137
Ukrainian disarmament aid by, 89
unification of, 42–43, 45
U.S. response to reunification of,
66, 214*n*2
U.S.-Soviet rules and, 40–41,
42–43

*Germany Unified and Europe Trans-
    formed* (Zelikow and Rice),
    214*n*2
Glasnost, 144
Gligorov, President Kiro, 115
Global economy, local autonomy
    and, 137
Global war, nuclear weapons use and,
    20
Goodpaster, Andrew J.
    on Eisenhower's firmness,
        208–209*n*34
    on Eisenhower's strategy, 17,
        207*n*17
Gorazde
    Bosnian cantonization plan and,
        126
    Dayton agreement, 132
    1995 attack on, 129
Gorbachev, Mikhail
    diplomatic revolution by, 142–143
    European missile withdrawal and,
        41
    "glasnost" program, 144
    miscalculations by, 145
    motivation of, 63, 143, 144, 145
    "new thinking" paradigm, 143, 144
    nuclear disarmament and, 9, 68,
        71, 74, 142–143, 146, 147
    resignation of, 72
    Reykjavik summit with Reagan,
        144, 150
    Russian criticism of, 143
    START I treaty and, 68, 144,
        146–147
    USSR breakup and, 70, 71, 72
Gore, Al
    Gore-Chernomyrdin Commission,
        102, 103
    trilateral accord and, 86
Gore-Chernomyrdin Commission,
    103, 109, 217–218*n*10
Gottmoeller, Rose, 80

Grachev, Pavel, 80, 128
"Grand design"
    Clinton and, xi–xii, 3–4, 10–11,
        181, 182, 200, 204
    in Cold War, 3
    Eisenhower and, 16–19
    feasibility of as goal, 198
    importance of in times of change,
        14, 38
    in long-range policy plan, xi, 3,
        10–11, 181–204
    NATO enlargement and, 176,
        177, 200
    Truman and, 15–16
    U.S. public opposition to,
        196–197
    U.S. public support for, 193–195,
        202–204
"Grand strategy"
    economic component in, 187, 188,
        192–193
    Eisenhower's development of,
        16–19
    Kennedy's "flexible response,"
        29–32
    in long-range policy plan, xi,
        10–11, 196–204
    needed in times of transition, 14
    nuclear disarmament and, 157
    success of, 181
Great Britain. *See* United Kingdom
The Great Illusion (Angell), 187
Grinevsky, Oleg, on opposition to
    Gorbachev, 143–144, 222*n*2
Grotian society, Europe as, 183, 224*n*3
Group of Seven plus Russia (Politi-
    cal 8), Moscow summit, 106
Gulf War, chemical weapons use in, 96

The Hague, 1991 Yugoslav peace
    conference in, 115–116
Halperin, Morton, on arms control,
    145, 222*n*4

Hegemonic domination zone, Eastern Europe as, 42
Helman, Gerald, 212n25
Helms-Burton bill, 189
Helsinki Clinton-Yeltsin meeting (March 1997)
  Clinton's "grand design" at, 3–4, 177
  Euroatlantic community and, 164
  nuclear disarmament and, 9, 148, 152–153, 155, 175
Helsinki Final Act, 46–47
  See also Conference on Security and Cooperation in Europe
  human rights issues and, 7, 46–47, 53–54, 55, 171
  NATO and, 48–51
  OSCE founding at, 46, 171
  precursors of, xi
  as seeds of change, 63–64, 171
  three "baskets" of, 57–58
  trilateral accord and, 88
  Yugoslav failure and, 112
Herzegovina. See Bosnia-Herzegovina
Highly enriched uranium (HEU) purchase, 73–74, 75, 215–216n11
  advance payment on, 87
  revenue-sharing agreement with, 86
  Ukrainian negotiations and, 79, 83, 85, 86
Hillenbrand, Martin, 212n25, 212n28
Holbrooke, Richard, 129, 130, 132, 135
Holloway, David, 206n4
Humanitarian aid
  collective security model and, 167
  Yugoslav conflict lessons, 138
Human rights issues
  CSCE and, 46–47, 49, 53, 54–55, 56–58, 171

diplomatic approaches to Bosnia and (1991–95), 119–126
  Eastern Europe and, 41–42, 53
  introduction of, 6–7
  normative change and, 144
  shared values and, 63–64, 214n50
Humphrey, George, 20, 21, 22
Hungary
  NATO enlargement and, 161, 165
  UN Charter and, 38
Hussein, Saddam, 95, 96
Hyde Park summit (October 1995), 103, 105, 219–220n10

IAEA. See International Atomic Energy Agency
ICBMs. See Intercontinental ballistic missiles
ICFY. See Geneva International Conference on the Former Yugoslavia
IFOR. See Implementing Force
Immediate deterrence, ix, x
Implementing Force (IFOR), Russian participation in, 128
Imprinting norms, 104, 217n3
Indiscriminate destruction, weapons of
  international norms and, 95–96, 104–105, 107
  Nunn-Lugar-Domenici legislation and, 107
Individual rights, Bosnia intervention approaches and, 119–126
Indochina, Eisenhower and, 18
Information access, revolution and, 63
INF. See Treaty on the Elimination of Intermediate Range and Shorter-Range Missiles
Inspection on demand, as requirement for disarmament, 157
Intelligence, Euroatlantic community ties and, 190

Intercontinental ballistic missiles
(ICBMs)
nuclear disarmament and, 9
Ukrainian crisis and, 77, 81,
216n15
Interdepartmental Commission for the
Protection of State Secrets, 99
Intermediate-range ballistic missiles,
U.S.-Soviet rules and, 41
International Atomic Energy Agency
(IAEA), 72
U.S.-Russian cooperation with, 96
International organizations
collective security and, 10, 171–
173
importance of in times of change,
38
in long-term strategy, 182, 185–
186, 203-204
International Science and Technology
Center (Moscow), 100–101
Intervention
See also Enforcement
by "coalitions of the willing," 176,
201
collective security model and, 167,
169, 171
decision-making dilemmas, 114,
167
justifications for, 139
OSCE results, 172
in stable peace, 178
Intrastate conflicts, collective security
model and, 166, 167
Iran, Russian nuclear aid to, 96
Irreversibility in nuclear disarmament,
153, 156
Irwin, John, 57, 213n36
Isolationism
post–World War I organizations
and, 185–186
in U.S. public opinion, 194
Yugoslav conflict lessons, 139–140

Israeli relationship with Arabs, as
"precarious peace," ix
Italy, Ukrainian disarmament aid by, 89
Izetbegovic, President Alija, 115
cantonization plan and, 121
decentralization plan and, 124

Japan
atomic bomb use against, 26,
208n26
international vs. internal security
and, 216–217n3
Ukrainian disarmament aid by,
88, 89
Joint Chiefs of Staff (JCS), nuclear
weapons use debate, 20–22,
23, 24, 27
Journalism issues, CSCE preparations
and, 55, 57
Jupiter missiles, withdrawal of from
Turkey, 41

Kahn, Herman, on nuclear war, 13,
206n2
Kampelman, Max, on self-determination, 137
Kantian international community, 183
Karadzic, Radovan
Bosnian Serb support for, 118
decentralization plan and, 124–125
Russian influence on, 127
Kazakstan
Lisbon Protocol and, 74–75, 147
nuclear disarmament aid to,
71–72
nuclear weapons control issues,
66, 72, 74, 78
START I treaty and, 89
U.S. uranium purchase and, 73, 75
Kennan, George
on future hope for Russia, 195
grand strategy and, 15
on nuclear deterrence, 151

Kennan, George *(cont.)*
  nuclear disarmament and, 146
  on spheres-of-interest policy, 41,
    163
Kennedy, John F.
  European policies and, 30–31
  firebreak doctrine and, 40
  "flexible response" strategy, 29–32
  leadership of, 43
  1961 summit with Khrushchev,
    31–32
  nuclear age policies, 14, 29–32
  nuclear deterrence and, 33–34
  nuclear weapons use authorization
    and, 29, 31
  U.S.-Soviet relations and, 6, 31–32,
    39, 43
Keohane, Robert, 215n3
Khrushchev, Nikita
  Berlin threat, U.S. policy and, 28,
    32, 39
  Eisenhower and, 32
  1961 summit with Kennedy, 31–32
  status quo challenges by, 44–45
Kissinger, Henry
  on Concert of Europe, 186
  CSCE and, 46, 51, 58–59, 60–61,
    211n19
  détente and, xi, 45
  on European-Russian differences,
    224n4
  on NATO-Russia Founding Act,
    173, 223n6
Korea
  troop withdrawal from, 21–22
  U.S.-Soviet rules and, 39
Korean War
  armistice, 20
  beginning of, 15
  nuclear weapons use debate, 20, 22
Kosovo
  intervention in case like, 178
  Serbian annexation of, 117

Kostenko, Yuri, 77
Kozyrev, Andrei, 127
Krajina Serbs, 128, 129, 130
Krasnoyarsk-26, nuclear security at,
  218n10
Kravchuk, Leonid, 66–67, 73
  challenge to authority of, 76–77
  defeated in election, 89
  Lisbon Protocol and, 75, 76, 83
  meeting with Clinton, 85, 87
  nuclear missile deactivation and,
    85
  Russian politics and, 84
  trilateral accord role, 76, 86, 87
  U.S. negotiations with, 84
  Washington visit by, 89
Kuchma, Leonid, 89
Kupchan, Charles A., 225n12
Kurchatov, nuclear security at,
  218n10
Kurds, Saddam Hussein and, 95, 96

Lake, Anthony, 129
Latvia, NATO enlargement and, 161
Law enforcement
  Euroatlantic community ties and,
    190
  international, recommendations
    for, 106–108
Leadership
  consensus on values and, 64,
    214n50
  importance of, 43
  for nuclear security, 107–109
  for rules enforcement, 111–112
Ledogar, Steve, 212n25
Levi, Primo, 224n4
Libya, effect of internal affairs in, 95
Limited Nuclear Test Ban Treaty
  as explicit rules, 43
  policy impact of, 29
The Limits of Safety . . . (Sagan),
  207n18

Lippmann, Walter, on strategy of containment, 195
Lisbon Protocol (1992), 74–75, 76
 Clinton policy and, 78–79
 Massandra accords and, 83, 86
 normative change and, 147
 Ukraine and, 74–75, 76, 78–79, 84–85, 87, 88, 216n12
Lithuania, NATO enlargement and, 161
Local autonomy, Yugoslav conflict lessons, 137
The Logic of Accidental War (Blair), 207n18
"Logic of peace"
 defined, 4
 for Euroatlantic community, 191–193
 German unification and, 45
 nuclear restraint and, 90–91
 presidential policies and, 14
 as stable peace requirement, 178
 tacit U.S.-Soviet rules and, 44
London Conference on the former Yugoslavia (August 1992), 127
Long-range policy planning
 advantages of, xi
 elements of, xi–xii
 goal for, 181–182
 "grand design" and, xi, 3, 181–204
 "tests" of, xii
Lugar, Richard
 See also Nunn-Lugar umbrella program
 nuclear disarmament role, 71–72, 76, 79, 142
 on top-down approach, 104

Maastricht Treaty on European Union, 219n4
 currency conversion and, 187, 190
McCone, chairman of AEC, 27–28

Macedonia
 See also Yugoslavia, former
 confederation plan and, 115
 historical context, 114–119
 NATO membership and, 161
McGuire, Ralph, 212n25, 213n44
McNamara, Robert S., "flexible response" strategy and, 30, 32
Madrid Declaration (July 1997), 161, 162, 177
Malenkov, view of nuclear war, 206n4
Maresca, John, 62, 212n25, 212n26, 213–214n45, 214n50
Markovic, Ante, 114–115
Massandra accords, 82–83, 86
"Massive retaliation," 18
 authorization to use nuclear weapons and, 23–24
 "flexible response" strategy vs., 29
Mayak, nuclear security at, 103, 218n10
MBFR. *See* Mutual and balanced force reductions
Mendelevich, Lev, 62
Metastable peace, in former Yugoslavia (1995), 131, 221n42
Middle East
 "precarious peace" in, ix
 U.S. participation in Europe vs., 202
 U.S.-Soviet rules and, 39
Mikhailov, Viktor, 102, 148
Military aid, Eisenhower's views on, 18–19
Military budget
 conventional force buildup and, 32
 nuclear weapons use debate and, 20, 21, 22
 overseas forces and, 21, 22
 transparency requirements for, 161
Military intervention, Eisenhower's views on, 18–19
Miller, Bill, 85

Milosevic, Slobodan
 diplomatic approaches to, 129, 130
 EC peace plan rejected by, 116
 encouragement of aggression by,
  138
 support for, 118
Ministry of Atomic Energy
  (MINATOM), 97, 217n4
 cooperation with U.S. by, 97–98,
  105
 top-down leadership and, 109
 uranium purchase and, 75
Minority groups. See Ethnic pluralism
Minority rights, Bosnia intervention
  approaches and, 119–126,
  136–137
MIRVs. See Multiple, independently
  targeted reentry vehicles
Missile defense systems. See Antiballistic missile systems
Mladic, General, in 1995 fighting,
  129, 130
Moldova, NATO enlargement and,
  162
Monroe Doctrine, 184
Montenegro, historical context,
  114–119
Morgan, Patrick, ix
Morgenthau, Hans, on collective
  security, 168–169, 223n3,
  223n4
Morozov, Ukrainian defense minis-
  ter, 80
Moscow summit (1972), CSCE
  and, 61
Moscow summit (1994), trilateral
  accord and, 87–88
Moscow summit (1995)
 Euroatlantic community and, 164
 nuclear security and, 102
Moscow summit (1996), Group of
  Seven plus Russia, 106
Mostar, 133

Mueller, John, on obsolescence of
  war, 223n1
Multilateral organizations. See Inter-
  national organizations
Multiple, independently targeted
  reentry vehicles (MIRVs), 34
 START II treaty and, 68
Munich, lessons of, Bosnia and, 120
Munkki, Olavi, 212n28
Mutual and balanced force reductions
  (MBFR), CSCE and, 60–61

Nagorno-Karabakh dispute, OSCE
  and, 167
Nationalism
 European Union and, 186–187
 inevitability of conflict with, 184,
  194
 revival of after Cold War, 137
National Security Council (Bush administration), USSR disintegration response, 70
National Security Council (Clinton
  administration), Ukrainian
  crisis and, 80
National Security Council (Eisenhower administration), 16
 Net Evaluation Subcommittee,
  27, 30
 nuclear war objectives paper,
  26–27
 Project Solarium findings, 16–17
National Security Council (Truman
  administration), NSC 68 statement of objectives, 15–16
National Security Study Memorandum (NSSM) 138, 58–59
NATO. See North Atlantic Treaty
  Organization
NATO Combined Joint Task Force,
  191
NATO-Russia Charter. See NATO-
  Russia Founding Act

NATO-Russia Founding Act, 174
  collective security and, 173–174
  expansion models and, 161
  long-range goals and, xii–xiii,
    165, 175, 191
  OSCE peacekeeping role in, 172
NATO-Russia Permanent Joint
    Council, 174, 175, 189, 201
Nazarbayev, Nursalton, 74
Nechai, Vladimir, 98
Negotiations. *See* Diplomacy
Neo-Sovietism, Ukrainian crisis and,
    77
Nerve gas attack
  See also Chemical weapons
  by Aum Shinrikyo sect, 8, 94
  on Kurds, 96
Net Evaluation Subcommittee (NSC),
    27, 30
Netherlands, The, Ukrainian disar-
    mament aid by, 89
"New medievalism," 109
"New thinking" paradigm, 143, 144
New Transatlantic Agenda, 188
New York, ICFY meetings in, 124
New York World Trade Center
    bombing, 94
Niles, Tom, 212n25
Nixon, Richard
  CSCE and, 49, 51, 56
  détente and, xi
  "Era of Negotiations," 37, 47,
    48, 49
  1972 summit with Brezhnev, 61
  SALT I agreement and, 68
  and seeds of change, 46–47
Non-first-use policy, 107–108
Noninterference in internal affairs
  See also Intervention
  collective security model and, 171
  terrorism control problems, 5–96
Nonuse of nuclear weapons, 28, 34,
    209n35

Norms
  See also Rules
  bipolar order maintained by,
    210n1
  force required for enforcement
    of, 8–9, 111–112. *See also*
    Enforcement
  Gorbachev and changes in,
    144–145
  "grand design" as basis for, 3, 4
  Helsinki Final Act and, 46–47
  methodology of imprinting, 104
  new international obligations and,
    97–100, 103
  nonuse of nuclear weapons, 34
  and nuclear terrorism prevention,
    95–97, 106, 107–109
  for post–nuclear weapons era, 141
  in UN Charter, 38
Norstad, Lauris, on nuclear deter-
    rence, 18
North American Free Trade Agree-
    ment, 188
North Atlantic Council, 48
  CSCE and, 49, 50, 52, 60
  détente process and, 48
  "freer movement" declaration, 50,
    52, 53
North Atlantic Treaty Organization
    (NATO)
  Acheson report to Kennedy on, 31
  Article V relevance, 201
  associate membership in, 161
  Atlantic Union proposal and,
    225n12
  Bosnia conflict role, 126, 127, 129,
    130, 131
  Bosnia conflict lessons, 135, 136,
    137–138
  Brezhnev doctrine and, 53, 54
  "coalitions of the willing" within,
    176, 201
  as collective defense system, 168

North Atlantic Treaty Organization
(NATO) *(cont.)*
as collective security–collective
defense system, 173–174, 200,
201–202
conflict resolution goals for, 11
CSCE and, 48–51, 52–63
denationalization of defense policies by, 175–176
enlargement issues, xiii, 10, 11,
160–166, 173–177, 191, 197–
198, 200–204
German reunification and, 66,
214n2
Gorbachev and, 143
"grand design" and, 176, 177, 182,
200
importance of in times of change,
38
importance of U.S. participation
in, 186, 190
intermediate-range ballistic missile deployment, 41
McNamara speech to (1962), 32
Madrid Declaration (July 1997),
161, 162, 177
on mutual and balanced force
reductions, 60
nuclear deterrence role, 18, 19,
30–31, 33–34
OSCE and, 172
peacekeeping role for, 172–173
proposals for transforming,
191–192
Russia and, 11, 161, 163–166,
174, 175, 197–198, 200–204,
224n4
Russian nuclear weapons and, 149
START III treaty and, 148
transformation in, 175
U.S. "sphere of interest," 41
Yugoslav conflict lessons, 135,
136, 137–138

North Korea
See also Korea; Korean War
Soviet support for, 15
U.S.-Soviet rules and, 39
Norway, Ukrainian disarmament aid
by, 89
NPT. *See* Treaty on the Nonprolifer-
ation of Nuclear Weapons
NSC. *See* National Security Council
NSC 68 (1950) statement of objec-
tives, 15–16
Eisenhower policy and, 24–25
NSC 162/2 (1953), 17–18, 23–24
"critical date" and, 25
NSC 5440 (1954), preventive war
policy rejected in, 25
NSSM 138, 58–59
Nuclear deterrence
Cold War policies and, 5–6
concept of, 6
conditional peace and, 153
Eisenhower's views on, 16–19,
26
explicit arms control rules, 43
fissile materials trafficking and,
7–8, 108–109
future negotiations on, 156–157
Kennedy's "flexible response"
strategy, 29–32
NATO role in, 18, 19, 30–31,
33–34
non-first-use policy, 107–108
Russia as nuclear power and,
148–149
stable peace prevented by, 151, 200
U.S.-Russian relationship and,
141–142
U.S.-Russian-Ukrainian negotiations and, 7
Nuclear disarmament
See also START *treaties*
aid to Ukraine for, 71–72, 76
Bush and, 68, 71, 74, 76, 146–147

Nuclear disarmament *(cont.)*
    challenge to nuclear restraints
        and, 68–70
    going beyond, 153–157
    Gorbachev and, 9, 68, 71, 74,
        142–143, 146, 147, 150
    "grand strategy" and, 157
    irreversibility requirements, 153,
        156
    need for, 9, 145, 156–157, 199
    other nuclear powers and, 155–157
    Reagan and, 9, 68, 145–146, 150
    Reykjavik summit as beginning
        of, 150
    Russian-Ukrainian negotiations
        on, 82–83
    transparency requirements, 153,
        155–156
    trilateral accord, 86–88
    in Ukraine, 88–89, 90
    U.S.-Russian cooperation and,
        141–142, 150–151
    U.S.-Ukrainian negotiations on,
        80–82, 83–84
    U.S. uranium purchase and, 73–
        74, 75, 79, 81, 83, 85, 86, 87,
        215–216n11
    verification techniques, 157
    weapons scientists and, 100–101
Nuclear era
    beginning of, 13, 14–15, 206n1
    presidential policies and, 13–35
Nuclear material. *See* Fissile material
Nuclear nonproliferation treaty
        (NPT). *See* Treaty on the
        Nonproliferation of Nuclear
        Weapons
Nuclear restraint, post–Cold War, 7,
        65–91
    as decisionmaking framework,
        90–91
Nuclear security. *See* Fissile material;
        Nuclear terrorism

Nuclear succession crisis, diplomacy
    in, 67, 70–71
Nuclear terrorism, 93–109
    cooperation to prevent, 7–8, 106,
        150–151
    fissile material protection, 65, 69,
        93, 98, 101–103, 105–106,
        217n6
    international norms and, 95–100,
        106, 107–109, 216–217n3
    P-8 summit on (1996), 106
    recommendations for preventing,
        106–109
    USSR disintegration and, 69
Nuclear test ban, other nuclear pow-
    ers and, 156
Nuclear war
    avoidance of in "grand design,"
        3–6, 14
    "critical date," 15–16
    Eisenhower's views on, 17, 26–29,
        208n26
    "firebreak" and avoidance of, 40, 44
    hypothetical outcome of, 27
    Kennedy's views on, 30
    as unthinkable, 182, 223n1
    as unwinnable, 14, 24, 27, 208n31
Nuclear weapons
    authorization for use of, 19–24,
        28–29, 30, 31, 39–40, 208–
        209n34
    "conventionalization" of, 28
    defensive use of, 23–24, 207n18
    European ownership of, 31, 32
    firebreak doctrine, 40, 44
    first-use policies, 23, 30, 33–34
    increasing numbers of, 28, 34
    limiting future role of, 154–157
    nonuse of, 28, 34, 209n35
    predelegation to use, 23–24, 31,
        40
    reciprocal withdrawal of, 71
    retaliatory use of, 23–24, 207n18

Nuclear weapons *(cont.)*
  Russian attitude toward, 148–149
  Soviet fears about, 40–41
  tactical, McNamara on, 32
  terrorism and, 94
  in Ukraine, 77, 81, 216*n*15
  U.S.-Soviet rules and, 39–40
  USSR disintegration and control
    of, 65–66, 70–74
Nunn, Sam
  nuclear disarmament role, 71–72,
    76, 79, 142
  top-down approach advocated
    by, 104
Nunn-Lugar-Domenici legislation
  (1996), 104, 107, 142
Nunn-Lugar umbrella program,
  71–72, 76, 214*n*1, 216*n*13
  nuclear security and, 218*n*10
  Russian Congress and, 78
  START III proposals and, 153
  Ukrainian negotiations and, 80,
    81, 83, 84, 85
Nye, Joseph, 216*n*2

Objectives, importance of, 134
Obninsk
  fissile materials protection train-
    ing at, 101
  nuclear security at, 103, 218*n*10
Obsolescence of war, 182, 223*n*1
Oklahoma City federal building
  bombing, 94
Okun, Herbert, 138
O'Leary, Hazel, 102
On-site inspections
  Gorbachev and, 143
  Russian opposition to, 143–144
"Operation Cerberus," 102
"Order"
  in international relations, 4,
    205*n*2
  nuclear succession crisis and, 67

Order-building diplomacy
  See also Rule-building diplomacy
  by Gorbachev, 144–145
  in collective security model, 168
  Yugoslav conflict lessons, 136–
    137, 168
Organization for Economic Cooper-
  ation and Development, Rus-
  sian membership in, 192
Organization for Security and Coop-
  eration in Europe (OSCE)
  Baltic states and Ukraine in,
    177
  Bosnia intervention results, 172
  collective security model and, 166,
    167, 170, 171
  Helsinki Final Act and, 46, 171
  long-range goals and, 10, 164,
    191, 192
  peacekeeping role for, 172
  Russia as member of, 175
  U.S. cooperation with, 190
Ostpolitik
  as challenge to bipolar order,
    37, 47
  CSCE preparations and, 60
  German unification and, 42
Overseas forces
  authorization for nuclear weapons
    use by, 23–24, 30
  Bosnian conflict and, 131, 132,
    136
  CSCE preparations and, 60–61
  Eisenhower's position on, 21, 22
  Kennedy's position on, 30–32
  military budget and, 21
  U.S.-Soviet rules and, 40–41
Owen, Lord David, as ICFY cochair,
  122–124, 135–136
Owen-Stoltenberg plan, 120, 133

P-8 (Political 8), 1996 Moscow
  summit, 106

Pale
    Bosnian Serb withdrawal to, 118
    NATO attack on, 129
PanAm Flight 103, 107
Partnership for Peace, 161
    Baltic states and Ukraine in, 177
    joint training and, 106
    long-range goals and, xii–xiii,
        164, 175, 176, 191
    peacekeeping role for, 172–173
Peace
    "logic of," defined, 4. *See also*
        "Logic of peace"
    metastable, in former Yugoslavia
        (1995), 131, 221*n*42
    risk-avoidance required for, 44
    types of, defined, ix–x. *See also*
        specific types
Peace enforcement. *See* Enforcement
Peacekeeping forces
    OSCE and, 172
    Russian participation in, 128
    UN, in Bosnia, 116–117, 118
Peace of Westphalia, 184
Perry, William, 86, 90, 128, 133
Pickering, Thomas, 85
Podolsk, nuclear security at, 103,
    218*n*10
Poland, NATO enlargement and,
    161, 165
Policy planning. *See* Long-range
    policy planning
Political 8 (P-8), 1996 Moscow
    summit, 106
Political exchanges, CSCE and, 53
Politics among Nations (Morgenthau),
    168
Pompidou, Georges, and seeds of
    change, 47, 48
Post–nuclear weapons era, rules of
    behavior for, 141, 199
Powell, Colin, on need for objec-
    tives, 134

"Prague Spring"
    as challenge to bipolar order, 37
    CSCE and, 51–52
    Nixon's "era of negotiations" and,
        47
Precarious peace, defined, ix, 206*n*3
Predelegation to use nuclear
    weapons, 23–24
Presidential leadership, importance
    of, 43
Preventive diplomacy, 70–71
Preventive war, 13, 15, 16
    Eisenhower's rejection of, 25, 28,
        29
    Kennedy's rejection of, 30
    Reagan's rejection of, 14, 208*n*31
Project Solarium, 16–17
Prompt launch. *See* Rapid launch

Qadhafi, Mu'ammar, 95
Quadripartite Agreement on Berlin,
    CSCE preparations and, 60
"Quick fix approach," to nuclear
    security, 102

Racism, state-sponsored, 119
Radford, Arthur
    "dynamic" policy example by, 26
    nuclear weapons authorization
        debate and, 20, 21, 22
Radio broadcast jamming, CSCE
    preparations and, 55, 57
Rapid launch, reducing reliance on, 154
Reagan, Ronald
    CSCE opposed by, 46
    Gorbachev and, 146
    nuclear disarmament and, 9, 68,
        145–146
    on nuclear war as unwinnable, 14,
        34, 44, 208*n*31
    Reykjavik summit with Gorbachev,
        144, 150
    Soviet changes and, 144–145

Reddy, Leo, 212*n*25
Redman, Charles E., 128
Refugees
    Dayton agreement and, 132
    as destabilizing element, 119
    Yugoslav conflict lessons, 134, 137
Regional conflicts. *See specific regions*
Restraint, bipolar order maintained
    by, 45, 210*n*1
Retaliatory use of nuclear weapons,
    23–24, 207*n*18
Retreat from Doomsday (Mueller),
    223*n*1
"Reviving the West" (Kupchan),
    225*n*12
Revolutions in Eastern Europe,
    acceleration of, 63–64
Reykjavik summit meeting (1986),
    144, 150
Rice, Condoleezza, 214*n*2
Ripe for Resolution (Zartman), 221*n*44
Risk avoidance, as requirement for
    peace, 44
Rogers, William
    challenge to status quo and, 37
    CSCE preparations and, 50, 62,
        214*n*47
Romania, NATO enlargement and,
    161, 162
Roosevelt, Franklin, security plan
    by, xi
Rosenfield, Stephen S., on policy
    strategy, 224*n*4
RPM. *See* Office of Regional
    Politico-Military Affairs
Rule-building diplomacy, 97. *See also*
    Order-building diplomacy
Rules of behavior
    See also Norms
    bipolar order based on, 37, 199
    in collective security model, 168
    in Concert of Europe, 186,
        224*n*7

conversion of strategy to, 182
explicit, efforts to codify, 43
force required for enforcement of,
    8–9, 111–112, 139–140
Gorbachev and changes in,
    144–145
governmental decisionmaking
    simplified by, 90–91
"grand design" as basis for, 3, 4
Helsinki Final Act and, 46–47
implicit U.S.-Soviet, in Cold War,
    38–43, 44
as irrelevant, 65
methodology of imprinting,
    104
nuclear security cooperation and,
    101–103, 217–218*n*10
nuclear succession crisis and, 67
for post–nuclear weapons era,
    141, 199
terrorist activity and changes in,
    94, 97, 216–217*n*3
U.S. presidents and development
    of, 13–14
Yugoslav conflict lessons, 138,
    139–140, 199
Rumsfeld, Donald, 212*n*25
Russell, Bertrand, 13, 206*n*2
Russia
    in biological/chemical weapons
        agreement, 96
    Bosnian conflict and, 126–128,
        136, 137–138
    in "contact group," 170
    differences with Europe, 183,
        224*n*4
    economic goals for, 192–193
    in Euroatlantic community, 164
    international vs. internal security
        and, 97, 98–99
    Lisbon Protocol and, 74–75
    long-range goal with, xi, xii,
        10–11, 195, 197–198

Russia *(cont.)*
  Massandra accords with Ukraine, 82–83, 86
  NATO enlargement issues, 11, 161, 163–166, 174, 175, 191, 197–198, 200–204, 224*n*4
  nuclear disarmament aid to, 71–72
  nuclear redeployment to, 74
  nuclear security successes in, 105–106
  nuclear weapons control issues, 66, 72, 73, 107–109
  nuclear weapons priority in, 148–149
  in OECD, 192
  as OSCE member, 175
  START I treaty and, 89, 147
  START II treaty and, 146–147, 148, 175
  START III treaty and, 148
  trilateral accord with U.S. and Ukraine, 76, 82–83, 86–88
  Ukrainian negotiations with, 82–83, 216*n*16
  Ukrainian nuclear weapons and, 66–67, 70, 77–78, 79–80, 216*n*14
  U.S. interests in, 197–198
  U.S. uranium purchase and, 73–74, 75, 79, 86, 87, 215–216*n*11
  in World Trade Organization, 192
Russian Federal Counterintelligence Service
  on internal security vs. international cooperation, 98–99
  top-down leadership and, 109
Rutskoy, Alexander, 78

Safe and Secure Dismantlement of Nuclear Weapons (SSD), 214*n*1
  fissile materials protection and, 101

Ukraine and, 81, 85
Sagan, Scott D., 207*n*18
SALT I agreements, 40–41, 68
Sarajevo
  1995 fighting in, 128, 129
  Dayton agreement, 132
  effects of attack on, 126
  ethnic pluralism in, 118
"Satisficing," 70, 214–215*n*3
Schelling, Thomas
  on arms control, 145, 222*n*4
  on nonuse of nuclear weapons, 28, 34, 209*n*35
Schmidt, Helmut, 212*n*24
Schumann, Maurice, CSCE and, 50, 60
Scientists, international aid to, 100–101
Security
  See also Collective security
  assurances to Ukraine on, 88, 89
  general deterrence and, x
Security
  noninterference in internal affairs and, 95–96, 98–99
  policy goals for, xii–xiii
  substate entity problems, 95–96
"Seeds of change," 63–64, 171
Self-determination
  Bosnia intervention and, 113, 119–126
  limits of, 137
Self-fulfilling prophecy, Russia's differences with West and, 183
Serbia
  See also Yugoslavia, former
  collective security model and, 168
  conflict with Albania, 178
  declaration of independence by, 116
  diplomatic approaches to Bosnia and (1991–95), 119–126

Serbia *(cont.)*
"ethnic cleansing" strategy of, 119, 122
historical context, 115–119
Sevastopol, Russian-Ukrainian conflict over, 77, 78, 80
Shakespeare, Frank, 57, 213*n*36
Shevardnadze, Eduard, 142–143, 147
Shultz, George, 146, 150, 151
Simon, Herbert, 70, 214–215*n*3
Slessor, John, 19
Slovakia, NATO enlargement and, 161, 162
Slovenia
    See also Yugoslavia, former
    confederation rejected by, 115
    in Dayton agreement, 132
    declaration of independence by, 116
    historical context, 114–119
    NATO enlargement and, 161, 162
    1995 fighting in, 128
Smuggling of nuclear materials, 93, 106. *See also* Fissile materials; Fissile materials trafficking
Sorensen, Theodore C., on first-strike briefing, 30
Southeast Asia, U.S.-Soviet rules and, 39
South Korea, 1950 attack on, 15. *See also* Korea; Korean War
Sovereignty, Yugoslav conflict lessons, 137
Soviet Union. *See* Union of Soviet Socialist Republics
Spain, Ukrainian disarmament aid by, 89
Spheres of interest, 160–166
    Cold War understandings, 6, 41–42
    collective security and, x–xi, 10, 160, 165–166, 179, 199–200
    conditional peace and, 165–166, 173–177

in conditional vs. stable peace, 177–178
defined, 200
human rights issues and, 6–7, 41, 42
NATO enlargement and, 163–166, 176–177
U.S. Russian relationship and, 173
U.S.-Soviet rules and, 41–42
Springsteen, George, 212*n*25
Srebrenica, fall of, 129
SS-19s ICBMs, in Ukraine, 81, 82, 83, 216*n*15
SS-20 intermediate-range ballistic missiles, 41, 44
SS-24 ICBMs, in Ukraine, 77, 81, 83, 84, 85, 216*n*15
Stable peace
    Cold War remnants and, 4–5, 177
    defined, x, 4, 205*n*3
    democracy as required for, 178, 183–184
    Euroatlantic community proposals and, 191–193
    feasibility of as goal, 198
    historical change and, 184–186
    moving from conditional peace to, 150–157, 177, 179, 204
    nuclear deterrence and, 151, 199
    spheres of interest and collective security in, 178
    strategies for, xi, xii, xiii, 177, 182–184
    as U.S.-Russian goal, 10–11, 150–151, 191
Stalin, Joseph
    bipolar order and, 45
    death of, 16
    German unification and, 42, 211*n*10
Stalin and the Bomb (Holloway), 206*n*4

START I treaty, 68
  CIS and, 72, 73
  Clinton policy and, 79
  Gorbachev and, 68, 144, 146–147
  Lisbon Protocol, 74–75
  Massandra accords and, 83
  ratification of, 67, 89
  Soviet disintegration and, 69–70,
    74–75
  Ukraine and, 73, 74–75, 84–85,
    87, 88, 89, 216n12
  U.S. economic aid and, 71–72
  U.S. uranium purchase and,
    73–74, 75, 80, 81, 87
START II treaty, 68, 150
  Bush-Yeltsin signing of, 146–147
  Russian opposition to, 143, 152,
    175
  strategic warheads and, 74
  Ukrainian and, 79
START III treaty
  issues arising from, 153–157
  key components of, 152–153
  Yeltsin and, 148, 153
Status quo
  collective security model and, 171
  cooperation to preserve, 43–45
  Helsinki Final Act and, 171
  long-term strategy for changing,
    183
Steel, Ronald, 196, 226n21
Stoessel, Walter, 212n25
Strategic arms reduction treaties, 68.
    See also specific treaties
Strategic concept. See "Grand
    design"; "Grand strategy"
Strategic nuclear systems, in CIS,
    74
Strategic warfare, Kennedy policy
    on, 32
The Strategy of Conflict (Schelling),
    209n35
Strategy for the West (Slessor), 19

Streator, Edward, 212n25, 213n41
Structural changes in Europe
  effects of, 184–185
  "grand design" as basis for, 3, 4
Substate entities
  international norms and, 107–109
  terrorism control problems,
    95–96
  U.S.-Russian cooperation and,
    97–103
Suez crisis, stable peace and outcome
    of, x
Summit meetings
  Helsinki (Clinton-Yeltsin), 3–4,
    9, 148, 152–153, 155, 164,
    175, 177
  Hyde Park (Clinton-Yeltsin), 103,
    105, 217–218n10
  Moscow (Clinton-Yeltsin), 87–88,
    102, 164
  Moscow (Group of Seven plus
    Russia), 106
  Moscow (Nixon-Brezhnev), 61
  Reykjavik (Reagan-Gorbachev),
    144, 150
  Vancouver (Clinton-Yeltsin), 79,
    101, 218n14
  Vienna (Kennedy-Khrushchev),
    31–32
Surprise attack, authorization to use
    nuclear weapons and, 23
Sverdlovsk-44, nuclear security at,
    218n10
Sweden, Ukrainian disarmament aid
    by, 89

Tacit understandings, "logic of peace"
    and, 44
Tactical nuclear weapons
  McNamara on, 32
  reciprocal withdrawal of, 71
"Tactics," in long-range policy plan-
    ning, xi

Talbott, Strobe
  on Russian transformation, 201–202
  trilateral accord role, 86, 87
  visit to Kiev by, 80
Tarnoff, Peter, 129
Taylor, Maxwell, 22
Territorial integrity, Bosnia inter-
      vention approaches and, 113,
      119–126
Territorial politics, as outmoded,
      165, 166
Terrorism
  See also Nuclear terrorism
  fissile materials control and, 7–8,
      93–94
  government-sponsored biological/
      chemical weapons programs
      and, 96–97
  international norms and, 107
Theft of nuclear materials, 93
  international norms and, 106
Timbie, James, 86, 216n11
Tito, Marshal, internal collapse after,
      112, 115
To Helsinki (Maresca), 62, 212n26,
      213–214n45
Tokyo, nerve gas release in, 8
Tolubko, Volodymyr, 77
Tourism
  CSCE and, 49, 53
  in Helsinki Final Act, 55
Trade, long-range goals for, 11, 188,
      225n11
Transatlantic Free Trade Area, pro-
      posal for, 188
Transitional periods, "grand design"
      needed in, 14
Transparency
  in defense budgeting, 161
  future negotiations on, 155–156
  in nuclear disarmament, 153
Travel restrictions, in Helsinki Final
      Act, 55

Treaty on the Elimination of Inter-
      mediate Range and Shorter-
      Range Missiles (INF), 68
Treaty on the Nonproliferation of
      Nuclear Weapons (NPT)
  as explicit rules, 43
  other nuclear powers and, 156
  Russian-Ukrainian dispute and,
      79, 80, 81, 216n14
  substate entity problem, 95
  Ukrainian accession to, 67, 70,
      87–88
  U.S.-Russian cooperation on, 96
  USSR disintegration and, 65, 69,
      70, 75
Trilateral accord (U.S.-Russia-
      Ukraine), 76
  Massandra accords and, 82–83, 86
Truman, Harry
  firebreak doctrine and, 40
  nuclear age policies, 13, 15–16
  U.S.-Soviet relations and, 6
Turkey, Jupiter missile withdrawal
      from, 41

Ukraine
  Lisbon Protocol and, 74–75, 76,
      78–79, 84–85, 87, 88, 147,
      216n12
  Massandra accords with Russia,
      82–83, 86
  NATO enlargement and, 161,
      162, 175, 176–177
  nuclear disarmament aid to,
      71–72, 76, 81–82
  nuclear disarmament completed
      by, 88–89, 90
  nuclear restraint norms and, 7,
      65–66, 91
  nuclear weapons control issues,
      66–67, 69–70, 72–73
  Russian negotiations with, 82–83,
      216n16

Ukraine *(cont.)*
    Russian politics and, 77, 84
    START I treaty and, 73, 74–75,
        84–85, 87, 88, 89, 216n12
    trilateral accord with Russia and
        U.S., 76, 82–83, 86–88
    U.S. negotiations with, 80–82,
        83–84, 85–86
    U.S. uranium purchase and, 73,
        75, 81, 83, 85, 86, 87
Ukrainian Science and Technology
    Center, 100–101
Union of Soviet Socialist Republics
    (USSR)
    "atomic archipelago," 93
    Bosnian conflict and, 126–127, 136
    disintegration of, nuclear restraint
        threat and, 65–66, 68–69
    end of (December 1991), 147
    as expansionist, 15
    Gorbachev's impact on, 142–143
    human rights issues in, 6–7
    relationship with U.S. *See* U.S.-
        Soviet relationship
    systemic failure in, 63
United Kingdom
    in biological/chemical weapons
        agreement, 96
    Bosnia conflict role, 129, 131
    in "contact group," 170
    CSCE preparations and, 60
    disarmament negotiations and,
        149, 155–157
    nuclear weapons development
        by, 32
    Suez crisis and, x
    Ukrainian disarmament and,
        88, 89
United Nations
    behavioral norms established by, 38
    in Bosnian negotiations, 126, 127
    Bosnia peacekeepers, 116–117,
        118, 128, 129, 130, 131

    British-French rapid reaction
        force and, 129, 131
    as collective security system, 168,
        173
    ICFY meetings at, 124
    nuclear security role for, 106, 107,
        108
    OSCE and, 164, 170
    peacekeeping weakness of, 116–
        117, 118
    terrorism prosecution role for, 107
    U.S.-Russian cooperation in, 97
    Yugoslav conflict lessons, 135
United States
    Bosnian cantonization plans and,
        121, 126
    Bosnian decentralization plan
        and, 125–126
    Bosnian partition plan and, 120
    Bosnian referendum call by, 118
    confidence in government in, 194
    in "contact group," 170
    Dayton agreement, 131–133
    as Euroatlantic community mem-
        ber, 185–186
    Euroatlantic economy and, 188,
        189, 225n11
    Euroatlantic politics and, 189–
        190, 203
    European security role, 139, 185
    public support for "grand design"
        in, 193–195, 197-198,
        202–204
    Vance-Owen Bosnia plan and,
        124, 125–126
    Yugoslav conflict lessons, 135,
        136, 137, 138
"Universal alliance," in collective
    security model, 168, 169
Universality
    in collective security vs. collective
        defense system, 168
    in OSCE, 170

Uranium, U.S. purchase of, 73–74,
75, 79, 81, 83, 85, 86, 87,
215–216n11
U.S. Congress
See also U.S. Senate
Bosnia conflict and, 129, 131
fissile materials control and,
141–142
NATO issues, 137–138, 161
U.S. Information Agency, freer
movement issues and, 57
U.S. Mission to NATO, CSCE
preparations, 50–51, 52, 54,
56–57, 58
U.S.-Russian relationship
agenda for improving, 153–157
Clinton administration and,
147–148
as conditional peace, 173
"contact group," 170
demarcation agreement (August
1997), 155
international vs. internal security
and, 97, 98–99
nuclear disarmament and, 141–142,
150–151, 153–154
nuclear security recommendations,
107–109
nuclear security successes, 105–
106
nuclear terrorism prevention and,
7–8, 97–103, 150–151
stable peace as goal of, 150–151,
191
substate entities and, 97–103
top-down leadership and, 109
trilateral accord with Ukraine,
76, 86–88
Ukranian conflict and, 67
weapons of indiscriminate
destruction and, 96, 104–105
Yugoslavian conflict and, 8–9,
127–128, 133, 136, 137, 199

U.S.-Russian-Ukrainian trilateral
accord, 76, 86–88
Massandra accords and, 82–83,
86
U.S. Senate
See also U.S. Congress
Bosnia conflict and, 129
chemical weapons debate in, 96
NATO enlargement and, 200–
201
nuclear disarmament role, 71–72
START II ratified by, 147
U.S.-Soviet relationship
bipolar order challenges, 37, 46–64
Cold War cooperation, 43–45
Cold War rules, x, 38–43
as conditional peace, x
CSCE preparations, 50–52, 61
"dynamic" policy proposals, 26
Eisenhower policies and, 24–26
Gorbachev and, 68
Kennedy policies and, 31–32
Truman policies and, 15–16
USSR. See Union of Soviet Socialist
Republics
U.S.-Ukrainian negotiations, 80–82,
83–84, 85–86
U.S.-Ukrainian disarmament aid, 89

Values, importance of in Western
diplomacy, 38, 63–64, 214n50
Vance, Cyrus
as ICFY cochair, 122–124, 135–
136
Serbian-Croatian conflict role, 138
UN peacekeeping and, 118
Vance-Owen Bosnia plan, 124, 125–
126, 132
Vancouver summit meeting and
Declaration (April 1993), 79,
101, 216n14
Verification of warhead dismantle-
ment, 157

Vest, George, 62, 212*n*25, 213*n*46
Vienna, Kennedy-Khrushchev summit in, 31–32
Vietnam, U.S.-Soviet rules and, 39
Vojvodina, Serbian annexation of, 117
Vukovar, Croatia, "ethnic cleansing" in, 119

"Walls in our minds," Clinton on, 8
War
    See also Nuclear war
    as "abolished," 19
    avoidance of as U.S.-Soviet rule, 39, 44, 45
    "general," Eisenhower policy on, 19, 20, 22
    global, nuclear weapons use and, 20
    preventive, 13, 15, 16, 25, 28, 29, 30
    strategic warfare, Kennedy policy on, 32
    as "subrationally unthinkable," 182, 223*n*1
War Crimes Tribunal, Dayton agreement and, 132
Warsaw Pact
    Budapest Appeal (March 1969), 47
    Budapest meeting (June 1969), 53–54
    CSCE and, 50, 52, 53–54
    Gorbachev and, 143
Weapons of indiscriminate destruction
    international norms and, 95–96, 104–105, 107
    Nunn-Lugar-Domenici legislation and, 107
"The West"
    defined, 3
    proposals for strengthening, 187–190
    prospects for stable peace in, 185–186

Western Europe
    American military presence in, 40–41
    nuclear deterrence for, 19
    U.S.-Soviet rules and, 39, 40–42
    U.S. spheres of interest in, 41–42
Western European Union, peacekeeping role for, 173
West Germany
    See also Germany
    challenges to bipolar order in, 37
    CSCE preparations and, 58, 60
    U.S.-Soviet rules and, 40–41
Westphalia, Peace of, pessimism since, 184
Wilkinson, Ted, 212*n*25
Wilson, Charles
    containment and coexistence and, 25
    nuclear weapons authorization debate and, 20, 21, 22
World Trade Organization, Russian membership in, 192
World War II, U.S. influence after, 185
"Worst plausible case" analysis, European view vs., 33

Yalta Conference, 41
Yazov, Russian defense minister, 144
Yeltsin, Boris
    Clinton's "grand design" and, 181
    on "Cold Peace," 176
    domestic opposition and, 147, 148
    Helsinki meeting with Clinton (1997), 3–4, 9, 148, 152–153, 155, 164, 175, 177
    Hyde Park summit with Clinton (October 1995), 103, 105, 217–218*n*10
    on international organizations, 171–172

Yeltsin, Boris *(cont.)*
  Moscow summit with Clinton
      (January 1994), 87–88
  Moscow summit with Clinton
      (May 1995), 102, 164
  NATO enlargement and, 161,
      174, 176, 177
  new international norms and, 99
  nuclear disarmament and, 71, 148,
      175
  on nuclear security, 101, 105
  on nuclear weapons, 148–149
  Nunn-Lugar program and, 100
  OSCE and, 170
  START II treaty and, 68, 146–147
  START III treaty and, 148, 153
  trilateral accord role, 76, 87–88
  Ukrainian crisis and, 66, 77, 78, 84
  Vancouver summit with Clinton
      (April 1993), 79, 101
  weapons scientists and, 100
Yugoslavia, former, 111–140
  collective security model and,
      168, 169
  Dayton agreement, 131–133
  diplomatic approaches to
      (1991–95), 119–126
  disintegration of, 114–115
  failure of norms enforcement in,
      8–9, 111–114, 117–119, 159–
      160, 199
  historical review, 114–119
  humanitarian aid in, 168
  intervention delay in, 159
  lessons learned in, 133–138, 159,
      169, 199
  1991 peace conference (The
      Hague), 115–116
  1995 fighting in, 128–131
  noninterference in internal affairs
      and, 95
  Russia and, 126–128
  UN peacekeepers in, 116–117, 118
  U.S.-Russian relationship and,
      8–9, 127–128, 133, 136, 137
Yugoslav Collective State Presidency,
      115
"Yugoslavia with nukes," 69

Zagreb, 1995 fighting in, 128
Zartman, William, 221*n*44
Zelikow, Philip, 214*n*2
Zepa
  Bosnian cantonization plan
      and, 126
  fall of, 129
Zimmerman, Warren, 115
Zone of hegemonic domination,
      Eastern Europe as, 42

James E. Goodby is a distinguished diplomat and scholar, whose work has focused on U.S. relations with Europe, both East and West. His many posts include principal negotiator and special representative of the president for nuclear security and dismantlement, 1995–96; chief U.S. negotiator for safe and secure dismantlement of nuclear weapons, 1993–94; vice chairman of the U.S. delegation to the START talks, 1982–83; U.S. representative to the Stockholm Conference on Confidence and Security Building Measures and Disarmament in Europe, 1983–88; and ambassador to Finland, 1980–81. He has served as a member of the State Department's Policy Planning Staff; with the U.S. Mission to the European Community and to NATO; and as deputy assistant secretary of state for European affairs. Winner of the inaugural Heinz Award for work in public policy, Goodby has taught at Stanford, Georgetown, and Carnegie Mellon Universities. He was named Distinguished Fellow by the United States Institute of Peace in 1992, and was Payne Distinguished Lecturer at Stanford University's Institute for International Studies for 1996–97. His publications include *The Limited Partnership: Building a Russian-U.S. Security Community* (1993; coedited with B. Morel), *Transforming Nuclear Deterrence* (1997; coedited with Hans Binnendijk), and *Regional Conflicts: The Challenge to U.S.-Russian Cooperation* (1995), as well as numerous articles in edited volumes and journal

Jennings Randolph Program for International Peace

This book is a fine example of the work produced by senior fellows in the Jennings Randolph fellowship program of the United States Institute of Peace. As part of the statute establishing the Institute, Congress envisioned a program that would appoint "scholars and leaders of peace from the United States and abroad to pursue scholarly inquiry and other appropriate forms of communication on international peace and conflict resolution." The program was named after Senator Jennings Randolph of West Virginia, whose efforts over four decades helped to establish the Institute.

Since 1987, the Jennings Randolph Program has played a key role in the Institute's effort to build a national center of research, dialogue, and education on critical problems of conflict and peace. More than a hundred senior fellows from some thirty nations have carried out projects on the sources and nature of violent international conflict and the ways such conflict can be peacefully managed or resolved. Fellows come from a wide variety of academic and other professional backgrounds. They conduct research at the Institute and participate in the Institute's outreach activities to policymakers, the academic community, and the American public.

Each year approximately fifteen senior fellows are in residence at the Institute. Fellowship recipients are selected by the Institute's board of directors in a competitive process. For further information on the program, or to receive an application form, please contact the program staff at (202) 457-1700.

Joseph Klaits
Director

The Arthur and Frank Payne Lectureship
Institute for International Studies, Stanford University

The Institute for International Studies (IIS) seeks solutions to real-world, international problems through contemporary policy research in three areas: international security, the global environment, and international political economy. IIS brings Stanford experts from a variety of disciplines together with visitors from other academic, government, and corporate institutions to create a collaborative, interdisciplinary research environment.

The Arthur and Frank Payne Lectureship on the Global Community and Its Challenges was endowed at IIS to raise public understanding of the complex policy issues facing the global community and increase support for informed international cooperation. Payne Professors typically deliver up to five public lectures at Stanford in the course of preparing a publishable manuscript. Ambassador James Goodby, who served as the 1996–97 Payne Professor, was the third distinguished internationalist to hold the position. For more information about the Institute, please call (650) 723-4581.

Walter P. Falcon
Director

Europe Undivided

This book is set in Caslon; the display type is Futura. Hasten Design Studio designed the book's cover, and Joan Engelhardt and Day Dosch designed the interior. Pages were made up by Helene Y. Redmond. The text was copyedited by David Sweet and Wesley Palmer, and proofread by Catherine Cambron. Elinor Lindheimer prepared the index. The book's editor was Nigel Quinney.